PREFACE

As a seven-year-old child, I did not appreciate that there might be anything unusual about my grandmother, hanging by her knees upside-down from the trapeze at the bottom of the garden. Her face was close to mine. I saw her grey eyes, fanned at the corners with laughter lines, her beads falling across her face, and from my angle her smiling mouth turned down at the corners instead of up. Her little grey plaits had come unpinned and fell, like wispy straw horns, from either side of her head.

My mother and I had just arrived back from mainland China, seeking sanctuary with my grandparents in the weald of Sussex, and re-joining my sister Catherine who had been living with them for the last two years. The trapeze was fixed between two tall firs and my grandmother was demonstrating what fun it could be, to a dubious child who had been brought up spotlessly by a Chinese amah and was unused to the rough and tumble of English country life. This early memory of mine was in 1953.

It was not until 1985, when I came across her handwritten journal long after she had died, that I realized that my grandmother, Elf, was perhaps not quite a normal grandmother. The journal she wrote covered the period during World War II from May 14 to June 27 1943, when she undertook the gruelling task of travelling from the extreme foot of Africa up to its uppermost tip. She was aged sixty-four, alone, and accompanied by a huge pile of luggage. It was a trip of over 6,814 miles, using many modes of transport. Curious, I typed up a copy of her scrawling journal, verbatim, as a gesture to give to each of her three daughters. And I did my maths! Elf must have been seventy-four years old when she swung from my trapeze, just ten years after she made the African journey!

As grandparents, Elf, Teddy, and the German Shepherd dog Leila II, were always there in rural England for my sister and me. Grandie, as we called her, taught me to ride, taught me the names of all the garden birds, and taught me to be independent. She also taught me how to make Palestinian yoghurt in the hot airing cupboard, a staple unheard of in England in those days. Grandpa drove us to boarding schools and instilled a love in me for photography and snooker! We adored both grandparents. With parents who were frequently absent because my father's career was based overseas, they supported us over holidays from boarding schools.

Elf's extraordinary journal was written as she travelled and is the basis of this book. Her descriptive powers and observational skills were all amply in evidence in her original hasty scribblings and in her later writings when it was obvious that she had worked and reworked the account she wanted to give. It was certainly interesting, but something was missing. I am sad that, for whatever reason, she did not manage to publish her account for her own sake, but I found myself frustrated by what she did not say about her feelings on those pages. Inevitably she was restricted by being a product of her generation, with social obligations limiting what she felt free to say.

I have no such restrictions. With the backing of considerable research, I have been able to fill in Elf and Teddy's fascinating 'back story', and with love and respect I have allowed myself to do what she felt unable to. I have delved deeper than the social niceties would allow her, and based on my knowledge of her character, imagined her emotional journey. I have changed not one step of her odyssey, and the considerable difficulties she courageously undertook, but I have attempted to paint her inner journey too. This is Elf's story.

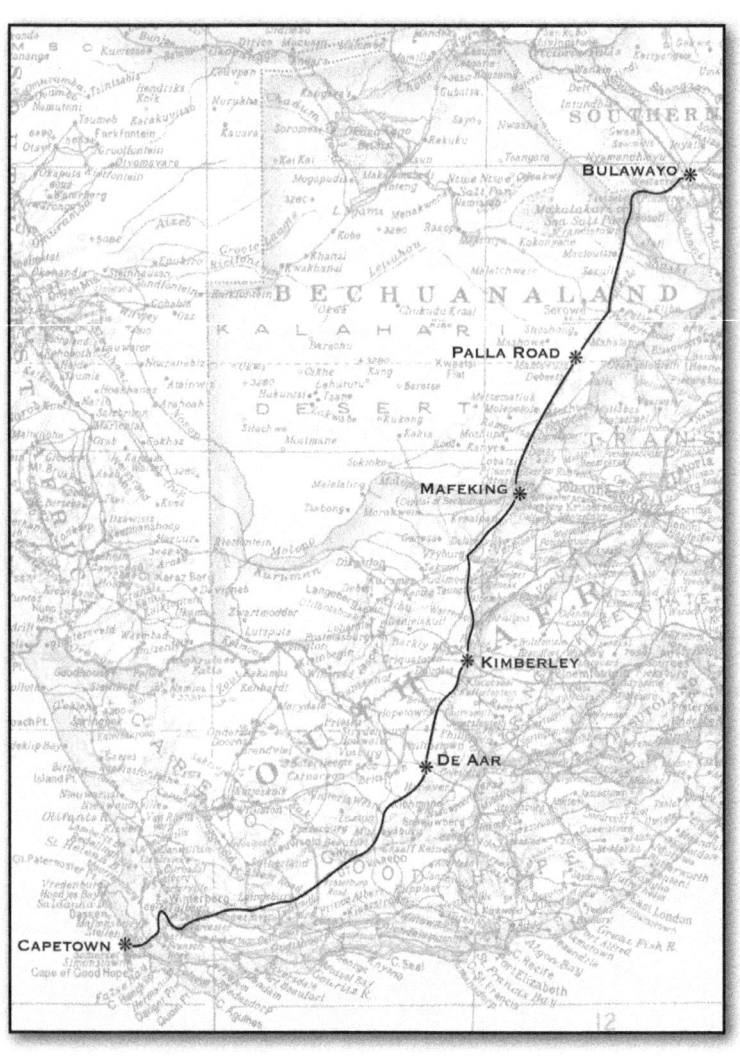

ONE

May 14 1943

There was nothing more I could do. I had reached those unreal minutes between weeks of frantic activity and the next irreversible step. I was about to leave the lovely Cape Province of South Africa, and the shadow of departing day, my last there, hung heavy on my heart.

From the window of my little flat in Cape Town, almost overhanging the small rocky bay at Sea Point, through wind and heavy rain, I watched my cormorant acquaintance funereally perched on the rocks below me. Evidently digesting a heavy meal, his big black banana-leaved wings whose grooming he fussed over daily, were damply enfolding him. I hunched my shoulders in sympathy, shivered and leant my forehead against the glass. How had I suddenly found myself placed in such a position?

This recurring tragedy of being separated from friends, family and country that was so dear to me was happening again and I had only myself to blame. At this moment of departure, I did not want to leave. I wanted to stay with 'my' cormorant and watched him carefully. Truth be told, I did not know for certain that he was my special one, the one I had once found helpless on these same rocks. With the aid of my cigarette lighter, petrol bottle, soap, and hot water in a flask, I had struggled to remove the crippling oil from his left wing. Finally, he had wrenched himself free and, to my relief, flown away from my inexpert handling, more grateful, surely, than he appeared. Since then, I liked to imagine that he allowed me to approach nearer to him than anyone else, but I suspect that was unrealistic. I whispered goodbye to my cormorant and turned again to face the room and the mountain of suitcases awaiting collection.

Phyllis alone remained of the dear friends who had spent the last week helping me reduce and pack up over two years of Cape Town life. There was little logic in my compulsion to leave this comfortable and rewarding existence, to be reunited with my husband in a distant country. My patient supporters were now resigned to my impetuous decision and no longer tried to talk me out of my undertaking. I desperately did not want my move to be seen as a rejection of their generous friendship; rather, as an instinct that I needed, once again, to take my place by Teddy's side.

So, through the rain, Phyllis drove me away from a life I loved. I was leaving my cherished flat, my SAWAS war work with all its political difficulties attending to the welfare of military personnel passing through Cape Town, and the vital companionship of friends who filled my life with laughter and mini adventures. Along streaming streets, shrouded houses, and shuttered shops we, and an assisting taxi, passed through the fallen darkness of night. Complete blackout desolately obliterated this last of my almost daily trips between Sea Point and Cape Town docks.

Two years of hard but rewarding work with the South African Women's Auxiliary Service lay behind me as close to twenty thousand troops had passed through the city in that time. Alone, one bright note struck across this sombre world; the brightly lit interior of a fast-moving crowded tram. The passengers, white and dark faces illuminated, could never know how momentously for me this day was distinguished from theirs. The journey had taken on the feel of an out of body experience. I supressed the overwhelming urge to call a halt, to admit to having made a huge mistake. At sixty-four years old, I must have taken leave of my senses to be undertaking so challenging a journey.

At the crowded station Phyllis and I were confronted by wet and hurrying people struggling to find their luggage and trains. Passengers and porters thronged around a large notice board solitarily lit and shaded, and the odour of wet clothes hit me. To my astonishment I found that, braving the heavy rain and hardships of unlit, unevenly paved streets, friends had come to see me off. My inner circle of local chums had all arrived and any chance of backing down disappeared completely in the face of their support. How I loved them and would miss them. Phyllis smiled at me through tears.

"God speed, Elf", she said. She had been my close ally in my life in Cape Town. We had learned to overlook huge cultural differences between us and had enjoyed each other's company. I bit back tears as we hugged and said our goodbyes. I left my South African life at the barrier.

My coupe was duly found and stolid smiling porters began stacking my fourteen pieces of luggage, including my trunk, into the space. On the table lay a beautiful gift, a great basket heaped high with fruit and blossom, its fragrance filling the air. I was pleased to note that an extra mattress had been placed on the bed, pre ordered for the princely sum of three shillings.

Checking my watch for departure I was distracted by a commotion on the platform as a group arrived outside the next coupe. Ambulance men were carrying a seemingly ill wraith of a woman to deposit next door. There seemed to be much discussion going on which ended with a knock on my door.

"I'm so sorry to bother you. My name's Reynolds and my wife's in the next cabin. We seem to be having a problem and wondered if you'd be kind enough to be of assistance." My intruder was a flustered but pleasant-faced man of about my age.

"Of course, if I can."

He was clearly distracted. "Goodness what a wonderful scent!"

I replied, "The Spirits of Air live on the smells of fruit!" His eyes widened in consternation.

"William Blake?" I compounded my mistake.

He returned to his mission. "My wife's ill and has been released from her nursing home so she can return to our home in Mafeking. The ambulance men were settling her, but it seems that the bed has its back to the engine. We didn't realise when we booked it. She's in some pain and this would be an unbearable position. We've been informed that your cabin is identical to hers, but with the bed around the other way. Would it be too much of an imposition to ask if you'd agree to change cabins?" He watched me anxiously as I hid my irritation at the upheaval.

I smiled, "I'd be happy to help but as you can see, I'm not travelling lightly! Even if you have the manpower, can it be done before the train leaves?"

"I'm sure that there'll be enough hands willing to make this a smooth transaction. My wife and I would be so very grateful to you."

With ambulance men in attendance, and an army of porters tripping over themselves the exchange was accomplished with only a minor delay to the train's departure. I hung onto my beautiful basket of fruit, and my mattress! Probably we both benefitted from this exchange as the activity lessened the void left by my supportive friends. As the train pulled out, for good or evil, I was off on my travels! The next few weeks would be spent in the hands of strangers crossing the entire length of Africa, from the tip of South Africa, all the way up the continent to Palestine and my husband Teddy.

The momentous decision to take on this journey and the hot weather trials involved was undoubtedly a rash one. I knew I had been driven by a compulsion in the last weeks which I now queried. The demands of working out the exact itinerary had entailed countless visits to the South African Railways offices. Endless negotiations for visas and permits almost derailed me. Packing and getting rid of my flat and its contents had appeared at times an almost insurmountable emotional struggle. But facing those challenges had a pace of its own and, like preparing for a funeral, it had given me little time to consider the full implications. Of the obstacles, only one had proved impossible to master, my precious Palestine Entry Visa. It might, or it might not, catch up with me en-route. However, I was given a Visa for Iraq, beyond Palestine, which was the best the authorities in Cape Town could provide. This involved a circuitous route via Bagdad! The ill effects of inoculations, especially that for yellow fever, had nearly wrecked my plans. But here I was, courtesy of South African Railways and I now had time to reflect on my decisions.

As the train gained momentum I walked about my roomy coupe, turning out the light and trying to distinguish through darkness and rain familiar glimpses of the country I had grown to love. Even Table Mountain's famous outline was totally hidden. I made my way to the dining car but had little appetite and returned to make the best of a poor night's sleep.

I thought back on my two years in Cape Town and the work there that had so involved me. What had initially appeared to be a fun way to add my bit to the war effort, had in fact been far more complicated. I thought lending my organising skills to be part of the team arranging teas, dances, concerts, and accommodation for the Allied troops passing through would be simple, but immediately stumbled over the political situation. The intention of the SAWAS was to provide entertainment for the influx of mostly young, unattached men and steer them away from the seedier neighbourhoods, with their brothels, illicit drinking, and dagga smoking dens. I was unfamiliar with the conventions of South African segregation and had no idea that welcoming Allied servicemen and women of colour would be such an issue. I was surprised by how engrained was the belief that troops of colour might radicalise the local population and create conflict for white women acting as their hosts. Phyllis and I had quite a falling out over it. It seemed grossly unfair to me that white troops would be granted unrestricted shore leave, whilst troops of colour were so closely supervised. I worked mostly with the recuperation of the sick and injured, ferrying them to appointments, befriending them, writing letters for them, and helped in a dockside canteen. Despite Phyllis's horror and my advancing years, on a matter of principle I put my name on the rota of white women willing to attend dances and concerts as hosts to our coloured Allies. It turned out that many of the troops appreciated the mothering I provided.

How I grudged the hiding darkness of night. I knew we would be passing interesting scenes, Worcester among them, with its fertile fruit growing soil, and the Little Karoo plateau. I would also miss the beautiful scenery of the Hex River, where Phyllis and I had spent a pleasant weekend on a houseboat with friends. How they had laughed at my delight in spotting the magpie shrike birds they were so used to! I would miss the vast view from the heights forming 'the buttress of the Great Karroo tableland' above, where the train had risen by very steep gradients.

Later, away on our right, would lie the 'Great, Grey-Green, Greasy Limpopo River' of Rudyard Kipling's Elephant Child fame. Between wooded banks in its upper reaches, but then through great level plains, well populated and growing rice, sugar and cotton, the river flowed to the sea a hundred miles above Lorenzo Marques. On our left we would have passed the Kalahari Desert with greener and denser looking scrub than the Karroo. Through this desert once flowed a great river, a tributary of the Orange, whose bed has long been dry and silted up. In the rainy season, salt pans and brackish water pools are found in this Kalahari Desert. I am told there are also curious limestone depressions caused by countless herds of elephants, who for ages have formed these hollows when taking their mud baths.

All this was blanketed in Africa's night as the train progressed in unexplained fits and starts, and my overloaded mind cried out for the sanctity of sleep to soothe it.

May 15 1943

A woman attendant, polite and smiling, brought the coffee and later returned with my breakfast, tea, and toast. I had a heavy head from the anxieties of the previous night and inertia slowed me. As the verdant landscape rolled by, I faced those next few weeks of travelling with some trepidation. It was late morning when, as a distraction from my thoughts I decided to check on the invalid next door.

Mrs Reynolds, her translucent face drawn in pain, propped up in bed and wrapped in layers despite the stuffy coupe, was glad of company.

"I'm so grateful to you for changing berths last night. It would have been an impossible journey to make otherwise." I shook her dry birdlike hand gently, frightened of crushing it.

"My name's Ethel Warmington Reed. Of course, I'll do anything I can to make the trip more pleasant. It's a shame your husband couldn't accompany you."

"Yes, he's a busy man. I'm sure he would have liked to assist me. He spends so much time in Cape Town nowadays, I sometimes wonder how our farm manages to run without him!" She stopped. "Oh dear, that sounds disloyal. He means well I'm sure, it's just that I think in my condition I'm unable to run the farm the way it should be. The boys do need a firm hand." I had been in Africa long enough to know that 'boys' did not mean family.

"I'm sorry to hear that. You must be pleased to be going home. Have you been in Cape Town long?"

"Far too long! I'm sure the nursing home did their best, but I always knew that my medical problems were beyond their help. I've lived with my asthma most of my life and this other wretched business was beyond repair. I begged and begged the doctor to send me home. I think I must have finally frightened them into letting me go as my weight's dropped to less than seventy pounds. They didn't want to take responsibility for me anymore!" She laughed a small bitter laugh and I wondered how reconciled she was to her condition. She looked as if she had once been a tall woman, but her extreme emaciation and the translucence of her skin looked alarming to me.

"What help are you getting on the train?"

"Oh, they've been very good, and I can't fault their attention. I just want to be in my own bedroom surrounded by all my familiar things and I'm sure that'll make me feel much better."

"You sound as if you originally come from England, as I do. Have you lived here long?"

"It must be thirty years, but I still miss England. I was bought up on the South Downs and I miss the gentleness of the landscape, the soft curves."

"It's hard to define, isn't it? The sun on the backs of the sheep and lambs? The passing of the seasons? The pace of life that was so gentle it was reflected in peoples' voices. The English villages with their warm stone and village ponds? I was bought up in Gloucestershire, on the edge of the Cotswolds. I could get boring!" We both slumped into reminiscing silence. "I've a favourite book with me, W.H. Hudson's 'Nature in Downland'. It's brimming with lovely home atmosphere, so completely unlike anything here. I'm happy to lend it to you for the rest of your journey."

"A kind thought my dear, but sadly my eyesight isn't up to reading. A shame as I would have loved to pass the time that way." Her failing energy had been taxed already, but we made a pact that I would pop in to read to her for a while after lunch.

We pulled into De Arr station and by leaning out of the train door I managed to buy a local paper. I had been lucky in Cape Town as war news was always readily available, but I imagined that might not be the case over the next weeks. It was important to me to track what was happening in London where two of my daughters were living. Joy was a physiotherapist in the Brompton hospital, and Felicity worked in a draftsman's office and drove ambulances. Both had continued working right through the Blitz in 1941 but I knew that English life was still fraught with daily difficulties. The Battle of the Atlantic recently had been the daily headlines, but my attention was divided between London and the Philippines. In Cape Town I had been able to communicate by letter with Joy and Felicity, but I was aware that German bombings of the capital were not a thing of the past. The fate of my middle daughter Ronny equally tormented me. I assumed she and her husband Pat were prisoners of the Japanese in the Philippines but had received no news from them since before Christmas '41. Ronny had been expecting her first child, my first grandchild. Despite badgering the Red Cross, I had heard nothing. I did not know if Ronny was alive! Foolishly, I had been convinced that if I took my eye off the ball something too terrible to contemplate would happen to one of my family.

Der Arr appeared to be a growing town and an important junction. The paper was full of sheep farming statistics as the town was noted for holding big stock fairs. All snippets of those insular interests were disappointing, their news was not war news. Turning my thoughts away, I gazed over the vast cattle and sheep-rearing land we passed through and concentrated on that privileged view of the landscape. I noted a splendidly built high bridge of nine spans over the Orange River. In about 1860, somewhere near here, the first South African diamonds were discovered including the famous 'Star of South Africa', which was valued a few years ago at twenty-five thousand pounds.

My reading sessions with Mrs Reynolds passed the time and stopped me worrying about what lay ahead. In comparison to her I was lucky to have my health and that made so much difference. It wasn't until the evening that my carefully judged visits seemed to give her permission to speak of personal matters.

"Now it's so close I'm becoming nervous about my return." she sighed. "My boys are all pretty rough and unskilled. When my husband originally worked the farm, we considered ourselves lucky to have such good and loyal help. He was lucky to inherit the estate but in recent years everything's changed. There've been disappointments and financial problems and my husband has lost interest in the land now. I don't blame him, but I've never had the authority that he had and it's difficult to make the boys listen to me when he isn't there."

"Who'll be there for you and your needs?"

"Well, although the farm's a bit remote, my doctor in Mafeking can come out if needed. I'm told there'll be a district nurse who can call in once a day."

"What about your local friends and neighbours? Will they be able to support you?"

"I don't really know anyone locally. To be honest, my husband's always disliked company. We never had children and kept pretty much to ourselves which was fine originally. When he started to spend so much time away, I would've enjoyed more company, but it's too late now."

"Mrs Reynolds, I'm really concerned for you. Are you sure that you want to go back to the farm?"

"I expect I've made it sound worse than it is. The boys will take care of me. I love my own home, and I'm sure we'll muddle through somehow." I was not so sure.

Our conversation was interrupted by our arrival at Kimberley station.

"I understand there's a famous mine here called the 'Kimberly Hole'. It was believed to be the deepest hole in the earth ever made by man. I wonder how deep it actually is?"

Mrs Reynolds didn't respond.

"Have you ever visited the museum here? I'd love to see the prehistoric bushmen's paintings they exhibit."

Mrs Reynolds was not interested.

I gently took my leave. I had seen before how the world of the terminally ill shrinks, so they have no interest, understandably, in anything not directly related to themselves. My acquaintance had not asked one question about me in the hours I had spent with her. It had suited me.

May 16 1943

Another restless night was due to my concerns about Mrs Reynolds as well as about myself. I had learned the name of her doctor and was determined to write a note to be delivered to him when we arrived at Mafeking that morning. I hoped it would give him some insight into Mr Reynolds' neglectful absence and his wife's vulnerability. In other circumstances I might have broken my journey to help. The South African Railways, who had planned all the arrivals, departures, hotels, money etc. en-route, had warned me that my ticket through to Palestine via Cairo was the very last being issued that season. If I missed connections and became stranded, I might have to remain wherever it was for, probably, a very long time. This was partly due to the war conditions, the requisitioning of hotels and movement of troops, but chiefly to the time of year. It was possible that even now the extreme lowness of the Nile this year might hold up the passage of the river steamers. Breaking the schedule was not an option.

Mrs Reynolds had also had a bad night. "I don't know how I'm going to manage. I don't blame my husband but it's so inconvenient that he can't be at home when I need him most."

It was clear that blaming her husband was exactly what she did. I had decided I disliked the man but wondered if she had always allowed him to make the decisions, which cleared her of all responsibility. Too many women did that in my experience, and it just wasn't fair. My husband liked to think he made the decisions in our household, and I went along with it to a degree for peace, but if there was ever something that I felt strongly about, I made sure it happened.

In the next hour I pointed out several small bucks fleeing from the railway and a few big, steel-grey birds flying together low over the bush, to try to distract her.

On reaching Mafeking station I watched as a bevy of officials and an ambulance collected my now reluctant companion, and my letter to her doctor. I was relieved to see her treated with care. She was no longer any responsibility of mine. I had enough problems looking after myself.

Leaving Mafeking we passed through dry, dusty thornbush country. I saw several wonderful community nests of the social weaver birds, but wildlife naturally avoids noisy trains. I so wanted to see the grey lourie birds that form large groups foraging in the tree-tops or dust bathing on the ground. Their distinctive go-away calls, of course, could not be heard above the roar of the train. Upon advice about regulations, I had not brought my binoculars, which I was already regretting.

The sun had just set as we stopped at Palla Road, 3,095 feet above sea level and 1,062 miles already from my beloved Cape Town. I was feeling alone at the thought of the distance between me and my South African friends, so was pleasantly surprised when the guard approached me to share my coupe with a charming fair-haired girl who had no berth. I had been warned that this could well happen, and my unrequired luggage efficiently disappeared into the depth of the train, hopefully to be seen again!

The pretty girl smiled at me. "Hello. My name's Rue, short for Rowena. I'm so relieved that you're happy to share with me.

They seemed to have mucked up my booking and I did wonder if I was going to have to sit up all night."

"You're welcome. As we're to be bed fellows, please call me Elf." I noted the accustomed rise of her eyebrows, and qualified this, "Shorter and infinitely preferable to Ethel! Where are you heading?"

"To see the Victoria Falls! I'm so excited. I've worked here for eight months now, and this is the first chance I've had. And you?"

"Sadly, I'm making a much longer journey, all the way to Palestine. But, like you, I'm making a break at the Falls, as I couldn't possibly pass by without seeing them." I studied my pretty companion with the slightly husky South African voice. Rue must have been in her early twenties, younger than my daughters, and I wondered why she was travelling on her own.

She was apparently wondering the same thing! "That's a huge journey! Surely you are not on your own?"

Rue turned out to be an easy companion. Johannesburg born and bred, this job in Palla Road was the first of her life adventures. Our conversations dwelt in that region of non-committed pleasantry when people are trying to weigh up if they can find anything in common. With Rue, aged a sheltered twenty-three, there were limitations!

That night was disturbed time and again. The wind was fresh at this elevation so Rue and I, thoroughly chilled, struggled to close one of the windows. The effort managed to warm us up considerably and we finally settled comfortably for sleep.

I was just drifting off when a slight noise and movement focussed my attention. Somebody, very stealthily, turned the handle of our safety-locked door. I froze in horror. My eyes were not deceiving me as the handle turned again, a little more persistently I thought. Sitting up, I reached across the void and touched Rue's arm and she responded immediately. Now the two of us watched silent and fascinated. A third attempt was made, and I considered what options we had. I wasn't sure how flimsy the door was to a determined attempt to get in and we had no hope of getting attention from the staff. Then, as silently as it had started, nothing further happened.

I was reminded of an incident when two of my girls were little, and Teddy was away from home on some war training exercise, as he often was. I woke to hear a noise downstairs in the kitchen and, as mother tigress, knew that I had no option but to investigate. I remember my heart hammering as I crept down the stairs a heavy candlestick firmly in my grasp. Time stood still. I wished myself anywhere but there, as I saw a shadow of a man bending over the sink. I don't know who was more surprised and relieved, Teddy or me, as he escaped having his head stoved in by moments! He never again returned in the night without warning!

Later when I was nearly asleep again, blessing the softness of my extra mattress, the looking-glass lid suddenly sprang a loud rattle. I tried to ignore it but eventually had to take matters into my own hands and the fractious lid was soothed with a towel gagged tightly round it, and at last comparative calm reigned. Rue was sound asleep, charmingly childlike and withdrawn. It had been a long time since I had shared an intimate space with one so young. In her face I imagined I saw an uncomplicated acceptance of what life had thrown at her. Nothing stood between her and her need for sleep. At my age, life was more complicated. During the night there were also several long halts when I struggled with window obstructions and stiff blinds in my efforts to glimpse the outside world without disturbing Rue. I have no idea how she slept through it all. At one enforced stop hammering started, accompanied by scraps of English conversation between men outside the train. "If you've got grease, I think I can mend this leak." The engine threatened failure to pull its weight, but after judders and groans we appeared to be staggering once more through the night. As I drifted off, I kept imagining that I could faintly hear the beginning of the distant roar of the Falls ahead.

TWO

May 17 1943

In the early morning we reached Bulawayo, in Southern Rhodesia, 1,360 miles from Cape Town. The name means "The Place of the Killing", but there was little to remind the passer-by of the fiery stronghold of the last of the Matabele kings, old Lobengula. Towards the close of the nineteenth century, he used to sit there in red-handed judgement under his 'indaba' tree which was said to be still standing. Only a hundred miles or so east of Bulawayo lay the famous Zimbabwe ruins, their history still wrapped in mystery, though archaeological experts believed them to have been Arabic or possibly Semitic in origin. How I wished I could take a detour to see them. Everyone had to disembark here for a few hours while the trains were changed. This was quite an endeavour with my trunk and cases, but finally, Rue and I in one taxi and my luggage in another, we were driven to the Grand Hotel.

To my amazement a parcel awaited me. Mr Reynolds, the invalid's husband, had ordered some quinine tablets for my use which had been delivered by the post office. These were unobtainable in Cape Town, and I had a dim recollection of mentioning my anxiety to him as we waited for the coupes to be exchanged. I would soon be needing these and was stunned at his generous gesture. So convinced was I that he was an uncaring character, it was a shock to realise that I had got it so wrong.

As I lazed in a welcome bath, I wondered what else had I got wrong too? The journey had been triggered by a warning from an old girlfriend, someone who had known me well in the days when Teddy and I had lived in Palestine before the war. Easing out two nights of aching bones, I thought about my previous life in Palestine. I remembered it as a glorious existence of long warm days and balmy nights in our cool, spacious house at Mount Carmel, the hill looking down to the Haifa docks in the distance. Our time there was one of the least stressful of our lives, with horses to ride, our German Shepherd puppy Leila to train, picnics and a social whirl supported by the most caring of staff. It had been a lot of fun, until in 1940, the Italians, having aligned themselves with the Germans, took everyone by surprise and sent their bombers over to torment us. Suddenly we were in the front line with their constant bombing. I would have remained in place despite lengthy arguments with Teddy but eventually the government gave me no choice as all English women were ordered out of Haifa. Very reluctantly I had to agree to evacuate and leave Teddy at his post. After much discussion, I travelled by boat down to Cape Town only taking with me possessions too precious for us to risk, along with my personal wardrobe. Now, so far secretly, I was returning.

Revitalised, Rue and I set out for a stroll in the clean and spacious town and stood before a splendid bronze statue of Cecil Rhodes.

"I was told that he had a hut here in the early days of Rhodesia. He was much loved. Apparently, it's thanks to him the streets were made so wide. Have you seen his memorial on the mountainside in Cape Town?"

Rue smiled. "I've only been to Cape Town once to visit relatives, and sightseeing was not on the agenda. Perhaps, next time?" Rue was sweet and inexperienced, but somehow a little scared of life. She appeared inhibited, which was sad, but a streak of originality in her delighted me.

"It's worth seeing. It's up the broad steps behind Watts' man-and-horse statue of Energy. I remember the inscription 'To the spirit and life-work of Cecil Rhodes who loved and served South Africa.' I personally think he was a controversial character. I'm curious, Rue, what did you learn about him educationally?"

"A fair amount of class time was spent on him. Born in England. Very wealthy businessman, head of De Beers diamond firm. Politician responsible for annexation of lots of Africa. I can quote,

'The immense and brooding spirit still
Shall quicken and control.
Living he was the land and dead
His soul shall be her soul.'" Rue intoned

"Goodness, I never expected to hear Kipling's words coming from your generation!" I was genuinely surprised. We were taught poetry at my first boarding school in Durham. We had to learn one poem a week to recite in class, and it ignited a love of poetry that stayed with me all my life. I still try to write some. I could recall no African history taught at the bastion of English education I later attended, Cheltenham Ladies College.

"Our history teacher was obsessed with Cecil Rhodes. We nicknamed her Cecil! To be honest we became tired of hearing his name."

"Well, that's enough of him then. I think it's time we headed back for lunch!"

On the way back, in a deceptively well-stocked shop I bought a few things including a fine world map with, to my surprise, Woodrow Wilson's Fourteen Points listed on it. It was extraordinary that a copy of the momentous document left over from the end of the World War, should be found in this backwater of Africa. I could only remember five of the American President's points by heart. 'Open covenants of peace openly arrived at. Freedom of the seas. The removal as far as possible of all economic barriers. The reduction of national armaments to the lowest point consistent with domestic safety. Impartial adjustment of all colonial claims.' Recently Roosevelt and Churchill had tried to base an eight-point statement of war aims on them with no success. Glancing at the document I wondered if I had the energy to learn the rest of them, 'The evacuation of all Russian territory. An independent Poland to be established with free and secure aspect to the sea. The evacuation and restoration of Belgium.' were some of the simpler points. I felt that Roosevelt and Churchill were as far away from achieving these principles of peace as when Woodrow Wilson declared them in January 1918.

I bought a tiny native 'piano', a little wooden frame with metal tongues which clanged quite melodiously. I was going to have to be careful adding to my luggage, but this morning I couldn't resist! My fellow travellers and I left this attractive spot after a good lunch to continue our journey. The luggage, all collected from the hotel by lorry, awaited us on the platform.

There was confusion on boarding as I found my name on two separate sleeping compartments. Porters were stacking my luggage into one compartment, where I was confronted by an elegantly dressed woman who was obviously horrified at my intrusion and the quantity of bags being unloaded. She demanded that they be removed forthwith. Her penetrating voice cut through the air, and I instantly decided that my second berth, no matter who I was coupled with, would be an improvement. There was no time to lose and after ordering the confused porters to move my luggage to the second compartment, with a sigh of relief I followed them.

Bee, short for Beatrice, who hailed from the fair city of Durban, was my new companion. Aged in her early thirties, her fair curls lit by the travelling lamps, she was very attractive and radiated gaiety and vitality. I knew immediately that I had drawn the lucky straw and this next stage of my journey would be relaxed with such a companion.

Bee and I talked long in the dark of the night. She was curious as to why I left Haifa at the start of war, and the reality of living through that time was a complete surprise to her.

She said "I had absolutely no idea that the Italians were responsible for such carnage. The tale I've heard is that they have had a disastrous war, with an almost unrelieved succession of military disasters. They really picked the wrong side to fight on."

"They came closer to total victory in '40, than anyone gives them credit for. Their bombing attacks on Haifa were devastating and took us totally by surprise. Tel Aviv suffered too."

"Why bomb there? It seems a long way from home for the Italians."

"Strategically, the oil refineries, only built in '38, were very important to our British and American forces in the Mediterranean and Middle East. The British built the Mosul – Haifa Oil pipeline stretching from the oil fields near Kirkuk in Iraq, controlled by the British. In Haifa we're talking about an annual capacity of producing two million tons of crude oil. We were so far from the front line, no one realised that we would be such an attractive target."

"But surely the British aircraft were more than a match for the Italians? They don't have a reputation for competency."

"The Italians sent their bombers from their bases in the Dodecanese Islands. They bypassed the British bases in Cyprus so widely that we had no warnings. And they did it time and again bombing us. We never seemed to put up our aircraft from Mount Carmel in time."

"And you and your husband were in the heart of this? That must have been terrifying!"

"Our house at Mount Carmel looked down on Haifa and I'll never forget the fires. They burned for days. The nights were red with the flames. Some of the refinery staff that Teddy worked with were killed. It went on for months, two or three bombing raids a week, and the British never seemed able to do anything about it. Teddy was convinced that the refinery would continue to be a target until it was destroyed beyond patching up. I would have stayed if not for the Government ruling that all women had to leave."

"Why didn't you go back to England?"

"That would have been risky. We decided that I'd ship down to South Africa with the Union Castle Line. Teddy had some connections there. As the refinery manager, he couldn't leave his job. We sorted out some of our possessions which came to Cape Town with me."

"It must have been hard for you to leave him."

"Yes, but these are the times we live in! I've spent a lot of my life on the move! I joined the SAWAS in Cape Town, which gave me instant access to a group of friends."

"Don't tell me! The South African Women's Auxiliary Service! Universal Aunts! I've heard some mixed stories about them in Durban!"

"What stories?" I asked, knowing exactly what she might refer to.

Bee was embarrassed, "In Durban a group of SAWAS ladies got into trouble for being a little too available to visiting servicemen! I'm sorry, I shouldn't have said anything. I'm sure it wasn't like that in Cape Town."

"I imagine there was bound to be the occasional breakdown of boundaries in the war. It's a volatile situation. I found that I could be helpful as a mother figure. The part that I found difficult to manage was the colour segregation. I never got used to it."

"Yes. It's something you grow up with and don't question unless you've seen more of the world. It needs an outsider to challenge it."

"I grew up in a traditional rural part of England so was naïve on that subject but mixing with troops, coloured or white, presented me with no difficulties. It was certainly an issue there. The difficulties with hospitality covered Indians and even Maori servicemen. I was told that when the West African troops first came through Cape Town, they were made to stay on board ship! No longer, thank goodness, but they're still restricted. The Cape Coloured Women's Organisation did most of the hosting and we white women who were happy mixing, were placed on a special roster to attend events with our coloured troops."

There was a pause and I wondered if I'd said too much. I'd learned from Phyllis, that for those brought up in South Africa this was a hot potato. I couldn't begin to understand the long-seated discomfort. I diverted, "I loved working with all those brave lads. It was the least I could do. Part of my job was to help those who wanted to write home, and it's been an eye opener that so many young English soldiers can barely read or write! What does that say about the British education system!"

My story was one of good fortune in comparison to Bee's. She showed me a photograph of herself and a young man with a handsome strong face, and a wisp of a child about a year old. Written below it was "To my lovely wife".

"I can't believe you've been married for seven years! That's ridiculous! You look far too young!"

"Ah looks can deceive! Geoffrey was fighting in the South African Army."

"Was, my dear?"

"Oh, it's a long story. We had a tough few years. We lost our only child to polio when she was one. That took a long time to come to terms with." She stroked the photograph gently as I struggled to regain my composure. "Then Geoffrey was wounded in the fighting near Cairo. We thought he was getting better, but he became ill with dysentery in a camp near the Red Sea. It was touch and go, but he survived that and was waiting to be sent back to South Africa. Finally, with many other sick and wounded men, he was loaded onto the 'Nova Scotia', and they sailed for Durban." Bee's voice tripped on the rawness of emotion. "The ship was torpedoed and out of several hundred men and many Italian prisoners, less than two hundred were rescued."

"I'm so sorry, my dear. He didn't survive?"

"No. He didn't survive. But that's not the worst part. Do you know the part that stops me sleeping? All the time he was ill, I received every one of his letters. Not one of mine reached him. Not one. Each letter of his stressed how he was longing to hear from me. He said he totally knew that I was writing very often, but no letters came." She broke off. "That's the toughest part."

There was nothing I could say. I suspected that even time would not change her perception that she had let her husband down when he needed her. Bee was such a lovely girl and had suffered two tragedies in her young life. I was certain that the time would come when she would begin this life again, and that her young husband would not have wished it otherwise. I tried to tell her, but I do not think she could hear. Bee's vitality seems to have an almost spiritual quality in it, a courage, and a warm interest in life. She was a star.

May 18 1943

Hot coffee at daybreak was a shock to the system, but we had to be dressed and packed quickly. Bee and I walked along the corridor to the open end of the coach. Rue, who had been a frequent visitor earlier last night, joined us as we had made a pact to miss nothing of the glory ahead. Shivering in the cold breeze, but thrilled to the core, we stood there watching the dawn breaking, awaiting our earliest glimpse of one of the wonders of the world – the Victoria Falls. In the pale clear light, we could see a solitary dark cloud below the clear sky. We knew it to be lying over the Falls, their very own permanent spray shadow. The train slid to a halt for a minute or two, and in the silence, listening with awe, we caught the roar of the Falls. Then we started again, ever nearer to the increasing, continuous thunder, and once more came a brief halt, tantalising, yet precious in delaying the exquisite moment. The wind flattened us out against the coach rails, and we shivered in it, but agreed that we dare not take the risk of missing anything while fetching more coats. Suddenly, however, from behind me, I was enveloped in a rug! Rue had slipped back into the compartment after all and seized the nearest warm things. So thoughtful of her, I felt ashamed not to have done it myself. Round the stationary cloud just ahead, the sky grew lighter and at last we came to the Victoria Falls station.

Smart and courteous porters in fresh uniforms took our luggage and off we all walked, a straggling procession, into the adjoining hotel grounds. By the booking-office a line of servants in spotless white was drawn up, and as we wrote our names in the register, we were assigned one of these, who showed us to our rooms. Number nine was mine, and William my excellent attendant. Before anything else I could not resist strolling through the hotel to its grounds beyond, so green in the bright, soft, morning light, drawn in the direction of the thunder and the sleeping cloud. Victoria Falls themselves could not be seen from here, though the bridge, that great engineering feat spanning their tremendous chasm, was visible. The cloud overhanging was radiantly lovely now with the sun, still low, shining through it.

I was alone and to my surprise met a party of baboons! They were chasing each other, careering over and under the tree's gateway, while an older one sat solemnly watching. They saw me approaching apparently without fear but imperceptibly withdrew from any tentative neighbourliness on my part. On trees against the hotel, I saw a pair of carmine-breasted, gold-capped bee-eaters, a miracle of lovely colour! I had yet to spot the trumpeter hornbill often seen, I understood, near the bridge or further up the Falls. Golden breasted buntings and chaffinches with much white on the wings, could also be seen. How impossible it was to describe that most beautiful location, and how I longed to have even one of my family with me to share the deep delight and the calm in the core of the thunder.

Bee and Rue met me for breakfast in the great dining room. We were talking about the importance of trying to get to know the local population better. I told them that when we lived in Palestine, I used to dress up in Arabic clothes to go to the market and just mingle and observe, in a way I could never have done as a European.

Bee was intrigued "Weren't you terrified you'd be found out?"

"It gave me an enormous feeling of freedom and helped me understand the locals better. The throbe and libas are so loose, they're easy to wear. And the keffiyeh covers your hair and you can pull it across your face. It was easy to hide. I did it on many occasions and it was liberating. You both know a white face means you are always being scrutinised. I became invisible. If somebody spoke to me, I just turned away."

"The throbe? The libas?"

"Sorry! The throbe is the dress, the libas are the pants underneath. The throbe can be highly decorated, and very attractive as it indicates your social standing. I used to borrow one from my cleaning lady."

"I had imagined that you were wearing one of those black cover all garments. Did you feel hot with all those layers?"

"I did find early evening for my adventures was best."

"What did your husband think?"

"Oh, Teddy used to turn a blind eye on my little jaunts. There was only one time when he was adamant that I wasn't to risk it, and that was a long time ago, September '33. King Faisal had died suddenly at a health clinic in Switzerland aged only forty-eight. His body was bought in a British cruiser from Europe into the Haifa port. We learned that his casket would be escorted across town to Haifa aerodrome, where the RAF would fly him to Baghdad for the funeral. Faisal was loved and esteemed by the Arabs and something of a hero to me. I desperately wanted to see the procession."

"What was so special about him?"

"It's complicated. Living in Palestine we were surrounded by the Arab-Jewish conflict. It was part of our daily life. As King of Iraq, Faisal represented the Arabs and their alarm at Jewish immigration to Palestine which seemed unstoppable. He was putting pressure on the British to limit Jewish migration and land sales. Talk at the club was that Swiss doctors said Faisal was perfectly healthy when he arrived. It was just his annual check-up. But something happened. They said he had a heart attack, but his private nurse reported that Faisal complained of pains in his abdomen, not his chest. She reported signs of arsenic poisoning. The body was quickly mummified so there was no proper autopsy to find the exact cause of death. A lot of frightening rumours were flying around. Teddy was concerned that the grieving crowds would turn ugly at the funeral procession."

"I can imagine it would be highly likely."

"Yes, of course. But it was too good an opportunity to be missed!"

"You didn't?"

"I did, and it was an event like no other." I described to my two young friends, the pomp and ceremony of the transportation of the body, against a background of weeping and emotional crowds. It was an event rich with tradition. They released twenty-five white Arab stallions that were driven in front of the cortege. The crowds were overwhelming but of course it was totally forbidden to foreigners. What I did not tell them was that I had been very naïve and was lucky to have survived that day. What had started off as an adventure, quickly turned into an unforgettably frightening and claustrophobic experience. I had thought I could just observe but soon found myself unwillingly pushed into the mass of people following the coffin. I was jostled and crushed in a sea of frantic and hysterical bodies. I was terrified of being discovered and knew that any non-Arab in this crowd would be lucky to get away from the mob with their life. Finally, I managed to shove my way onto a bus for protection from the ebb and flow of the mourners. I re-joined my driver hours late. Teddy suspected my stupidity and became very frightened for me. I remember his face had aged with fear when I finally returned. He wouldn't stop raging until I promised I would never take the risk again. The truth is that I could see nothing. My description of the event was based on a news reel.

As we enjoyed our breakfast I couldn't resist. "I know one of the men who was responsible for building this bridge, opened in 1904!"

"Why does that not surprise me, and I've only known you twenty-four hours?" Rue laughed.

I continued, "Well, I know the man's wife! Actually, her claim to fame is even greater than his as she was the first woman to cross Victoria Falls!"

"How did she do that?" Bee queried.

"She was slung across in a basket on a Blondin-type of rope cable. The bridge itself is 660 feet long and is one of the highest in the world."

"Blondin? You've lost me again Elf!" said Rue

Bee interrupted "Wasn't Blondin the man who was the first to tightrope walk across the Niagara Falls?"

"Yes, that's him. In 1859 Charles Blondin tightrope walked across Niagara Falls! He used a hempen cable secured on both the American and Canadian sides. He used guy ropes at twenty feet intervals attached to the cable and secured on both banks to try to lessen the swaying. The cable he walked on looked like a giant spider's web, but it was still very dangerous."

Bee continued, "I saw a photograph of him doing it, dressed in pink tights covered in spangles. I think he did it many times, each time increasing the degree of difficulty. He was a major showman."

Rue laughed "I assume he never fell, or it would have been a different story!"

"He died at a ripe old age, and they estimated that he actually walked over the Falls over two hundred times!"

We walked across the beautifully planned grounds and climbed on to the little trolley which runs, or is pushed by attendants, towards the still invisible Falls. Their cloud, as though tethered to the sky, still hung over them, and the roar became even more impressive before we finally beheld them. All could not be seen at once. Walking and climbing were necessary to reveal one entrancing, magnificent vision after another. Before we had more than a breath-taking glimpse we were interrupted. Knowing no better, having overlooked a notice in the hotel, we had walked along the bridge, all damp and shining with spray, that carried the railway line and spans the Falls. We were stopped by sentries and asked for our police passes. Excuse of ignorance was brushed aside politely but firmly; passes were essential. There being no alternative we had a tiring walk back to the hotel and beyond it to the police station, where the passes were produced. This time, thankfully we hired a car to take us.

From the bridge we were only seeing part of the Falls because they curve about, zigzagging in a most bewildering way, roughly running east and west at right angles to the Zambesi. Curiously the level of the plain above and below the cataracts was much the same. The Falls were like giant cracks or fissures occurring in that level country. We drove on to the Eastern Cataract and I stood absorbed in its terrific power and beauty.

At last, we tore ourselves away and drove on to the Game Reserve. Here we were among various unfrightening creatures of the wild, koodoo, sable, zebra, warthog, and finally when we thought we had missed them, giraffe. These we stopped to photograph. We left the car but stood near it, warned by the driver to be aware of giraffe's legs which can kick forwards as well as backwards. One giraffe seemed very tame and stood quietly besides us with a nearly full-grown young one at her side. They apparently wanted sweets, but we had only cigarettes, and when Rue produced one it was rejected! Leaving the girls taking snapshots, I retired inside the car. The mother giraffe followed me and all but put her head in at the window and I wondered if she might bite. At such close quarters she appeared a vast height, her knees, so near me, seemed colossal, her ears so wide, her great brown eyes, soft and luminous, appeared friendly, but about her enquiring mouth so near my own, I felt not so sure!

All too soon we left the Reserve, some of its inhabitants still undiscovered. We drove on a few miles to Livingstone, once the capital of Rhodesia, a pleasant, green-bordered little town. Here we had fun buying curios. I was restricted by the fear of running short of money, as much as by having something else to carry. Bee was particularly captivated by a handsome silver jackal fur cape, but practicality got the better of her. A pushy shop owner presented me with bits of copper, smelted and un-smelted, which his workmen were chopping from two huge chunks of copper. What a lovely metal, first such a rich green, and when smelted glowing with bright bronze light. Wet, these colours gleamed still more vividly. I also saw the fruit of the ivory or Dom palm. The ivory kernel can be lathed into an attractive ball-shape, and ivory buttons and suchlike were made from them. In the local museum the highlight for me was Livingstone's notebook with a sketched map of the Falls made by himself. Apparently, he exclaimed on seeing the Falls for the first time, "They must have been gazed on by Angels in their flight!" Other artifacts included a fossilised elephant's molar tooth and some local devil costumes, uncanny and crude. A display of cave and rock paintings, some of them good in line were laid out on a greased surface. We were pleased with the few shillings' worth of sightseeing the car had cost us and drove back to the hotel for lunch.

Later Bee, Rue and I found a bus running past the Eastern Cataract, so, with more time on our hands we went to see it again. This time, we saw so vividly, the Falls' own wonderful rainbow, always there, created out of its misty atmosphere. Its reflection, with colours reversed, was an unforgettable unique sight. We bought a few souvenirs from locals sitting on the grass behind a row of carven images, whips, and pipes. I found a large locust bean pod. This is an emblem of good luck, each bright red bean in its black case neatly filling one of the pod's serried compartments where it had grown. Rue bought an elephant and a hippo carved out of Rhodesian teak, big heavy animals, strong simple work, which I took back for her when I caught the bus back by myself later. Bee and Rue, tall and slim in their white shorts above long sun-tanned legs, preferred to walk. How glorious they looked, and how I envied them. The days when I too walked with the confident stride of youth, attracting appraising glances as my right, were long past. Sadly, the skimpy white shorts would not have been permitted in my day. I certainly don't enjoy this aging process!

A bottle of Cabernet Sauvignon at dinner that night led us three women to a promising night's sleep. That night I greeted, after two years without it, my old friend, the stuffy but indispensable bedfellow, mosquito netting!

May 19 1943

After breakfast Rue, Bee and I took the trolley to the tiny river launch destined for Zambesito Kandahar Island and its monkeys and birds. Several young men in RAF uniforms were already on the launch. I was pleased that amidst their serious endeavours they managed to have this break. As we parted from the bank, an athletically built man with an attractive face, arriving late, came running toward us. I watched in amazement as he hesitated for one second on the bank and then leapt with agility on to the launch.

"Goodness, you took a chance!" I spoke.

"I'm so sorry for holding you up". He was not embarrassed and laughed. "My time keeping is atrocious!" We had noticed this man the day before, clothed in sou'wester and long enveloping mackintosh, setting out by himself to visit the Falls through the Rain Forest.

The Zambesi here was wide and very deep, the dense green of its banks overshadowed by trees. A hippopotamus near us in the water, just its incredible head showing, yawned colossally. The gargantuan red interior of its mouth only just clear of the water caught my eye and I could not imagine at first what it was. Many others were seen, singly or in groups. These enormous, vegetarian creatures seldom attack man, but when on land, they will savagely trample anyone who accidentally comes between them and their natural retreat, the water.

Kandahar Island itself was deeply jungled. We found some old ivory palm nuts on the ground and watched monkeys ribboning up and down the creepers and drooping tree branches. The launch official had given us a handful of nuts to feed them, but no matter how I coaxed, only one was confident enough to take from my hand. There was little to see, partly because we made too much noise. How impossible it was to get away by oneself. Time was too short, and the island was too small! To my disappointment I saw no birds as we wandered about the island's scrub-bordered, tree-roofed narrow paths, greeting and losing each other again. Before returning we walked through the greenery to an immense baobab tree with a mighty trunk. These great and aged trees are known locally as 'Kerra Matata' from the acid of their fruit, which mixed with water makes a pleasant and safe drink. In their huge, often hollow, trunks, water lay and could be stored, and sometimes local men were seen up in the trees letting cans down inside to collect it. Another less happy use of these vast interiors was as hiding places for live or dead men, or tombs. Back on the launch I saw grey heron in the rushes and weaver birds' nests. The RAF men, with many a jest, came in useful pushing our trolley back to the hotel.

A thrill after lunch was to be our walk through the Rain Forest to the Falls. The kind hotel people, knowing I was leaving that evening, had insisted that I should not miss the sight. So, wrapped in hotel mackintoshes and sou'westers, with shoes lent to me by the sweet office girl, we set off again. Leaving the trolley after a brief run, we began the walk through the trees. Enveloped in mackintoshes as we were, we found it rather hot and exhausting. Open glades led us along muddy, wet approaches to wonderful views of the Falls. Several times we were in what appeared to be heavy rainfall, but it was only the continuous spray and mist rising and descending from the precipitous sides of the chasm below. We met some people wearing no coats, their summer clothes soaking and their faces chilled and we felt sorry for them and thankful we were suitably protected.

Fine ferns grew in our path. I brought a tiny maidenhair root away with me, to the amusement of Bee, and she gave me some pretty pebbles with a laugh, to add to my luggage! Through the trees and falling mist we kept on catching marvellous visions of other aspects of the Falls, now and then walking out into the open right by them. It is impossible to describe their light, colour, and immensity. The rocks and stones were slippery, and, in some places, we had to step very carefully. We scrambled across wet, rounded rocks to see an imprint on one of them called 'Eve's footstep', to us, perilously near the Falls' roaring, boiling edge. There were cataracts and canyons right and left – Grand Canyon, Devil's Cataract – forty miles of canyons counting their curves and angles! The natives called the rising vapour of the Falls the 'Smoke that Thunders". They say it can be seen twenty-five miles away. "The end of the world" is the Arab's name for the Falls, - "Muaa i nunya". There were a few little islands just above the Falls and to go there in a hired canoe and sit almost on the brink of them was possible, I was told, when the Zambesi was very low. How sad I was that this, realistically was my first and last visit.

Back at the hotel I had to pack quickly and do a little washing, socks and stockings being caked in mud. William, my room boy, took it all away to dry. I expect he baked them as they returned surprisingly quickly, dry, and rather stiff!

The agile man who had jumped on to our launch had attached himself to us for a purpose. He had developed a poisoned heel, and requested that we 'Three Musketeers', as he called us, would dress it for him. We went to his hotel room and Rue provided the disinfectant and lint and a comedy sequence emerged. Bee and I sat facing each other on the sides of the twin beds and I saw a completely different aspect of the man! Our victim, at his suggestion, lying on the floor on his back between us. An awkward but adequate position! He had a good sense of humour, laughing harder even than us at the ridiculousness of his situation. He was good company although we learned nothing as to why he was at the hotel. I noticed that he had a very distinct circle of brown hair surrounding a bald patch like a monk on the very crown of his head only to be seen when looking directly down on it. We held his foot in a steely grip and bathed and bandaged his heel. There was an ill-timed knock on the door and his boy came in during the operation. He stood stock still, his eyes nearly popping out of his head before he retreated slamming the door in his haste. It must have been an odd sight. All he could see of his hotel guest was a foot, firmly held, sole up in four strange hands! Our patient rewarded us with ample gin and tonics!

Dinner at the hotel with Bee and Rue, who were staying on, was a difficult one for me. Once again, I was being torn away from an experience, and people whose company I was enjoying, to continue my solitary journey.

This was the pattern from my early childhood in County Durham, when I was torn from my family to go to boarding school at seven years old. I remember my mother crying, and begging my father to let me stay, but my father drove me himself to the teaching convent and told me that I was not to embarrass him in front of the nuns. My reputation for being a tom boy was already established and I assumed it was the explanation for my punishment. Always fascinated by whatever crossed my path, my natural curiosity was my downfall. If it meant climbing a tree or muddying my clothes to study whatever caught my eye, so be it! My younger sisters, Grace and Maude were, in comparison, quiet girls, but it did not save them and in their time, both sisters followed me. I remembered the blue lit corridor dormitory and the black robed nuns glidingly patrolling it. Holidays spent with my mother became what I lived for. I did make friendships among other girls, but as one of the few Protestants in the convent, I was confronted by subtle differences in the way we were treated. It was clear that I was not one that Jesus would mark out as chosen.

I was eleven when I was taken to the kindly Mother Superior to be told of the greatest loss I could imagine. She informed me that my parents had died in a pony and trap accident. I cried for my mother, not for my father. I remember my awkwardness at being held close against the black robe of the nun, and realising the warmth of her embrace, when I had always thought the nuns were untouchable and ethereal. I was told it was my responsibility to replace my mother for my sisters and to be a good example for them. Memories of those days are confused. We left the convent a few days later, and returned to our home now filled with neighbours and strangers. We were told that we were to live with uncles, my mother's brothers whom I had never met, in their house in distant Gloucestershire, hundreds of miles away. This astonishing chasm threw my previous years into indistinct shadow. Survival and looking after my sisters became my early life.

Nothing could lighten my mood as I hugged my dear Rue and Bee goodbye at the station. My solitary coupe seemed overwhelmingly empty as I leant out of the window to feel the spray falling as we passed over the bridge across the chasm. Every train and every passenger may receive, as Rhodes had long desired, this benediction in passing. It was a long, bleak night. The bed seemed hard, sleep far away, train creaking and limbs aching, but I cannot imagine that it ever stood a chance of being otherwise.

THREE

May 20 1943

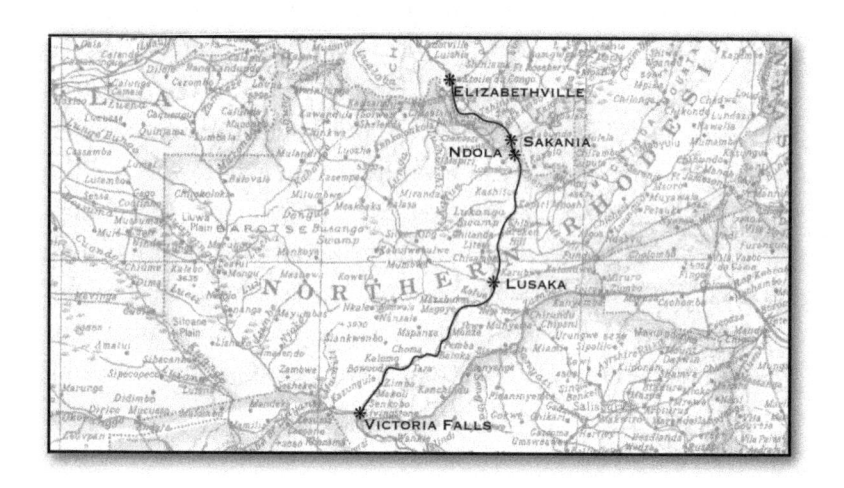

The conductor, his face screwed up against a bright shaft of sun, told me that when we reached Lusaka, I would have to change to a different coupe and share it.

He said "The train will be very full, Madam. We're sorry for the inconvenience." My mood was dark, and I only wanted my own company to consider this foolhardy enterprise I was engaged in.

"I wasn't told I had to share a coupe when I originally booked this stretch. Are you sure that will be necessary?" I smiled into his open, shining face. "I can see that you oversee the decisions round here, and I'd really appreciate it if you allowed me to stay where I am. You can see how much luggage I'm forced to carry with me!"

"Mrs Warmington Reed, I can see how troubling it is for you, but we do have an overcrowding problem. I don't know if I can help you."

I smiled trustingly again, "I am sure that it's in your power to let me stay. Of course, another conductor wouldn't be able to reorganise the coupes, but I can see that it wouldn't be so difficult for you." In both Southern and Northern Rhodesia, the locals have such pleasant, likeable faces. Wherever I met them they all seemed happily endowed with that quality of interest and friendliness I can feel, and happily return.

I continued, "You look to me something of a wizard!"

"Well, perhaps I am," he said laughing. "We'll see!"

How I hoped that I would not have to share my space. I had been so fortunate with Rue and Bee, who had lifted me out of myself without intruding. I did not rate my chances of finding easy going travellers like them again. I felt the need to reflect on my position and make some decisions as to how I was going to handle myself as I progressed overland.

That morning we went through the capital of Northern Rhodesia, Lusaka, and we did indeed have an influx of passengers. My wonderful wizard had fulfilled all my hopes in him, and I was able to stay alone in my coupe. I thanked him profusely as I pressed my mite on him in lieu of the more common currency of cigarettes.

I was becoming restless with the endless observation of the

landscape. My eyes were tired of the endless craning to see birds. I had been told to look out for grey and purple herons, hoopoes, bulbuls, hawks, ring doves and sea eagles, all to be spotted with binoculars, time, and experience, none of which I had. I tried to make a start on the books I had been lent, Wodehouse's 'Lord Emsworth', and 'African Handbook and Travellers Guide' by Otto Martens and Dr Karstedt, but neither appealed to me.

My dear Teddy was still not aware that I was making this journey. We had written lengthily to each other over the two years. I always enjoyed the flow and cursive beauty of Teddy's handwriting which put my scrawl to shame. Everything that he did was done with care and consideration, whereas my achievements always looked as if there was an element of having been taken by surprise! My strengths were different to his. Whatever Teddy took on he worked at methodically whereas I liked to think I was more intuitive and open to thinking outside the box. If his cavalier attitude to finance was irresponsible and tripped me up, the beautiful objects that filled our lives gave me pleasure too. I would be too cautious to indulge myself like he did. Often, I had to rescue our resources with ingenuity and hard work. In the long run we made a balanced team.

We had discussed my return, but with Egypt a field of war until now, travelling overland had clearly not been possible. With the threat of submarines, the long journey by sea to Haifa was also out of the question. In his letters Teddy always said how much he missed me, but it is easy to get used to any lifestyle. After two years, my life in Cape Town had become the normal one, why should I expect it to be any different for my husband? There was danger to our marriage, just in that. I had now been assured by the railway people that they understood the conflict in Egypt was over. I hoped so! I had deliberately kept Teddy in the dark because I knew that he would have tried to dissuade me. My husband in a temper was not to be trifled with, and I knew that he would not be happy that I had taken this decision on my own. He would think it was premature to travel and would see all the practical reasons for not risking it. At some point he would have to be warned, but not yet.

At Ndola we had two or three hours' wait, for no explicable reason, and whilst I was idly glancing down the platform which lazed in the midday torpor, I was astonished to see the man with the poisoned heel from Niagara Falls on the platform. I blinked and looked again. It was him, without a doubt. I had no idea what he was doing there. I couldn't imagine why he hadn't told me that he was on the same train. I watched him covertly, not wanting to embarrass either of us should he become aware of my gaze. His heel appeared to have made an astonishing recovery and he hung around the excuse of a platform until a black car swirled to a stop in a cloud of dust, whereon he hopped in with alacrity and was driven off. I was totally baffled, but finally assumed that he must have been involved with some sort of war work. I had never learned his name.

At Sakania, a long wait was made easier by an excellent Portuguese dinner in the dining coach. Then immigration and customs people brought three forms to be filled in. Nobody so far had wanted to inspect my luggage. They took my passport away despite my objecting to such high-handed procedure, promising to return it next day. It was late evening before we moved off again and I could settle to sleep.

May 21 1943

Elizabethville in the Belgian Congo was reached punctually next morning. My passport had been duly returned and I was met by a young, polite, and very tall railway representative, Monsieur Guislaine of Belge Maritime. He walked with me the little distance to the hotel. The young porters trailed behind in the gathering heat carrying my trunk and luggage. The cool sophistication of the interior of the hotel was a welcome refuge, but my relief was short lived. Something had gone wrong with my accommodation, and we were told that the only room available to me was in the annex, at least a quarter of a mile away, and that would have to be shared with two American ladies. I was annoyed, and Monsieur Guislaine was furious.

I had insisted that my trunk was stored in the hotel but in the steadily increasing heat of the day, with the poor boys carrying most of my heavy luggage, we walked over to the annex, through an overgrown courtyard and up an outside staircase. The annex had evidently been the upper part of an ancient hotel, and the allocated room was sparsely furnished, housing two beds, two chairs, one dressing table, one wardrobe and one washstand. How were three ladies supposed to share two beds! An old man with shuffling gait and only one tooth was in attendance!

Back we went to the hotel, Monsieur Guislaine and me carrying oddments of the lighter luggage to re-register a strong protest. I was staying three nights here; they could only promise me a room in the hotel from the next day.

Monsieur Guislaine apologetically took me to his offices to regroup with refreshments. He was responsible for me as Belge Maritime represent South African Railways here. A charming Major, thin faced and long of jaw was relaxing there and immediately offered me his room in the hotel as, unbeknown to the staff he was leaving at midday. We returned to reception once again, my arm firmly through the Major's as he told them he was giving his room to me. To his amazement the receptionist said she knew he was leaving and had already relet his room! Had I not felt so drained of energy I might have appreciated the French farce this was turning into! I was preparing to withdraw when she suddenly asked my name again.

On hearing it she exclaimed "Oh yes! I had your name wrong! I didn't understand it was you!" She told me that a room was available in the hotel for tonight, and a very good one indeed was promised for the following two nights! I could have kissed her!

The kind Monsieur Guislaine, sensing my exhaustion, left me in the foyer to return to the discarded annex with a collection of porters and brought back my luggage. It was intensely hot by then and I watched the line of these immature but plucky lads staggering along with such burdens and felt intensely guilty. Settled in my room at last, my next visitor was Monsieur Guislaine's friend Dr Cabou. Big, lion-maned, lion-hearted, the doctor's presence filled whatever room he was in. He insisted on driving me to the Immigration office to have my passport inspected and then round the town in his car.

The streets of Elizabethville were spacious and mostly level; the buildings uncramped with plenty of greenery growing in the spaces between them. We visited the cathedral, a fine building with much of the roof lined with copper, done before the war. We met a long procession of little girls rehearsing their march for a big review on Sunday to celebrate the victory of Tunisia. Summer and its rainfall had just ended and could account for the noticeably pale faces of the European children and adults here.

Finally, we visited the museum, Dr Cabou's museum, his child, created by him and grown into a very important part of life here. The best native material had been discovered and displayed and was now so valuable a collection that the Government was talking of taking it over and rehousing it. I saw fine works of basket, wood, and leather. A complete leopard-man's outfit, part of it in bark cloth, barbarously decorated in circles, with horrid little knives that were carried behind the ears. The leopard-like claws were finished off like gloves to be drawn over the hands. Remembering tales of terrorism by leopard-men, it made me shiver in sympathy with the Africans.

One of the most attractive collections was that of musical instruments; especially the small native 'piano' called the "Hazana", the metal prongs lying flat but raised from the slab of wood below. I had bought a diminutive one when passing through Bulawayo. There were also drums of all kinds and xylophones. These were big, grown-up instruments and if an empty box was attached underneath more volume was obtained. This increase in volume happened with drums too. My host showed me very long wooden drums with a hole slit lengthways that, when beaten alternately on the two sides with sticks, created two totally different sounds. These drums produced a rousing tingle and was said to have a hypnotic effect on its audience.

Dr Cabou could play all these instruments and bewitched me by playing on the pipes of Pan. He was certainly multi-talented being able to speak thirty-two languages including rusty Chinese and Japanese. I started to feel weary in his presence despite my interest and was happy to be returned to the hotel for lunch and a siesta.

That evening Dr Cabou and his corpulent wife took me for a drive to see the colossal copper-smelting plant, with its high chimney towering above the landscape. By its side was a cone-shaped hill entirely composed of slag, still rich in copper particles. On its peak a great "V" sign, illuminated at night, was visible over an immense distance. We watched the fires burning and the rivulets of lovely molten copper flowing out. It was hypnotising in the dark.

Dr Cabou explained, "This is the highest chimney in Africa. The second highest in the world we're told. The workers keep this up in day and night shifts non-stop and we're very proud of our war effort. This is the Allies greatest source of copper."

"I love the Victory sign. I imagine it must be impossible to imagine the devastation in Europe and the world, when surrounded by such a beautiful place to live."

We were driving along the so-called Lido by the river and near the bathing pools, through green and pretty avenues covered with acacia, bougainvillea, yellow jacaranda, and poinsettias.

Madam Cabou smiled "Everything is arranged for the benefit of people connected with the smelting plant. We really look after the large number of employees who work here. They own or rent pretty houses with gardens attached and have their own swimming pools, schools, clinics, and shops. There's great competition from Africans outside the Katanga district of the Belgian Congo to come and work in Elizabethville."

"If they are capable, they've a good chance of advancing in their field of work. They can become engineers and chemists. A real interest is taken in them and their children's future welfare." Dr Cabou added.

"This is so encouraging. I've witnessed extreme poverty in urban South Africa, and they could follow your example."

I was not being honest. I had heard the horror story of the miners' rally held here in the football stadium in '41. Not so long ago! It had got out of hand and led to police opening fire and killing numerous protesters. Certainly, the indigenous people I saw looked sleek, and happy in their clothes of bright colours. Two young men of splendid carriage and physique were walking by accompanying a strapping girl, handsome, and amply proportioned. Her gay dress cut high and slipping slightly from one shapely rounded shoulder made an arresting picture. But, surely, there were tensions here that my hosts would not acknowledge.

Madam Cabou positively beamed with pride. "They have everything they want. The houses are carefully planned with adequate accommodation for water, cooking stoves and sanitary arrangements. Obviously, everything is run by Europeans."

Dr Cabou cut in. "We make sure that the workers carry the responsibility of choosing their own inspectors who work under European supervision."

I noted that my comment about the unreality of war in such surroundings, had not been addressed. Perhaps concentrating on a future for their local people was the only positive thing that Dr and Madam Cabou felt they could do in this frightening world.

"I congratulate you. It's important, isn't it, to do something in your life that you hope will make a difference to those you leave behind." I surprised myself.

"I couldn't agree more." Madam Cabou enthused. "We like to think we're making a difference. Can I ask if you've done that? Created something you are proud of, in your life so far?"

I hesitated "My husband and I designed and built our own Arts and Crafts movement house which I hope will continue to be enjoyed by others, but I don't think that counts." I paused, "I wrote and published a book once, to help women."

"Tell me more!"

"I was living in the village of Painswick, in England, and was surprised at how ignorant the local girls were about any facts of life. I was friends with the local Doctor, and he asked me to give talks to them in the village hall. Writing the book was a natural progression from there, although I never imagined that it had such a strong future. 'Women and Marriage' it was called, under the pseudonym of Margaret Stephens. Teddy was rather alarmed at me disclosing any marital secrets, so he was insistent on the pen name! I'm rather embarrassed about having published the book."

"Why would you say that?"

"I was only thirty-one years old, with daughters of six and three! Looking back, I wonder why I thought I had the authority! I've always written poetry for myself, but this was a different matter and required a lot of research! Teddy was somewhat embarrassed by the whole endeavour."

"Men can be such children! I would be fascinated to read your book." Madame Cabou smiled at me.

"I could ask the publishers to send you a copy. It's still very much in circulation and seems to have become something of a textbook for the medical profession, which is a huge surprise to me. I imagine it just indicates that there was a need for it."

'How fascinating! Thank you so much. We would love you to do that." I saw Dr Cabou smiling fondly at his wife.

On returning to the hotel, exhausted from the heat, the decision to send the wire to Teddy about my intentions, was shelved once again. My nightly dose of five grains of quinine as protection against malaria made my head spin. I had taken them since leaving Bulawayo with no such reaction but that evening I decided to skip dinner and have an early night.

May 22 1943

The taxi drive to call on the British Consul, and then the South African one, went well. I am unsure of the purpose of these visits but just followed my itinerary instructions. In those troubled times, I was sure the Consuls had far more important events to occupy their minds. Honour satisfied I spent the morning grudgingly having my hair shampooed in a local salon. The trouble with having long hair is that it is such an effort to have it coiffured up. In that sticky heat it really did drive me to despair. If it was not for Teddy's admiration for my tresses, I would have had them all cut off years ago!

Back at the hotel I finally composed the difficult wire to

Teddy to tell him that I was on my way. I had learned to always present him with a fait accompli so that I was not swayed by his arguments. Teddy always assumed that he knew best, and I had learned over the years just to make my own decisions! I was running late by the time I had worked out the wording and took a gruelling walk to the post office only to find it shut! The heat was oppressive, and the town lay torpid in it. I sought refuge in Monsieur Guislaine's office and asked him to arrange for an advance of money. I needed francs instead of tickets, for meals and hotels as far as Kingoma, which he supplied me with, as well as giving me transport-and-bedding tickets.

I asked him about my trunk which I had reason to be anxious about. I was worried about it on many counts. Despite my careful insulation, my trunk's contents might be damaged by the extreme heat, extreme dryness, or humidity. I was also concerned that ignorant officials might damage its contents in their searches, or even worse, that knowing persons might recognise its content's value and deliberately remove it. Informing my husband that his prize possession was lost or damaged en route did not bear thinking about. I had left it at the station on my arrival, and Monsieur Guislaine leapt to his feet immediately to go to the customs office by the station. He did sometimes remind me of a nervous colt, or perhaps a giraffe due to his height! I wondered if this was his normal mode of behaviour or whether I was a novelty to him in a normally eventless life. The disheartened young man returned to tell me that the office was closed but that the trunk would still have to be opened there for inspection. He assured me that there was no need to worry and that he personally would collect the key early on Monday morning for the inspection. He told me he was doing his best to ensure that I would have a coupe on my own for the ongoing journey. I think everyone should have at least one Monsieur Guislaine in their lives!

It was good to be in the cool of my room again. I allowed myself to lie on the bed and think about my children, my daughters, all three independent women now with strong personalities. I had not told any of them that I had undertaken this journey and I considered what their response would have been.

Joy, my oldest would be full of concern and would fuss, creating difficulties out of ineffectual kindness. It amazed me that she could be such a disorganised flapper at home, but the minute she stepped onto her hospital wards, she became a person of calm efficiency. It was some sort of miracle. We had always had a complicated relationship. She adored her father who was driven mad by her kindly intentions and seemingly she could never please him. Teddy had seen off her only serious suitor. Now I wonder if Joy's chance to marry is past, the war has killed too many of our young men. Her last letter told me she had taken in a lame duck as a flat mate, a woman called Mary who had been buried for three days in a bombed house. I suspect that her caring needs would be channelled in that direction now. London has not seen the last of the bombings and I knew Joy would stick to her post no matter what.

Felicity, our 'mistake' baby, was also in London in the thick of it. At twenty-six she was no longer a baby. She would see this trek of mine as the interesting challenge it obviously was. I got the feeling from her letters that she views being stuck in central London in the war as an adventure. Although the drawing office where she was working was dull, driving ambulances gave her the excitement she always seemed to crave. I imagined she was good at it too, always strong, and decisive. I preferred not to think about the possibility of them suffering hurt or worse. That way lay madness.

This applied even more to my middle daughter, Ronny. She was the one most like her father with his temper and his fearlessness. The last letter I had from her from the Philippines, carried the news that she and Pat were having a baby, my first grandchild! But that was before Christmas '41! It was a lovely letter full of positive hopes and looking forward to Christmas. The baby had been due in March. Teddy and I received the news of the Japanese invasion of the islands with horror and had heard not a word of them since then, despite endlessly badgering the Red Cross for news. I could only pray that she, her baby, and Pat were safely in a prisoner of war camp and being treated well. I tried not to think about it. To change my mood, I roused myself in the cooler temperature of late afternoon and walked into the town to see the preparations for tomorrow's ceremony.

Everyone appeared to be out in the streets, hanging flags and erecting coloured street markers and stands overlooking the main thoroughfare. Women were doing most of the organisation and the air of gay anticipation for the Review bought a smile to my face. A group of men all dressed in dazzling white against their dark skin played a game in the street and I stopped to watch. I was informed that it was a Belgian or Walloon game called 'Muurke Klop', something like tennis but hands are used instead of racquets. People cheered with great enthusiasm and there was a lot of barracking from the side lines!

That evening at the hotel our dinner was served against the background of a small orchestra playing. They had managed to produce a double bass, a cello, two violins and a piano in honour of the next day. I did enjoy it and had certainly heard worse! Teddy and I had met at the Leipzig Conservatoire in Germany where he studied violin and I the piano. Music was core to our marriage, an important aspect of our lives together. We played well together, each intuiting the mood and pace of the other and it gave us enormous pleasure.

FOUR

May 23 1943

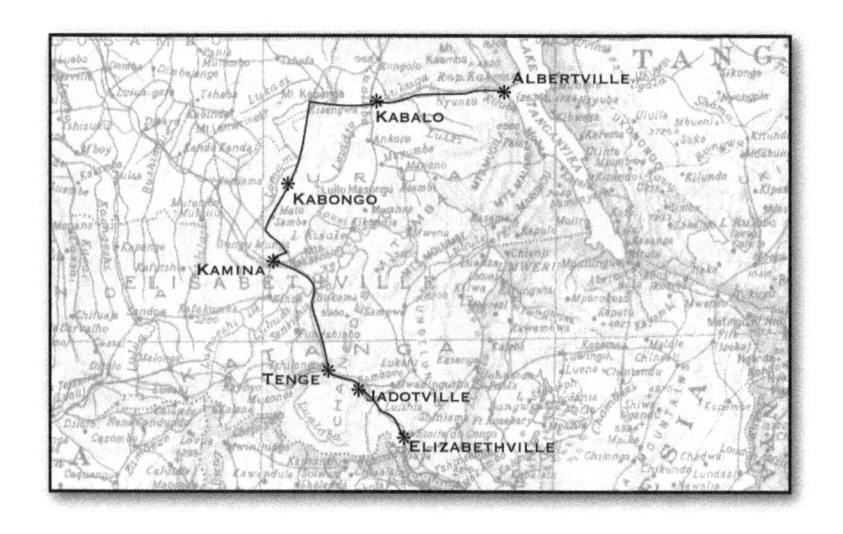

A gala day indeed with the world and his wife in their very best. The hotel had organised for their guests to watch the Review from the grandstand, but I preferred to watch at closer quarters at the edge of the tree-shaded streets. Despite raised eyebrows, I was ushered to the edge of a broad, shaded pavement, with great courtesy. This great Review, though requiring an immense amount of hard work, was considered worthwhile as propaganda as well as giving the community something enjoyable to focus on in these dark days.

It was expertly staged; the sapphire skies, shades of palm and acacia, wide roads, and broad clean pavements. Europeans were mainly on our side of the road, and masses of picturesquely dressed, smiling local people on the other, their children being pushed under the guard ropes to get a better view. Smart policemen, alive to their dignity and importance, kept order easily among the eager crowds, primarily of women and children, their menfolk mostly taking part in the procession. Many of these women had fine faces and some of the girls were a delight to behold. Often, they let their frocks slip off one or both of their splendidly moulded ebony shoulders to the armpits where they were tightly secured. What lovely figures some of them had! The beautifully toned legs of the men made me wish I were a sculptor. Alas, my talent was solely in the musical field but Teddy with his passion for photography would have been having a field day. The young women I was studying were aware of the picture they were presenting, and I reflected on how my age had forcibly withdrawn me from the competitive aspect of our biological natures. Where once I expected male attention, I had now become invisible however attractively I presented myself. I had to rely on charm for attention and be aware that younger women had the biological advantage. The tragedy occurred when men actively appreciated beautiful young forms and did not understand the boundaries. My dear Teddy could not be totally relied upon to take his appreciation of the female at a distance, which made my role as wife more complicated than it needed to be.

The long march past progressed, made up of schools, miners, old warriors, and every section of the populace. Naturally the military who remained in Elizabethville dominated the scene. I was standing next to a sweet Belgian family. The father was the only one to speak English, and the mother was pretty. Their well-behaved sons of nine and five were quiet and polite, but my attention was glued to a fascinating pet monkey sitting on the older boy's shoulder. It was tied by its waist and a long chain to the boy's wrist, and the sons took it in turns to control him. The monkey had a white sided nose and was called Pankashy, after Pan meaning flour or bread. I was amazed at how secure the monkey was, surrounded by so much activity and noise.

The father was keen to practise his English "The professional bands are away in Egypt with the regular troops, but these local bands are wonderful, don't you think?" I agreed wholeheartedly.

"Our oldest son is in the scout group, and they will be coming soon. They've been practising marching for weeks! I see you have nothing to sit on. You'd be welcome to use this spare stool we brought for when he finishes."

I was grateful as there were still a great many troops to pass, smart and highly disciplined, mostly with white officers. Great numbers of school children in neat lines marched past, martially erect and serious faced, a black section, a white one, then more black sections, all presenting a harmoniously blended pattern. Even the rows of distracted tiny tots had on clean white uniform, belted and very short. All marchers had bare feet, except officers, teachers, nuns, and white folk generally. We cheered loudly for the keen and correct boy scouts, followed by university lads in their robes. Old soldiers of all origins, proudly wearing their decorations received the warmest applause of all.

The procession went on for considerably longer than I had imagined, and I was starting to wilt. The family were most comfortable speaking French, so my fluidity in that language was getting exercised.

Fifty miners in starched blue overalls marched past pulling what turned out to be an immense open chariot. More were pushing it from behind. A mass of the richest, loveliest, un-smelted and smelted copper in two gleaming heaps were displayed on the upper and lower tier. Green and gold-bronze, its reflected sparkling lights from the gleaming sun and passing tree shades fell across us all. For passing minutes, we watchers were transported to fairy land, far from the heat, dust, and uncertainty of central Africa. Reality then reappeared when hundreds of other miners marched past, each carrying his own working weapon, axe, mallet, irons, crowbars, and other tools. It struck me how ugly all these tools could become if turned to fierce occasions. I remembered the bloodshed spilt here in the past.

It was strange to think that my father loosely belonged to that fraternity, as on my birth certificate it said he was a mining engineer. His name was Samuel Taylor Jones. I have a photograph of him and my mother on their wedding day and to my eyes, the image appears to lack the feeling of celebration I would like. I have no idea when my father died, but it was not when I was eleven, as I had been informed. My sisters and I were supposedly orphans, taken into the care of two of my mother's brothers who gave us a different way of life. But we were not orphans. I only learned of this fabrication in the days leading up to my own wedding, when my uncles thought I was old enough to understand. It was they who considered my father not suitable to parent their nieces and claimed us. He was rumoured to be an alcoholic, and certainly had made no attempts to see us that I knew of. I was upset and confused and toyed with the idea of returning to County Durham to try to trace him, but wedding plans were galloping ahead, and I allowed it to take a back seat. Since then, I have been haunted with questions. Did my parents love each other, as she obviously married 'out of the family'? Were there problems between them? I remembered tensions and being sent away to boarding school at an age when I would never have sent my own daughters. Samuel Taylor Jones, my father the mining engineer, was still an enigma to me.

The marchers must have been melting with the fierce heat of the parade and I was thankful I had made the decision to stay under the tree lined shade. It was a much bigger, better show than I had anticipated. I was told there were five hundred or so white people living here and forty thousand native Africans; the numbers varied greatly owing to the ravages of tropical diseases and above all, the War.

The Belgian family invited me to join them to watch a football match after a picnic lunch. It was generous of them, but the heat was terrific, and I wanted to retreat to the cool hotel.

Walking back through a garden park, bright with flowers and green lawns, the brilliant red of the poinsettias clashed with pink and white frangipani and scented the air against the background of green and golden cassia. Everything grew so luxuriously and everywhere the lacey foliage of fine waving acacia and gay jacaranda sprayed the sunlight.

The evening was spent writing letters to my sister Maude, and my daughters Joy and Felicity, not knowing when these would be delivered. I finished by writing to Mr Lambert of the High Commissioners Office in Cape Town for any news via the International Red Cross of Ronny in the Philippines. He was probably fed up with hearing from me, but I wanted him to know my change of address in case they learned something of her whereabouts. It was the least that I could do to relieve my anxiety.

May 24 1943

Dr Cabou's booming voice told me it was time to leave just as I was finishing my breakfast coffee. The hotel porters bundled my luggage into his car which I squeezed into; Madame Cabou already ensconced. There was no sign of Monsieur Guislaine, so we started for the station.

Leaving Madame on the platform to guard the luggage, we drove off to collect my trunk from customs a little way off. The customs officer had already agreed with Monsieur Guislaine to open half an hour earlier than normal so that I would not miss the train. Dr Cabou had only to explain, and the porters hurried about and heaved the trunk into the car without it being opened! I had nothing to declare at all. The Dr is a power in the land. Then Monsieur Guislaine arrived, panting on his bicycle full of apologies for missing me and we all hastened back to the platform. I was impressed to see how quickly and effectively Dr Cabou worked. He seems to know exactly how everything should be done. Madame Cabou gave me some deliciously juicy tangerines, and an informative book on African animals. As the train was pulling out, we shook hands warmly, and further down the platform my hero Monsieur Guislaine was waiting for a final handshake. Lucky me to have such a happy send-off!

The charming French woman I met in the observation coupe had two sons travelling with her. She was dressed chicly in co-ordinating purple and introduced herself, and her sons Jeanot, aged twelve, who unhappily had just had his tonsils out and his brother Daniel, aged fourteen. Madame Hyde had an abundance of grapes with her, and I exchanged some of my tangerines for them. I was able to contribute to Jeanot some of the good, boiled sweets my old friends had given me before I left Cape Town. I was astonished at how long ago that seemed! My French and I were renewing our old acquaintance with more ease, although Madame's husband was English, and the boys were bilingual.

The lady's husband, who was meeting her in Kamina, was the Agronomic Administrator in Ruanda-Urundi district, northeast of the lake. They would accompany me to Kigoma, where they would leave me to go by steamer to Usumbara and then to their second home in Costermanville on Lake Kivu where their boys are at school. Their home proper was at Kitega.

We spent much of the time passing through tangles of jungle, mostly of small trees, scrub, low hills, and innumerable high, red-earthed anthills. What great pests those white ants were hereabouts. They and human beings waged incessant war on each other, but the soil of their upright rounded abodes was most fertile and could also be made into good bricks. Some of the nest columns must have reached twenty or thirty feet high. I caught a glimpse of a little shepherdess on top of one, high above her browsing flock and wondered how she had arrived there. I had always disliked ants, despite their obvious group intelligence. It was the queen ant with her enormous balloon-like laying organ, that made them so repulsive to me. That and their bite which I have suffered from many times!

The time passed pleasantly enough, as the train stopped at several little stations, Chitembwe, Luishia and Kapolowe among others all basking and grilling in the sun, but always with greenery around and often brilliantly flowering shrubs. At Jadotville we all lunched together in the dining car which had been unexpectedly attached to our train.

After Katamonda station, we passed through forests, many of the trees with long bare branches, and waving green topknots of leaves, two or three feet in length. Some had horizontally interlaced boughs like green ceilings. Further on there was another variety of high tree, also bare except for crimson masses of lovely feathery leaves at the top. By the much-burnt scrub alongside the train, many varieties of very tall, beautiful grasses were growing, waving, and whispering in eddies of breeze.

We passed Luambo station, neatly kept. Among the leaves of a high clematis, rampant and green, I saw one perfect, giant, white flower had just opened.

In the early afternoon we reached Malungwishi. Daniel and Jeanot pointed out local boys selling small eggs, hens' apparently, although I thought they were pigeons', and little green tomatoes. I experienced a pang for my native Cotswold countryside which had absolutely nothing in common with this arid and harsh land of conflict, and I wondered if I would ever see it again. To accentuate this remoteness, on the platform I saw an indigenous man standing stock still by a brilliantly flowering hibiscus. He wore a spotless white suit and despite his colour had an entirely English-looking face.

At Mutaka station, many locals were on the platform and one white man with the usual topee. The peace of the silenced engines was broken by the continuous whine of a spoilt child next door. We passed much burnt grassland and a few trees, bare of leaves, rose out of it like shipwrecked masts. There was no sign of animal life, frightened off by the noise of our passing train. The villagers here, the women especially, seemed of a very fine type, virile, dignified, and pleasant faced.

Autumn tints abounded and more euphorbia trees. I caught

sight of a stretch of violet earth, irises perhaps, like swathes of some parts of the Loire sands at sunset. A marvellous colour! Low hills were succeeded by more open country. Then the railway cut through high ground. Vertical banks on each side screened the view, though some little rifts in them revealed patches of sown land, chiefly poor-looking maize. Then a strange screen of immense dimensions made of thatch interlaced with reeds appeared on our right side up the hillside. Madame and I couldn't understand it. A viaduct bridge was behind it and water flowed below.

At Tenge, all four of us took the opportunity to walk along the platform to the goods van attached, to inspect the Toulouse geese and white ducks the family had just bought.

"I'm please to see how well they're being looked after." Madame said

"They're certainly fine birds. During the Great War I ran a chicken farm from home in the Cotswolds with about a thousand laying birds, White Wyandottes. We sent the eggs to London. I bred ducks too. My husband was away a lot. My daughters were about ten and seven, and they always collected the hens' eggs for me." I remembered how seriously Joy used to take this task, sending Ronny in to get dirty and pick up the eggs while holding out her skirt for them to be placed in. Despite being offered more practical containers, this skirt holding became a ritual with the two little girls even if it meant several journeys into the kitchen. The hens could not outsmart my daughters who knew all their hiding places. I smiled at the recollection of their solemn morning faces.

Jeanot asked, "Which did you like best, hens, or ducks?"

"Ducks, without a doubt. My two favourites were called

Painswick Nancy and Painswick Fancy, after the village where we lived. I was very proud of them. Have you been to England?"

"No, but Papa says we'll all go to visit my English grandparents one day, when the war is over." Jeanot was a natural chatterbox, despite his very sore throat. He persevered, "I love to ride. Do you?"

"As a matter of fact, I do love riding. I started riding when I was about twelve in England and have always owned ponies and horses, since then. I think I enjoyed it most in hot countries like Palestine. You may find this strange, but I enjoy riding side saddle when I get the chance."

"Oh, I don't think I could do that! Mama doesn't ride, but we ride everywhere, and you could come and ride with us if you came to stay."

Madame smiled at me over her son's head. I felt as if I had finally passed some sort of assessment as she leaned over to suggest. "Mrs Warmington Reed, I have an offer to make you that would make one section of your journey much more pleasant, I'm sure. My husband is meeting us at Kamina to take us on by road to Kigoma where we board the steamer to take us to our home in Usumbara. We'll be in a convoy of our own and we'll have ample space for you and your luggage to do that section with us."

"What a generous offer," I cried, "But you haven't seen the amount of luggage I'm transporting with me. Much as I would love to join your company, my schedule is very tight."

Daniel cut in, "Our father has just bought six new horses, young ones. They are Nigerian. He's collecting them when he meets us at Kamina. We're lucky that we live in mountain country as there aren't any tsetse flies so high up. You are welcome to stay." I smiled at Daniel's generous hospitality and wondered if his father would be so welcoming of strangers.

But Madame persisted, "Your schedule wouldn't be affected

I assure you, and it would save you a particularly unpleasant experience. Trust me. I would not dream of undertaking the section you are intending to by public transport. Once was enough. Please join us."

After assurances I gave in to their kindness and counted myself lucky in my change in fortune.

We were passing through a vast plain, stretching for miles on either side as far as the eye could see. Madame told me of the quantity of cattle breeding here and as we passed the little station of Bianos we saw the great pens connected to the railway line for the easy entraining of stock.

After dinner was served at the following little station, it was not quite dark and our gang of four walked up and down the platform to stretch our legs. A bunch of English officers were doing the same thing. I would have loved to talk to them but imagined that they would have little they would be allowed to tell me on a siding in central Africa.

Looking up into the sky I saw my old friend the Great Bear! He had been missing from my life for over two years. How welcoming it was to see shining familiar stars from my past, and yet also see in the blue-black immensity of an African night, my South African acquaintance, the Southern Cross. I felt choked when I remembered my nightly ritual of going out onto my balcony to find it in the Milky Way above me.

May 25 1943

I was gasping for air, bolt upright in the berth, convinced that Ronny was in desperate need of me. Totally shredded and exposed, my fear for my middle child lay on my chest like a living presence. Wide eyed, it took me a moment to understand that I was in a railway coupe in central Africa, totally out of reach of everyone who knew and loved me. Not only was I beyond help, but I was also totally unable to help anyone I loved, and at this moment that meant my daughter Ronny, somewhere in a Japanese prisoner of war camp. Something in my dreams had triggered the suddenness of my fear, normally kept so closely wrapped and impenetrable. As my breathing normalised, so did my brain. I had obviously been deeply connected to these natural anxieties, and some deep-seated dream had broken through my normally carefully monitored emotions. Controlling anxieties had been vital to my survival as a child, so it was second nature, and I rarely allowed my guard down.

I knew the roots of my behaviour, brought about by the seismic change in my young life. The death of my lovely warm mother changed my life overnight. Immediately my sisters Grace and Maude, aged nine and seven became my responsibility, as I had to become mother to them. Supressing my emotions to look after theirs became part of my emotional habit. Memories of that time were confused. Returning home, I remember people I had never met before intruding into our home at Durham. We were taken away to stay with a kind neighbour without a backward glance. I couldn't understand it. We three girls were in shock, and very frightened. Within a couple of days, two tall, unknown uncles made an appearance and despite efforts to shield us, I remember raised voices and emotional tears. Grace, Maude, and I were taken to live with these uncles in a part of the country that was far away from our home, our schools, our friends and the only life we knew. My mother's funeral from Vale House, Stroud was a vague memory of black carriages pulled by black horses tossing their heads, silent crowds dressed in black and trying not to fidget. I was told that my mother would have wanted us to be good and do as we were told, and we were lucky that these uncles would give us a home.

I missed my mother enormously. She rapidly became a shadow for Grace and Maude, and they would get upset when I fiercely tried to get them to remember her. It seemed that I was alone recalling her face, her smile, and her attempt to give us a good life despite an atmosphere of anxieties. I tried to hang onto that. She had been a constant for me in a way that my father never was. A shadowy figure at best, I forgot him quickly. Certainly, my new family talked about my mother with love and sadness, but my father was a carefully managed blank. Uncle Henry and Uncle Frank meant well without a doubt and we three orphans were lucky in the support we received. The legacy I was left with was an inability to be moderate in my emotions, or perhaps I was always like that. As my recent nightmare showed, I was either determinedly in control of my emotions or completely exposed and raw.

It took time to go through the routine of my toiletries to regain my self-control, so I was ready when, as dawn lifted, our train reached the pleasant station of Kamina where it terminated.

Under an avenue of high trees, we walked to the simple little hotel nearby for breakfast. Madame's husband was a big smiling man, totally attentive to his sons' enthusiasms, to the detriment of his wife, in my opinion. I noticed how she deferred to his judgement in all things, whereas I had found her to be knowledgeable and a good companion in the last twenty-four hours. The boys left us after a pleasant breakfast of good white bread, eggs, butter, and coffee, before Mr Hyde turned to his wife.

He boomed, "Dear girl, I'm awfully stuck as the horses haven't arrived here yet."

"But I thought it was all arranged?"

"Yes, but the wretched men are walking them here! What can you do! It's so typically inconsiderate! I won't be able to join you!"

I stared at Madame's blanching face! She appeared completely overcome and close to tears. "But you promised that I could travel in the car with you. I saw the convoy parked outside!"

He continued unapologetically, "I simply must see that the horses are looked after correctly. They're far too valuable to leave to the locals. I'm sorry to disappoint you but, as they haven't arrived, it's impossible to join you. I'll catch up with you at home. Buck up my dear. I'm sure that the boys will find it an adventure. Good for character building! Can you order me another coffee, while I have a word with the groom?" He left the room and I turned to my distraught companion.

"Are you alright?"

Her voice shook, "You've no idea what's ahead of us! My husband promised he would travel with us. He knew just how tough it would be. This is not a journey to be undertaken by public transport, especially at this time of year! I would never have agreed to this if I'd known." I had never had an option other than public transport, so perhaps I was not as sympathetic as I could have been.

After breakfast we oversaw the packing of our luggage partly into the cars which were now carrying us on and partly into an immense motor van. There was a convoy of five or six carloads to undertake our long trek of three hundred miles to Kabalo where we would once again take the train as far as Albertville. Madame was very quiet, but the boys were excited. I made sure that I sat together with them on this next part of their journey.

The heat was tremendous and after travelling fast along the straight red road, the floor of the car became extremely hot. Nobody seemed to mind except me, and I tried to keep my feet off the floor but there was only 'mid-air' to rest them on and that became very tiring. Jungle and scrub came down either side of us, right to the road, and I wondered in how short a time they would join hands and obliterate our track, if continual work was not spent on them. Easy to talk of clearing bush or jungle to keep roads open yet how extremely laborious and unceasing such work must be to achieve.

We stopped two or three times to stretch our legs. Cicadas were buzzing loudly around us, the volume much greater than I had experienced in Palestine. With such heavy, luxuriant growth of vegetation in this humid heat, insect and all kinds of animal life increase in size for the same reasons; food, warmth, and space to grow. I considered that likewise most South African men I had encountered had been big men, unlike some of the British lads in the convoys calling at Cape Town, who were pale, undernourished, undersize city dwellers. These dear lads were still brim-full of mettle and cheery kindness despite immense discomfort and deep homesickness. I was proud of the endurance, staying power and pride of spirit, war-crippled Britain exuded.

As we pushed through dense jungle or slid through open cultivated plots, very few birds piped and twittered. We were told there were elephant in the neighbourhood and that rare animal, the okapi, but we saw none. Doubtless we travelled too noisily and too fast so that every living animal was scared away. How I wished to stop and stay quiet, but it was impossible. We passed cotton growing, fine palms, red fertile earth, and high anthills like landmarks. Sometimes our Lilliputian red road was almost hidden at its edges in the tall strong elephant grass and rampaging jungle which only seemed to pause above us, before joining its green fingers across and wiping it out. No wonder that its inhabitants should be large creatures with impenetrable hides and four stout legs apiece. They needed what nature had bestowed on them to push their way through such density of scrub and giant thorn bush. Festoons of creepers, brilliant yellow, blue, or red laced their hanging ropes, inseparably woven together, over every obstacle in their path. Besides growing upwards these luxuriant, hidden-rooted creepers appeared to grow down and along creating roots, curtains, and carpet all in one.

Once, stopping on the orange jungle road for a breather, but finding in the hot still air the very reverse, we heard some big animal threshing through the undergrowth. It became silent almost as soon as we did and nobody wanted to wait and see if it was a lion or an elephant, except my eager self! A pride of lions had been known to hold up cars for hours on this stretch while they leisurely strolled across the road. I would have happily jeopardised our inflexible travel connections to see that! As we drove off all I caught sight of was a gleam of black and white behind strands of soft yellow creeper and decided a colobus monkey was most likely to be the culprit, rather than something more dramatic.

At Kabongo, a wayside village, we stopped for lunch in a tiny restaurant. The few tables were crowded with us as the five cars disgorged their travellers into the long, thin dining room. Our host and hostess were an enormous couple, both tall and stout. He must have been handsome when thinner and she, anxious faced but pleasant, was insecurely fastened inside slacks and a low-cut blouse. Despite the heat most of us were hungry and they gave us a good, well-cooked meal, mostly fried as seems normal despite there being many other attractive, economical ways of preparing food.

If we had felt that we had experienced a long hot journey from Kamina, after Kabongo it grew much hotter and much, much longer. Our road was being mended so to the vocal irritation of our driver, we were waved onto an offshoot, and for some distance had to hang on tight to our seats. It reminded me of travelling in Romania in the thirties when the roads were usually so rough, so full of steep-sided potholes, that cars ahead of ours seemed to toss about as though on a choppy sea. Workmen waved friendly hands at us and shouted "co-lala, co-lala!" which means in their language "Bon voyage!"

Towards dusk we pulled up with the other cars at a river, or tributary of the Congo called the Lualaba. There lay a little tug, and a long wait for our luggage lorry to catch up with us. We thankfully trouped on board and sat on planked wooden seats. The flies were tiresome, and we could see many more skimming the river whose current ran sluggishly and darkly by. Mosquitoes abounded and there was nothing we could do. Tired and aching and so very hot we sat there for what seemed hours. One of our groups nursed a small baby who howled in such fretful misery that I felt desperately sorry for him and his poor mother. Older children had to be continually monitored to amuse them and keep them away from the water.

An hour passed before the lorry arrived, and then we were required to clamber back again on to the bank to try to sort through our entangled luggage. Each piece had to be carried individually by a river porter on to a barge which lay on the far side of our tug. The sun was setting as we reboarded and the little convoy chugged away wending past other river craft loaded, like ours, almost to the water line. We were all tormented by thirst. Flasks had long since given out. Mine, at

Madame's request had been filled at Kamina with milk-and-egg for Jeanot's sore throat.

I was reminded of a sunny day in Painswick during the World War, when a group of soldiers on leave bought eggs from me at the gate. They were happy and relaxed exchanging banter with me, and promptly broke the eggs and tipped them down their throats, raw. Apparently, no eggs came with Army rations! Madame had given the last of the egg mixture to the crying infant on the barge, who was promptly sick! We consoled ourselves with thoughts of tea or liquid of any description at Kabalo which was a little way down and across the river. It wasn't long before we realised our mistake!

After travelling for a short distance, the tug and its satellites came to a tiny quay. Broad steps led up from the lapping water's edge and another struggle with heavy luggage and clumsy porters began all over again. The low sun shone red over the broad river, now darkly bright behind us. Ahead lay Kabalo's small railway station. Nobody appeared as we explored its interior, so Madame and I sat on our luggage outside leaning against the wall. Madame's chic purple outfit was now covered in grey and red dust and looked beyond rescue. How I envied Daniel and Jeanot who roamed the river quay and munched sugarcane, but I assumed that it would not assuage the burning of my throat. The soft murmuring of the river mocked us, but none of the travellers felt confident enough to scramble down to its edge to drink from it. When at last a stationmaster appeared he deeply regretted telling us that until our train, which was due shortly, arrived there was no chance of drinking even water. The outlying village was without a doubt beyond our strength to reach so Madame and I continued to solidly sit on our luggage and wait, … and wait.

In the last of the twilight our train stole upon us, slipping quietly to the furthest end of the platform. Porters seemed to have vanished with the tug, and the two remaining had a mammoth task ahead of them, so taking one or two lighter cases, and leaving Daniel in charge of the remainder, we started off to find our compartment.

The conductor, in answer to the request for drinks, replied "Oh no. Nothing on this train". Drinks would be served in the restaurant car which would arrive shortly, all being well. I think it was at this stage that I decided that all my energy was to be devoted to just keeping myself alive and I gave up all hope of seeing my luggage again. I cared even less.

Madame showed pluck, or simply the advantage of being twenty years younger than me and insisted on going back to the station to supervise the porters bringing on the heavy luggage while I stayed in our berth to guard the bags we had already hauled on to the train. It was a long wait, and I was giving up hope of seeing them when the restaurant car, well-lit and inviting cut through the dark and drew up parallel to us. Jeanot made a dash for it and finally, we all gathered at an empty table, secured by the boy who was already halfway through a bottle of iced soda water. That delicious drink was the only one available but pure nectar! Dinner followed soon afterwards, a rough meal of fried odds and ends with service to match, but our appetites were undaunted.

We were joined by an odd-looking man who sat down and tried to engage us in conversation, however after a few unintelligible remarks, we found it best to ignore him. We were too tired to talk to each other anyway. Daniel and Jeanot watched him with icy, hostile eyes and at last he gave up. We thought the man was possibly mad as he was dressed in a thick warm suit, totally unsuitable in the near equator climate. At another time I would have tried to hear his story, assuming I could have understood it, but today was not the day. I now fully understood why Madame, who had made this trip before, had been reluctant to undertake it again.

My coupe was a broad double one equipped with a table and berth and nothing else. Not even a blind. There was only one little square room with washbasin and lavatory on this coach, so all the miscellaneous passengers had to queue up for it. The train was noisy and so bumpy that it was hard sometimes to remain in one's berth. Thanks to aspirin I slept several hours as the stifling heat grew cooler.

FIVE

May 26 1943

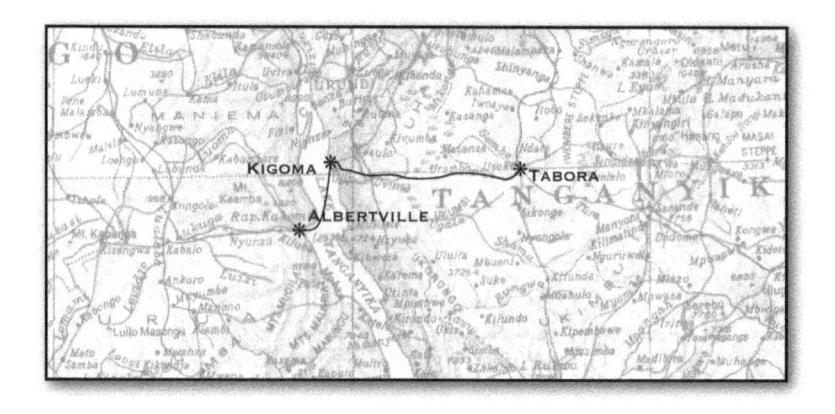

We reached Albertville at about 7 am and the family and I walked to the Hotel du Lac for breakfast. The hotel would be our backdrop to all the performance of transferring our luggage through customs but apparently there would be no porters available until after lunch. No such luxury as a taxi was available, so the walk had been grilling in the early heat. The town's one main street beside the lake had appeared interminable as we tried our best to keep to the scanty shadows thrown by high palm trees lining either side of the road. We had a day to occupy ourselves before our steamer for crossing Lake Tanganyika was due to arrive in the late afternoon. The hotel was totally booked out and families were occupying any available sofa and chair. We struggled for somewhere to settle ourselves.

Madame had pre-arranged to visit an old friend, so, leaving the boys in my care, I suggested a walk. Albertville is a pleasant little town, with a fine war memorial and a church on a small hill but we were rapidly beaten back by the crippling heat and settled for the view of the lake from the hotel balcony.

Jeanot and Daniel chose to entertain me from a schoolbook.

"Did you know, Mrs Warmington Reed, that originally the lake was 4,000 feet above sea level and now it is just under 2,600, so it is geologically very old." Jeanot raised big eyes to me, checking that I had appreciated this fact.

Daniel was not to be outdone, "Of 402 animal species of local life, 293 are peculiar to this lake. Did you see that man selling fish? We call that Seebu or 'poisson chat.'"

'Yes, I saw him. By the look of the fish, they could have been what we called Galilee catfish. They have a strange whiskered mouth and sometimes make a queer noise." I replied.

"What sort of noise?"

I tried to make a breathy, grinding noise to the boys' evident disbelief. "They make it by rubbing their spine fins together when they're alarmed." Jeanot tried to copy my imitation, but his sore throat immediately halted him.

Daniel read, "Historically this lake is interesting. In 1914, soon after the outbreak of that war, two British motorboats were bought here overland from Cape Town and managed to clear the lake of all German shipping. Both boats were salvaged and are now used for carrying cargo and passengers under the Belgian and British flags. The Germans won't dare to come here!"

"They could have submarines here for all we know!" his brother contributed.

"What gives you that idea?" I asked.

"This lake and Lake Baikal in Russia are the deepest freshwater lakes in the world. My teacher told me that." I could see that Jeanot was flagging and was pleased that lunch was announced in the dining room.

A strenuous afternoon was spent trekking from the hotel to the station and then on to the Customs shed ahead of a stream of porters supporting our luggage. It was another long walk in the unbearable heat. Madame, the boys, and I carried lighter packets, and after the formalities the same straggling procession was reversed. It seemed such an inefficient way of doing things! Then, only half an hour after tea, we were required to start walking again, there being no other mode of transport. Once again, we passed the Customs sheds on our way down to the quay. My head was aching, and I was pleased that Teddy was not experiencing this. His temper would have been short lived by now, and I would have had to be placating him as well as looking after myself. Africa had a way of doing things that feels set in stone, and it is useless to try to change it. Teddy would never learn this lesson and I was relieved that he was not there. It was an exhausting walk. I thought I would never reach the ship and was humiliatingly forced to rest several times along the blazing length of the quay. My heart felt constricted in my chest, and I wondered about my sanity, not for the first time.

When we finally reached the vessel, we were not allowed on board. For what seemed hours we sat on our suitcases alongside, everyone doing the same. There was no sun shelter, and I pitied my poor luggage, a strap missing or broken here, a handle off or sprung lock there, and its overcooked contents. We were grateful for our hats and had soon drunk all the iced water from our flasks. An elderly Moslem brought a young wife near our group; elegantly attired and tasselled, she sat on a gilded chair by herself, surrounded by highly coloured packets of all descriptions while he paced back and forth. Somehow, she retained a dignity that we Europeans had long ago lost.

Finally, we were allowed on board but first we had to visit the captain's office to show our passports and permits, and then queued again to see another officer who needed to check our medical certificates.

I appeared to be sharing a cabin with Madame and the boys. Between us we had six narrow berths in two tiers of three, one very close above the other, and a communal washbasin. We covered most of the floor and two bunks with luggage. Thankfully I lay down on my berth, but as there was no fan and the heat was unbearable, we were soon forced to leave the cabin. All over the ship there were recently painted bright red stools, still sticky as passengers were discovering to their cost. It might have been funny if we weren't already at the end of our tethers, having found neither food nor drink obtainable yet on board.

Across the lake and bordering hills to the west the sun was gloriously setting. All the sky and water lit, or deeply shadowed, made a beautiful sight. As it grew darker signs and sounds of departure arose, shouts, ropes creaking, hooting and at long last we began to move. To my surprise we appeared to be towing another steamer behind us!

Heat, hunger, and thirst drove us to the dining room to claim a table before too many passengers had the same idea. A long, long wait ensued.

It was nearly an hour before waiters arrived with a plan of just how seats had been allocated. By this time the room was packed, every chair full. After much expostulation to seemingly deaf waiters, we all got up and surged around looking for our named places. Most of us had been hungrily eating our bread and melted butter, so the waiters had to pursue each diner with his or her plate or knife. Unfurled dinner napkins became inextricably mixed, and glasses had been used, due to the discovery of water on the sideboard. Some of us had persuaded an early waiter to give us some beer and these glasses had a real game of hide and seek. It was all ridiculous, Gilbert and Sullivan, a noisy mix up with flustered waiters and ravenous diners. Tempers were rising fast when the sudden belated appearance of the captain with three guests put the brake on an impending riot. Still, we waited incredulously.

At last, the soup was served to the captain's table and then to the rest of us. Then we suffered another long wait while famished men drank and everybody gasped in the heat. Finally, we insisted on having the windows open, and waiters wrestled and struggled until two or three windows at last became unstuck, the mosquito netting with them, but anything for air! Doors were open by then too, each kept open by the foot of the nearest irate diner. As if on cue long, green-winged, green-bodied flies came flooding in, flying all over us. They were pretty things even though they were swarming in everybody's hair, plate and especially beer, and I considered them preferable to the stifling air before their arrival.

Eventually spinach with hard boiled eggs on slices of toast followed the soup. It was lukewarm and oily, and I could not touch it but watched Daniel and Jeanot tucking in with relish. After another wait which led to people thumping the tables and stamping, the next course of tough meat, damply fried potatoes, peas, and carrots arrived. I watched folk having two helpings of everything which I could barely eat. Thank heavens for some good fruit at the end. Doubtless coffee was being served later on the deck, but we four retired to bed. I had a cold shower and wished I could have put my hot, painful head under it.

Madame and Daniel settled quickly but Jeanot was as restless as me. The mosquito window would not stay closed and disappeared down its sash aperture, so there was no holding back the mosquitos. I went on deck and found staff who finally had it fixed. Not until later when Jeanot and I were up again trying to find a way of cooling the cabin, did the boy discover that the wretched staff member had closed the glass window as well as the mosquito netting. We struggled with it for some time before we at last forced it down.

For a brief respite, aided by a sleeping draft, I fell asleep, but at midnight, soaking in perspiration, head aching, heart violently thumping, I awoke. Experimentally I opened the door, but the strong deck light shining in directly made me shut it again. Madame awoke and we got up and found some deck chairs which we placed outside our door, both Jeanot and Daniel soon joining us. The noisy staff who had never ceased their chatter on our deck finally wore out their tongues and the deck lighting. Sometime between 1 am and 2 am all was dark and quiet.

I stayed on awhile after the others had retired to their berths. All was peace and in the soft darkness I could both hear and feel how different every night seems from each other. This colossal Africa, especially at night, seemed to fill and filter through every pore of feeling and spirit. As it fell through the blue dusk which deepened so quickly, each night seemed of an enduring quality. It seemed impossible that it must pass away and give birth to another day. I reflected on the dead I had loved and that they too faded away through the tunnel of their bodily lives. Somewhere in the world, the madness of bloody war was raging. I hoped there was a bright country beyond.

I tried my little berth again and dozed on and off. My kitbag was at the head of my bed, so I put my little pillow on it. There was just room for this without catching my hair on the berth above me. I wondered seriously during another wakeful period whether I would survive this trip and how I could ever have been mad enough to tackle it in the hot season.

May 27 1943

Kigoma was reached at 6 am and this was where I lost my dear little family. Mr Hyde's brother met the boat, and all was bustle and shouted orders. The boys were excited, and Madame immediately became anxious and in this state the niceties of saying goodbye were forgotten. The family rushed off into their normal life with barely a backward glance, which was hurtful even if understandable. Ships in the night indeed. I thought about the friends I had left in Cape Town and how my departure must be a distant memory now that their normal routines filled their lives. I had been on the move for thirteen days so far although it seemed much longer. It felt as if I was endlessly floating between one reality and another. I had to make the life I was heading for a thing of more substance, a solid renewal of the partnership and understanding within our marriage. I vowed that I would send Teddy the long-delayed telegram. I needed to alert him to my arrival. I had put it off too long.

No taxi was available to bring me to the Stanley Hotel, so I started to walk the distance carrying camera, flask, provision bag, one or two small packets from which I will not part, plus two handbags and my coat. I was overtaken by a delightful elderly Englishman who came to my rescue and insisted on carrying my things on up the hill and into the hotel. Bless him. I nearly wept with relief. The hotel proprietor took me across his garden under the shade of trees, passing hotel staff sitting on the grass, to a veranda opening onto rooms occupied by transients like myself. I could see a woman stretched out on a bed, very lightly clad. Next door a man was lying down reading, a mountain of luggage heaped outside on his share of the balcony. It was a very narrow little book he was holding up, and a wisp of dark moustache peeped out from each side of it. I had a ridiculous longing to see what kind of face remained so resolutely hidden!

By mid-morning I was sitting on a clean little bed in an almost bare room in the Stanley Hotel, very thankful to be still once more. After a refreshing semi-bath and a sorting out of papers, tickets, and notes, I was determined before travelling any further to try to get level with myself.

Teddy's cable had to be the priority and had to be dispatched. My anxiety about his response was complicated. I was reminded of Madame, that morning, who had allowed a clear head to be clouded in the presence of dominant males, always anticipating criticism. Teddy would surely have tried to dissuade me from coming, especially at that time of the year, and it was easier to present him with an action already in motion. Unlike Madame I prided myself on being an independent woman, capable of handling my own life, much to my husband's confusion. I couldn't help smiling as I remembered an occasion when Teddy came home from war duties unexpectedly to find me unloading a batch of unbroken ponies into our garden. I remember his shocked face as he strode up the drive, which was blocked by ponies threatening to spill onto the lane. I had been to Bampton Fair and had seen this opportunity to make money and could not resist it. I had every confidence that I could break them into reliable ride and drive horses and make a tidy profit. All it needed was some stout fencing and a bit of patience. Teddy was furious and called me irresponsible, but he was really worried about his newly planted roses. I managed to break the ponies and sold them at a considerable profit! He had to eat his words, but I did buy him new rose plants and promised not to do it again!

This marathon journey had been triggered by the warning letter I received in Cape Town from a concerned Palestinian friend. The letter's contents had to be addressed. It was time to return. I had been warned that my handsome husband appeared to be enjoying the company of a particularly predatory female, too much. I wasn't totally shocked. My two years' absence had become too long, and my marriage was threatened. I loved my husband, despite his shortcomings. We had a good marriage. We made a good team, and not just on the tennis courts and bridge tables and I was not prepared to allow anyone to threaten it.

My thoughts were interrupted by the arrival of a water wagtail, a quivering beauty of very black and very white, alighting on my windowsill. I froze in my tracks for all the ten seconds it lingered.

The heat was made more bearable at teatime as a slight breeze stirred which cooled the air a little. The proprietor told me that more rain should have fallen that May and the heat had come too early. I was badly in need of news, and he tried to get English news on his radio for me, but reception was almost unintelligible. We had bombed Sicily again, also Crete but that was all I could discover. Taking advantage of the lull in humidity I had to make my way to the customs office to see my luggage through. A polite fatherly Sikh oversaw it and warned me that I must be early to catch the train that evening.

I wished I had the time to go down the lake coast four miles from here to the little harbour of Ujiji where, after his long quest, Stanley at last met Livingstone in 1871. I smiled at the recollection that this was the historic moment when Stanley produced his famous remark, "Dr Livingstone I presume?" How very British!

I shopped and bought a packet of red pepper seeds for my garden in Palestine, an ebony walking-stick for Teddy, tortoise-shell dinner-napkin rings and saccharine. Most importantly I visited the district offices and changed some money and sent off the vital cable to my husband.

We finally left Kigoma station in the twilight. I had almost come to grief when boarding the train as an Englishman chose to board at the same time, with difficulty. Heat, doubtless, and native drinks certainly having affected him more than he expected. He was very apologetic at having almost flattened me, and I had to duck away from the overpowering smell of alcohol and hope that he didn't track me down to my carriage to apologise further.

My coupe had neither blind nor curtain in the windows. Except for my trunk and suitcases in the van, I had all the rest of my luggage safely stowed with me. This was thanks to the station master, his assistant and even the customs officer. Their eager attention compensated for the uncouthness of my own countryman!

As we slowly skirted the lake, it looked shimmering and intangible. What a spiritual quality water could hold, like Venetian glass! Little lights from the coast shone across it in a score of narrow paths. The day had been such a long one. Could it be only yesterday that we had left Albertville? Round the moon, like an egg in a cup, there was a circle. I wondered what that foretold of the weather. I felt quite at sea at this new aspect of my familiar star world. I missed the view over the bay at night from my little Sea Point balcony: Venus rising from the glowing western sea; Orion far above me; Castor and Pollux; Aldebaran: the Pleiades; the beautiful blue of Sirius; and stretching vastly overhead the great Milky Way and Southern Cross. We must have been travelling due east to Tabora via Uvinza and passed through the station of Mala Garazi, and then over a long bridge spanning the un-navigable river of that name.

In a big compartment near me an Indian family were travelling in state. Two little girls, two younger brilliant-eyed boys, all attractively and richly robed, came to my door and smiled. We made friends even though unable to talk. I opened their little hands and shook a few drops of eau de cologne onto their tiny palms, and then let them smell it, and closed their fingers so that the scent should last longer. They ran off with delighted giggles to tell their mother and then soon came back to have the performance repeated. The younger boy was a beautiful grave child with a slow smile, whose shining quality was entrancing to behold. It made me melancholy when I thought that somewhere in this world, I might have a grandchild. Ronny's baby if it was born when expected could be fourteen months old now. If it had survived. If my daughter had survived. A well of pain sprung up inside me and I hastily turned my thoughts away.

Mosquitoes in the train were very lively so, to restore my peace, I had to unpack my flit gun.

May 28 1943

Thank heaven we had a cool night and dawn! I was forced to dig out my rug during the night, and it grew so fresh my windows needed to be almost shut. I watched a pale rose sunrise, like an expanding blossom filling the sky eastwards towards which we were heading. It was grassy country around, rather flat, some trees, some cultivation. Maize stalks of poor quality and scrub abounded. No animals or birds were to be seen.

When my early morning tea was brought, the waiter, by way of knocking, rattled his foot up and down my venetian shuttered door. Such a funny unexpected noise. I thought it was the Indian children at first, then realised how noiselessly these children behaved, even as a bunch of four. Later I watched the waiter open the next door with his toes, his hands being full of a tray piled high with plates of food.

The station of the township of Mabana abounded with locals in all sorts of colourful costumes, the chatter of their voices filling the air. I bought through the window a crude little wooden cup from a clean, small boy with shining face, large smile, and half a white shirt over one ebony shoulder. On straw trays further down the platform scores of little, round, gold-green tomatoes were being sold. Red fez, or Indian turbans crowned heads, while polished bodies usually clothed from underarm downwards mixed well with boys in ragged loincloths. Women in white, rust, or black, their shining shoulders bare and often beautifully moulded, held babies bound low on their backs, little heads round and wobbling. I watched a tall stately gentleman in flowing robes wandering down the platform being followed by a little grey kid, as if it was a dog. All this movement and colour against a background of green brilliantly flowering trees, was an unforgettable vibrant sight.

After Mabana there was brush both sides of the line, then open land, brown tinted with trees similar to edible chestnuts.

Others had long hanging pods cup-curling, and fine high trunks with densely foliaged branches. There were many hill ridges with small trees growing on and up them. The ant hills looked old and grey and were not so numerous as in the Belgian Congo. We passed immense tracts of high, thin grass with densely wooded hills behind them.

As the train ran through a small nameless station, I saw some boys on the platform wearing white, round, decorated caps like many Palestinian boys. Long, thin cones of grass or rush, looking as if they could enclose tall wine bottles, were lying by them. I wondered if they were to be used to construct hut roofs.

So far, I had seen hardly any wild animals, just a few small bucks in Rhodesia and hippo in the Zambesi, and an odd lizard or two. We passed thatched little villages and one large one standing back from the line of low hills rising behind it. Perhaps here, as in Transjordan and Iraq, the villagers preferred to be away from the main track. Some of the huts were oblong. Among the dried up pools were a few full of muddy water. These had recently been disturbed by animals, judging from the criss-crossing of many marks in the earth surrounding them.

The coupe was becoming covered in a thick layer of tan dust, despite the closed window. I was sure that I too was beginning to look worse for wear, in contrast to the Indian children who periodically popped in to smile. They looked immaculate still! I imagined they spoke Hindustani. I had tried Arabic on them, and French, but they did not understand.

We reached Tabora mid-morning. It was here in Tabora in 1872 that Stanley and Livingstone had parted. Apparently after the Ujiji meeting they had explored together for a time, then, as Stanley could not persuade the great explorer to accompany him home, they separated. At that time Livingstone believed the Luala, the name for the upper reaches of the Congo River, to be the source of the Nile. He was determined to verify this.

I felt a little lost on the busy platform in all the bustle and clamour of boys shouting Swahili and competing for my luggage. The heat, colour, and noise were overwhelming, and I must have presented as a sorry sight, but fortune favours the brave. Standing by the exit was a good-looking police officer, who kindly offered to help me. The station master could not be found anywhere, but this guardian angel organised the storage of most of the luggage at the station and then insisted on taking me and the remaining bags in his gleaming car to the Park Hotel where I was staying until the following night. Major Harvey was my hero's name and I thanked him profusely.

The hotel was an attractive place, greenly and pleasantly situated. An ex-Austrian managed it, and he was all smiles and bows, and a cool room was ready for me. Apparently, the downcoming steamer on Lake Victoria had just run on to sands and the passengers all bound for this hotel including RAF personnel, were consequently delayed. They could be stranded for a day or possibly two. With time on his hands, the manager asked me to join him for a coffee which I enjoyed after a refreshing shower.

The course of the conversation turned to his tragic past.

"I was a landowner in Austria. I was fortunate to have hereditary wealth and had a good life with my wife and child in Vienna. Until the Germans arrived. They robbed me of everything except for my house." the manager disclosed.

"I'm so sorry. It seems a long journey that you've made to end up in Africa."

"Yes, it's been a bitter learning curve. Not content with confiscating all my land, the German officialdom ordered me to pay 30,000 Austrian shillings for my freedom! It was preposterous! I had no money by that time and didn't know where to turn. Fortunately, I managed to borrow the sum from a friend, and gave him my house as security."

"What possible excuse had the Nazis for doing that?"

This unassuming, courteous, rather old-world gentleman looked me straight in the eye and gave me the answer that I was mortified I hadn't already guessed. "I'm not a practising Jew, but my ancestry gave them all the excuse they needed to take all the money and possessions I had. When they had everything that they could squeeze out of me, they still threw me into prison. I would be there now if it hadn't been for the tenacity of my wonderful wife. She made daily attempts to get me released, until she finally succeeded. I don't know what changed their minds, but I owe my life to her. My wife had support from her family and with their help we immediately fled the country with our daughter and will never return. We made our way to Cyprus and, with my in-law's help, bought a hotel in Nicosia."

"What a terrible experience. And what fortitude to start again like that."

"Needs must! We poured all our hopes for the future into that hotel and gradually began to make a success of it. It was dilapidated when we took it on, but we worked hard and built up a good relationship with the Cypriots. We were just beginning to feel secure when we were warned that our family had better remove ourselves as there was trouble coming."

"But I thought that Cyprus was considered a safe haven from the Germans, on the assumption that it was geographically too far away for them to be bothered with?"

"You'll understand that I was not going to take any chances. I was no longer as naïve as when Germany invaded my home country. I wasn't going to wait. Perhaps it was a mistake. In great haste I sold the hotel for a ridiculous price, the price of one room. And here we are in Africa. I run this hotel for a Greek owner. My daughter goes to school nearby."

"And your wife?"

"My dear wife is ill and has been ever since we came here. She's always worrying about her mother who we had to leave in Vienna. We've heard no word of her of course. Although my wife is pure Aryan, she worries that her mother will be associated with me. Vienna is not the place to be, and her mother's wellbeing is a constant worry to her."

"I do understand what it's like to have so little information. I don't want to presume but, when I pass through Nairobi, I could go to the Red Cross there and ask if there is any news of her. I'm only too happy to do that for you if you'd like me to. I would just need her details."

"That would be most kind. To be honest I hold out little hope for my side of the family. I believe that the Nazis have imprisoned or killed all of them in Austria, but I am more hopeful that my wife's family have survived."

The manager's plight was a sharp reminder of how far away we were from enemy activity. In Cape Town I had been closer to the reality, with soldiers passing through, fresh faced and nervous on the way out; damaged, seasoned, and quiet on the way home. But cocooned here in central Africa it was hard to feel connected to the urgency in the world around. The clusters of English Army and RAF personnel that I kept coming across seemed unanchored and it was hard to imagine what they were doing there.

In the afternoon a note came from Mrs Harvey, the wife of my saviour this morning, asking me to dinner. I was charmed by their kindness. It was delightful to be in an English family's home again.

Major and Mrs Harvey's house was a lovely one, standing on

an eminence with far views, and an enchanting garden. A very lovely golden-trumpeted shrub flower, an allamanda apparently, with open petals and long shining green leaves dominated the garden. I regretted that I could not see any ripe seed or bean to take away. The house had been built by the late Kaiser for himself. I learned that my fine, spreading hotel had been intended for his son and heir. Inside the house was fascinating, with beautiful furniture, and treasure of all description. On shelves, around the frieze in one room, was wonderful carved woodwork done by local artisans. Groups of figures displayed Africans working in different occupations and one man's work was extraordinary in its sensitivity. I learned that he was from the Watuzi tribe and had never had a lesson in his life.

After a good and plentiful dinner, Major Harvey persuaded me to play on their finely tuned piano. I was a little rusty, but it was a joy to stroke the keys of such a fine instrument. We also had fun with a hunting horn, making the weirdest attempts to produce notes from it. Only Major Harvey succeeded in blowing it, by no means an easy thing to achieve. He made a great noise which naturally aroused the guard who came to see if all was well. It brought back memories of lively dinner parties in Palestine. My life then seemed to belong to another world of time, space, and experience.

Major Harvey oversaw the large camp of Italian prisoners there. It was an unlikely but happy place for the Italians to have found themselves. I was shown some of their artistic drawings and paintings. Included was one by a gifted prisoner who had copied and enlarged, beautifully, a little photograph of the Harvey's only child in England. He had also made a painting of Major Harvey's father. It must have been hard to be living so far away from their only child. At least my distant daughters were now adults. Teddy and I had tried to make their childhoods in Gloucestershire as secure and idyllic as possible. Despite whatever money problems we were struggling with, they wanted for little. They each had a pony when they were old enough to learn. Dina, our Dalmatian dog, and Moppety, the Irish Wolfhound were their constant companions. Having myself been sent to boarding school much too soon, I made sure that the girls didn't have to go until they went to Cheltenham Ladies College at secondary level. Since the children had been born, I was always balancing time spent with their father with time spent with them. I was away escorting Teddy on business and pleasure trips from time to time, but the girls had a much loved and trusted nanny and cook to look after them. I always felt that I had to support both husband and children and couldn't hope to get it right, so constantly lived with guilt.

Mrs Harvey drove me back to the hotel. Deep in conversation, a nightjar rising in front of the car in the black night, made us both jump. The night was fresh, and my room was a cool one off the long veranda, the windows netted against insects.

SIX

May 29 1943

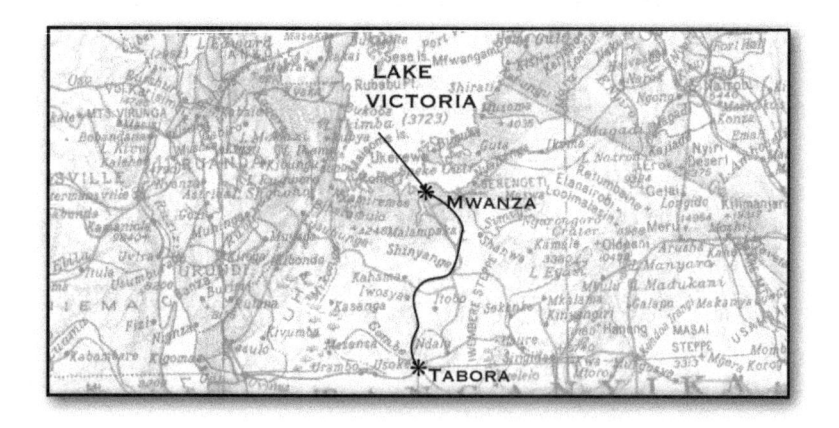

It was so peaceful in the hotel I wished I could have stayed longer. The compulsion to make this odyssey as quickly as possible had governed my initial decisions over timings on route. Many sights on this journey I would have liked to linger over. I doubted if I would ever see these places again in my lifetime, so it seemed a shame to be rushing past them, but this was in direct conflict with my growing need to get all this over. The heat that had still to be lived through and the burden of my luggage weighed me down. I wanted to be back in the security of my home in Palestine and, for better or worse, with my husband.

I was again invited to lunch with Mrs Harvey to meet her friends, which I accepted with pleasure. The continuous happy murmur of wind in the treetops in the heat of the day was pleasant and I found their home and garden a green and friendly spot. At the luncheon I was a novelty in the ladies' predictable lives and although life in Tabora appeared stress free and very pleasant for these families, I wondered if an element of boredom crept in. Competition on the domestic front abounded. One incident at table amused me. Course after course of a very attractive buffet luncheon was served by her attentive servants without any evident direction from my hostess. When I congratulated Mrs Harvey on the efficiency of her staff, she told me it was all due to a button on the floor under the table which, when pressed by her foot, rang a bell in the kitchen for service!

The conversation turned to the apparent bad famine in many parts surrounding the township. Apparently, food was being sent to many districts to relieve the suffering, but there was no evidence of any shortage in the Harvey household.

Leaving Tabora that night was a late and tiresome business. All was ready in the hotel, three luggage boys waiting, and others had already taken the well-travelled trunk to the station. At 10.30, after bidding adieu to the manager, I walked down the dark, dusty little road escorted by the porters. The stationmaster, whom I had been unable to find on arrival, was still not to be found. My trunk dominated every changeover of this journey, and I quietly cursed my original naïve belief that it would not create endless difficulties. There were times when I thought no content was worth the restriction it put on my movements. My trunk was brought out of the cloakroom, and with the help of a British officer, I found my compartment, not in the train filling the platform but in another alongside. I was tired and irritable by this time and was annoyed to find that my coupe was to be shared. A blousy young Belgian woman had already filled the space to overflowing with her luggage so my belongings would have to be stored in the corridor outside. It was a tight fit in the coupe, and I was dismayed further by being stifled by my companion's sweet-poppy scent that I would have to endure.

The ticket collector arrived at this moment, the usual turbaned Indian and I complained at first without avail. However, my charming British officer who had been politely standing back, stepped in and a few words from him to the ticket collector and, hey presto, it was agreed that I should have the empty coupe next door to myself! I was highly relieved, but also infuriated that the British officer had influence that, evidently, I did not have. Of course, I expressed my gratitude, but I was inwardly fuming.

The Harveys had nobly proposed to see me off, but I had dissuaded them as it was such a late hour. A wise decision as I was in no mood to make small talk while waiting for the train's departure. It was almost midnight when we started.

May 30 1943

Breakfast in the restaurant car proved to be a farce. There was fruit, pawpaw, and lemon, but good fish, sausage and meat was made uneatable by being soaked in odoriferous grease. I asked for bacon but there was none, nor marmalade. I had just started on bread and butter when a smiling boy whisked it away and produced, after all, a plate full of very hot bacon and fried potatoes.

The country we were passing through was level and marshy. Many stretches of it were under crops and much of it was burdened with horrid thorn scrub. Here and there patches of a high lovely red-gold grass grew. Scattered hamlets of huts and herds of black and white goats dotted the land. In twiggy clumps high in thick old trees on right angle branches, I could see stork nests and the occasional big bird with black tail in flight. We passed surprising groups of old grey rocks, some of them perilously balanced on smaller ones. The green plains came with crops of dark dead-headed maize, which again belied the talk of famine. Naked little boys, hump backed cows and pool hollows flashed past all morning, and I relished the kaleidoscope of swiftly vanishing landscapes.

There was a long halt at Shinyanga. This place has a reputation for being a difficult territory, although believed to be potentially rich in diamonds. Snakes are supposed to abound here and lions and other wild beasts. And fever. The land is marshy as one goes closer to Lake Victoria, so any development has yet to be achieved. On the platform I heard English people talking outside my window and through a chink in the blind saw a white-faced small boy with a group of Europeans. Odd how quickly one catches the sound of one's own language. How washed out we all looked in comparison to the local women. These statuesque women had their shoulders bare to the armpits, breasts covered, close cropped almost shaven heads and they wore identical black or white garments from breast to skirt length. Ankle bangles were the fashion. Many of the women carried a baby astride their backs, wrapped around in dingy black. The tiny, round heads of the babies reached up to just below the mothers' shoulder blades. One baby cried a little, its small face puckered up, universal in sound and expression. I watched as women balanced enormous bundles on their heads. One Junoesque young girl carried on her elaborately dressed hair, just one upright bottle. In her arms was a long narrow green banana leaved bundle, very neatly packed and bound. On her way to a rendezvous perhaps? The children here all seem to have protruding bellies, an indication of too much maize or starch in their diet, or certainly too little food variety.

I enjoyed these glimpses of humanity which made a welcome break from the endless passage of large plantations of maize, flocks of black goats, sheep and scrawny grey cattle, clusters of stones, thatched villages of huts and endless plains. All these sights passed too speedily to be able to enjoy, so they become a repetitious blur. The immense green plain, broken by patches of cultivation and islets of rock, stretched to the far horizon. I leant my forehead against the cool of the glass and closed my eyes.

Teddy would have received my cable by now. The earliest I could expect a response would be when I reached Nairobi by my calculations. What would he be thinking? Would he be delighted that his soulmate was returning to his side, or would he be irritated that a delightful episode in his life was being curtailed. Or worse, would he be forced into making a change of life decision because he had seriously involved himself with this predatory female. I would only know when I saw my husband again. Losing him was unbearable to contemplate. I clearly remembered the Teddy of long ago when we met. I was studying the piano at the Conservatoire, and Teddy, the violin. We, being English and far from home were naturally thrown together. He was so tall and handsome; I couldn't believe my luck when he declared his love for me. I was overwhelmed. What Teddy wanted; Teddy was used to getting but perhaps he got more than he expected with me.

We were both passionate and vocal, so life was never dull. I had grown up capable of looking after myself and had never accepted the role of wife as being a supportive wall flower. I had always pursued my own interests, as well as our joint ones.

Teddy's looks caused many a bosom to flutter and being a flatterable man, there were times he might well have wandered had I not been there to support and escort him. Sometimes keeping an eye on Teddy conflicted with my own interests and I hoped I had not pushed my luck too far this time.

We crossed a wide, marshy riverbed, most of it waterless, its side pitted with hoofmarks. Then came acres of dark-headed millet again, and handsome aloe sisal in high clumps, aloof, unfriendly plants used primarily as roofing thatch. Little loinclothed or naked boys ran laughing alongside the slow-moving train, near where I spotted the upright ruins of an ancient temple. I was struck again by the dearth of trees. There were so few around, yet it looked like good growing country, and I would imagine their shade might be most useful in this dazzling African sun.

Through rock-clad hills each side we approached the small station of Malampka, storks flying around it. Four donkeys laden with sacks appeared, the first I had seen for a long time. I do like donkeys! There was a long wait here. Indian women, with their easy gliding carriage, walked past. The police on the platform were all fine upright quiet men full of dignity, dressed in khaki with navy-blue tunics and white shorts, and all wore red fezzes. Local Africans wandered past carrying bunches of a curious purple hanging fruit, something like a fig with green calix, perhaps a variety of egg plant. The District Officers' luggage which was coming aboard with much fuss and agitation seemed responsible for the delay. I spotted the two attractive young Englishmen it appeared to belong to, casually laughing and joking as if they didn't have a care in the world. Oh, the confidence of youth!

A tall Indian servant walked by carrying on his shoulders

a little Indian girl in fine European clothes, her dark hair in a long plait. One of his arms stretched over his shoulder behind, carefully supported her back, like a little chairback. The unconscious stature of this small sedate person was a joy as she sat at ease and surveyed the strange world. She had large dark brown eyes in her tiny face. The last I saw of her; she was walking quietly away from the open platform on a gently rising road. She did not turn her head as the train whistle blew. Some paces behind her humbly walked her powerfully built servant.

We passed along a deep cutting through rock into scrub and then came rock again, immense boulders each side of the line. The train crawled dead slow; a big notice gave the warning that a lookout for boulders must be kept. There were many shrubs with little bright yellow hanging balls, and mauve flowers. When we were clear the view on the left was of immense, low hills rising against the horizon. We must have been passing a rich flower belt being so near the Lake. There were tall, bronze, orange flowers, like wide open daisies, their vertical stalk growing straight up the centre of them. Also, swathes of white daisies, their flat heads with their yellow centre looking up to the sky, then thousands of little yellow daisies and grasses of bright warm shades, ripe, flowering green of countless varieties. Among the maize crops was a lovely violet flower rather like a fine poppy on bare stems. Single, low growing light mauve flowers around them may have been the young ones of the yard-high, violet ones. I could bear my lack of knowledge no longer and went into the corridor and pointed them out to several people, but no one knew their name, and we passed all too quickly. I had never seen such a profusion.

We passed Bukimba station, and Fella. Great boulders again closed us in on both sides, almost like a tunnel, but not meeting overhead. We were just crawling through. A brisk walk alongside the train would have done me a world of good as I noticed that my ankles were swelling from the endless sitting. A lovely break finally came in the boulders, a little vale full of luscious greenness, then a glimpse of Lake Victoria just showing.

We finally arrived at Mwanza mid-afternoon. The now usual free fight between the porters over my luggage, was an embarrassment to me. Why didn't I know more Swahili? A stout Polish man came to my rescue and gave the boys their orders and finally we all headed towards the hotel. We walked quite a long way down a leafy avenue; in many places it was a tunnel of greenery from the trees each side meeting overhead.

At the hotel a dour man of grey complexion and clothing received me and showed me up an outside staircase to my small room. Two porters had to return to the station for my trunk and the rest of my luggage. I imagine they had to make more than one trip! This luggage business had been a huge hindrance to me, as well as the constant burden of tipping porters to have it looked after. Had I fully understood what I was letting myself in for? Surely, I could have reduced it? I wonder! It represented two unrepeatable years of my life in Cape Town, and the trunk contained something of great importance to Teddy. I would have struggled to reduce it further.

Later I lay on my bed under a net in the pale green room and had a rest, but it was too noisy outside to sleep, so I changed and went down to dinner. The stout Polish man joined me at the table and was a bit too familiar for my liking, so I was pleased when we were joined by an interesting man, a Mr van Lindner. He used to be a big game hunter who had grown tired of killing and now preferred to study game instead. He was employed in tin mining in the north and had some fascinating, if suspect, stories and made an entertaining dinner companion.

Bath and bed were most welcome as I was tired.

May 31 1943

The Marine Superintendent had a large brown mote in his eye. It was quite disconcerting as he was one of those men who holds your gaze for as long as he can, defying you to look away. I had arrived in his office after breakfast, to verify my booking on to Nairobi. I presented him with my 'T Series Exchange-Voucher' as my South African itinerary directed.

"All seems to be in order, Mrs Warmington Reed. Have you had a good journey to date?"

"It's been a fascinating journey, thank you. I'm amazed at how healthy your plains of maize are, considering there's talk of famine."

"Ah, you are mistaken," he corrected, "the maize you saw is in fact matama, or what you would know as millet, and there's much too little of it. My chief work now is famine relief and organising food to be sent out to all local districts. We've a major problem here."

"I'm sorry to hear that."

"It's difficult to educate the natives. Knowledge of the best methods of planting and the soils most suitable for each crop is handed down from father to son. Only one crop is traditionally grown, and if that crop fails it results in famine. It's hard to instil the practice of growing alternative crops in case of disaster to one of them."

"Is it millet, you are distributing?"

"No, most of it is manioc, also called hapogo or cassava."

"I thought manioc was poisonous?"

"Manioc roots are peeled, soaked in water to extract their poisons, dried up and used as flour. The natives mix this with water which makes a kind of porridge to which they can add meat or vegetables. With this drought, it's their main diet. We desperately need rain."

This seemed a strange notion, knowing that I was about to embark on a steamer to cross Lake Victoria which is said to be deeper than any other African inland water.

My next call was to the Head of Customs for the usual casual formality before I felt free to wander round the shops in the light breeze that blew off the lake. Mwanza was ringed with trees and graced with colonial architecture but there was a poor selection of things to buy. All the shops were the same: small, and dull, run by Indians with mostly uninteresting cotton materials for sale. At a photographer's shop the man complained that few of his goods were available owing to the war.

I passed a local school where, through the open door, I saw a lesson in progress. The bespectacled schoolmaster was saying solemnly, in English, to the attentive rows of little children, "What big ears you've got!". I hope they appreciated their 'Red Riding Hood' lesson. Later I heard indigenous soldiers singing "Clementine', and 'My Bonny lies over the Ocean', but in their own language! It would have been interesting to have known the words as they translated them. I wondered what they thought about our tunes, so very different in rhythm, quaver, or tone to their music. I struggled to find any thrill or charm or even relief in their monotonous chanting and imagined they found our songs as incomprehensible.

Back in the hotel bedroom I faced my own challenge. Against the high balcony outside my window a green leaved acacia 'Flame of the Forest' tree was growing. Hanging just beyond my reach was a huge pod. By pulling on other branches, and with the aid of a small suitcase to stand on, I managed to pick it. Probably the seeds were unripe as they did not rattle, but true to my reputation as a seed vandal, I felt triumphant and secreted the pod in a suitcase for future planting in Haifa.

The afternoon was peacefully spent in my room before I went down to tea, passing at the foot of my staircase an excitable crowd of men and boys squatting, waiting to fight over luggage. The polite, grey-clothed manager said he would instruct my room-boy to keep his eyes on them until I was ready. In due course my luggage was all shouldered or mounted on the head - what neck muscles - and with my room-boy in charge we trooped down the quiet, leafy avenue to the Customs. I didn't want my luggage to be examined and hoped the magic words 'In Transit' would do the trick. My cases passed without an inspection on an assurance as to what I had not got in them. Then we processed on to the quay where I noticed sacks of cotton and coffee beans lying about. Cotton bags had spilt some of their white balls onto the paving of the quay, and whoever was in charge was careless as the over full sacks of coffee bags also had beans spilling from them.

My deck-cabin on the 1,200-ton steamer was a roomy double one, and I learned that my fellow traveller was to be the matron of Mwanza hospital. My hillock of luggage carefully stacked, I emerged on deck to sit and watch passengers and cargo coming onboard. I was quickly joined by a young officer I had noticed on my last train leg. So far, he had looked very 'browned off' but now began to thaw. More army officers and a captain, a Scot by his accent, along with about thirty-two men, started pegging their claims and arranging their bundles on deck where they were to sleep. Several officers came up and sat with us and talked, which was pleasant if slightly frustrating. The reason for them being on Lake Victoria was the white elephant in the room, and understandably this was the last thing they were allowed to disclose. A major in the Pioneer Corps had a broken arm, tied up in a sling which I helped him readjust, but he said not a word as to how it got broken. Another interesting man, a major from Glasgow joined us. He was not young and looked delicate and is apparently living on bananas and coffee having teeth trouble and a distaste for the food provided. He was an entertaining man, loved nature and solitude and must have found this communal army life hard to bear, except by joking about it. He was busy buying from the locals on the quay and ended up brandishing a huge bunch of bananas bought for a song! He insisted on my eating some, so being hungry I had two! They were just ripe, delicious, and quite a different fruit from the usual, woollen, tasteless variety. Miss Morris, the nursing matron and cabin companion, and a young and pretty nurse from Zanzibar joined us. We and the Army became good friends immediately.

The laden steamer cast off in the deepening dusk. Dinner was in two sittings, and the Army apologetically had the first of them. When it was our turn, I found myself on the captain's left. He was nice, I am sure, but a dour Scot oppressed possibly by social requirements, or more likely, his responsibility. The soup, two courses, and coffee, were basic but better than the usual 'austerity' meal I have become accustomed to on this trip. Later, on the open deck space we played Rummy with the soldiers. I think all of us enjoyed each other's company. Around us flowed the quiet water of Lake Victoria and above us in the clearing mist the stars were shining out of a deep blue sky. A big bird on the water suddenly rose alongside and disappeared into the night. Of war news, I learned that the French navy in Alexandria had come over to us, a useful and timely addition to our forces. We ordered bottles of ginger beer to celebrate, the only drink except soda water available.

Miss Morris and I talked late into the night. She had recently taken an escorted expedition into the interior. How I wished I had gone too. We pass by this way but once, and life is so full of missed opportunities. She appeared to live a solitary life, seemingly without family.

"Have you got brothers or sisters?" she asked casually.

"I'm the oldest of three girls. My sister Grace married and sadly died quite young leaving two nieces, and my youngest sister Maude lives in Hastings, on the south coast of England. She never married but lived in India for many years as a governess. We were orphans, bought up by our two uncles."

"How hard for you!" She looked at me inviting more, but the complication in my history was not one to share with all.

"We were lucky. My uncles were wealthy and unmarried and gave us security and a good education. I can't fault the life they gave us." I remember our initial amazement at the huge Gloucestershire house and grounds we were brought to after the long journey south. The Vale House, Ebley was the largest house we had ever seen. It was big enough easily to get lost in! Being young, the excitement of this new fairy tale life quickly blotted out our past. We had ponies to ride, and dogs to enjoy, and our own maids. The uncles did not have children, so we were given a free rein to roam the grounds, and I was in my element. Grace and Maud settled down quickly, and I sometimes felt that I was the only one who remembered and missed my mother.

I smiled at Miss Morris "It was a long time ago, and another world!"

I was not going to elaborate on my loss, kindly as Miss Morris appeared to be. The story of my parents' death was more complicated and wounding than I had recounted. It had been an issue that could have ruined my wedding and destabilised my entire adult life if I had let it. Only time had been the healer, and life's challenges had finally given me a sense of perspective. This was a subject that was not open for casual discussion.

It was only in bed that I remembered that I had forgotten to look out for the long belt of the Sesse Islands stretching for over a hundred miles towards Jinja. These fertile isles were all sizes, some as large as forty square miles. They were the home of the rare Sittatunga antelope. They were rarely seen as they hide in the reeds and marshes until dark. They were the only almost-web-footed deer, very long and splayed in the hoof to suit the marshy ground they live in. It was a good thing they were rare, as they were said to be the hosts of the blood parasite of the tsetse fly which caused sleeping-sickness.

SEVEN

June 1 1943

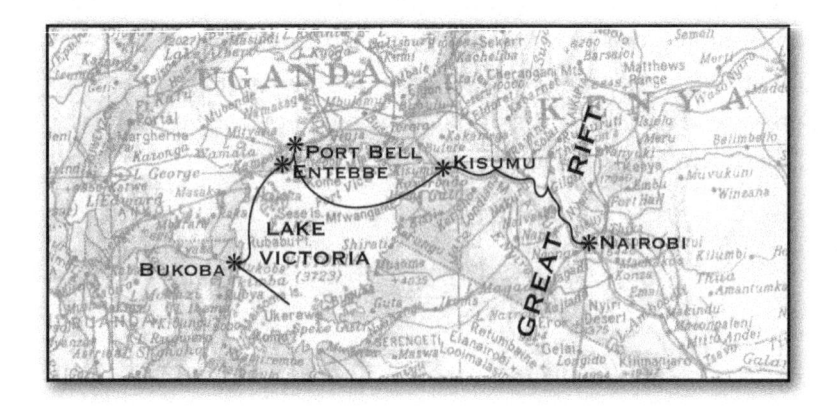

The lake was like an inland sea, bigger than Switzerland and often no land was visible from the steamer. Bright and early in the morning we came to the little port of Bukoba on Lake Victoria's west bank. It was a pretty, green port and the name of the tribe round here was the Wahai. I was told I had the time to go for a walk along the coast to find hippo as these good tempered, non-man-eating creatures were said to be numerous.

I really wanted to see crocodile but had to settle for hippo. The Chief Officer, Mr Wilkins who was paunchy and round faced, insisted on escorting me and took my arm with great gusto. I am sure he was a kindly man, a music lover he told me, with a wife and child in Kisumu, but he was less certain on his feet than me. I am sure I did more of the supporting on the treacherous coastal path than he did.

After a mile or so we found one hippo wallowing in the water, and many others further out in the lake. Hoping for a closer look, we waited patiently. The hippo was watching us as closely, it seemed, and it remained exasperatingly inactive. By the time we returned to the ship we were tired, discouraged and, as usual, extremely hot. Cool ginger beer awaited us.

The ship's departure was heralded by a hum of creaking winches and excited voices, and above all the hubbub, orders were being shouted. I noticed two young District Officers were boarding with all their luggage. They were the same officers, whose luggage had caused such a commotion being loaded on to the train somewhere between Seke and Malampaka. I was sure of it. How had they managed to overtake me? The endless activity of unexplained comings and goings intrigued me. It was wartime, a time when questions were frowned upon, but this was ridiculous! I clearly remembered the dapper man whose poisoned heel Rue, Bee and I had bound up in the hotel at the Victoria Falls. I had seen him days later from the train and it was an unexplained mystery as to what he was doing hopping on and off my route. These two young men presented an equivalent enigma and this time I was determined to learn more about them.

The tiny port of Bukakata was our first call in Uganda territory. Here the pretty nurse from Zanzibar left us for a holiday with friends living in the hills. As she departed, I noticed the young Corporal whom she had nursed with dysentery and malaria in hospital in Zanzibar, was overcome with grief. I believe the parting of the ways weighed far more on his heart than hers, and I felt sad for the young man. Miss Morris and I went on land to visit a little local souq. Fruit and vegetables were spread out on the baked ground, and we happily bartered for tangerines, small pineapples, poor bananas, and oranges. After being invited to handle beautiful shiny red chillies, I stupidly touched my lips, and suffered the burning sensation for at least an hour afterwards!

A beautiful little girl was seated on the ground next to a mat piled with native vegetables. She must have been about ten years old; her smile charming, and her ebony skin glowed with health. What was shocking was that her right arm was severed above the elbow and ended in an unsightly stump. Her father spotted me studying her and I averted my eyes embarrassed, but he was proud of his daughter, quite rightly, and by means of mime told me that she had survived a crocodile attack when she was little. I think this gave her some sort of kudos in the village as I noticed women surreptitiously touching her lightly on passing, as if she would bestow good luck. These villagers lived so close to the riverbank; crocodiles were something that they had to live with. I realised how little I knew about these frightening creatures.

Later in my cabin I dug out the book on African animal characteristics gifted to me by Madame Cabou in Elizabethville and found the relevant chapters. I was stunned! I had no idea crocodiles were so fascinating! The information was endless, and I had a treat in store. Crocodiles can stay stock still under water for up to two hours as they lie in wait for prey! Nile crocodiles kill between two hundred and three hundred people every year, as they will eat anything that moves. They primarily eat fish, birds, reptiles, antelopes, wildebeest, and zebras. They eat several times a month or can last a year without if necessary. A few of the facts I was to learn.

After a day in port, a late-sunset glow of gold lay over land and water and enticed Miss Morris and me to walk toward a bridge where two old boats formed a small breakwater. Our chat exposed an extraordinary coincidence, that she had once visited her sister who lived in the Cotswolds.

"I remember it well," she enthused. "The rolling green landscape and all those stone cottages and walls. They were such pretty, warm colours. You have some beautiful houses, with such history, and folk like you live in those houses! I couldn't get over it!"

I laughed "It's a different world, certainly. My parents in law lived in a beautiful old house in Painswick, and initially we lived with them, but the oldest house I ever lived in was Wickstreet House which was amazing. We rented it while we were building our own house, and my second daughter was born there. Wickstreet House dated back to 1633 and we felt privileged to live there. It was a treasure trove! It even had a priest hole, a trapdoor under polished floorboards leading down worn stone steps to a hiding place."

"Goodness, was it just as it was? Surely it had been modernised to some extent?"

"Of course, but very sympathetically. A stream running from below the house was the source of the water pumped up into storage tanks in the house and barns. I remember the moulded ceilings and stone mullion windows through which you had an incredible view. There was a music room and a little Gazebo that had been added in the late eighteenth century." I stopped suddenly, aware that I was painting an elitist picture that might alienate my companion.

I was transported back to a long hot summer there, heavy with pregnancy. I was looking after three-year-old Joy who loved nothing better than to play in the stream tumbling down to feed the small trout pool, shaded by oaks, that lay in the valley beneath the house. I often took a picnic for us and tried to write poetry, or read, whilst keeping an eye on my inquisitive daughter. Originally, I supplemented our picnics with watercress straight from the bed the stream wandered through. It seemed such an idyllic, romantic thing to do, but I was horrified later to learn of the existence of liver fluke, a parasite that attaches itself to watercress and can be easily ingested. Joy never exhibited symptoms, but my wild watercress days halted immediately. The climb back up to the house afterwards was always penance for lazy hours amusing myself.

Teddy was away so much that summer, either working at the mill or organising the building of our future home, The Knapp. He and his architect and artist friend, Charles Gere, were mad on the Arts and Crafts movement and designed our house along those lines with stylish doors, a fireplace, beams, and interesting corbels. When it was finally completed, he inserted a 1910 datestone in the sitting room. Teddy wanted it to be perfect for his family and I like to hope that the house we created gave future families the pleasure it gave us.

"What did your husband do for a living?" Miss Morris brought me sharply back from England to Africa and I apologised, as we walked on.

"He inherited his parents' business. A mill in Painswick, in the Cotswolds. It made hair pins, and snap studs, and later, war requisites. One hair product was named after me, Elf grips! But Teddy's heart was never in it. He was far more interested in photography, playing cricket, and making music. He pulled out of the business a few years after the Great War."

"A lot of men were disillusioned after the War. Did he serve overseas?"

I remembered the anxiety so well, the day Teddy volunteered for the army. He was determined and would not listen to any of my protestations. I have never changed my view that war was created by maniacs, totally out of touch with the horror it imposes. We had to present a united front and explained it to the children and all four of us walked up to the recruitment office together. My husband wanted to fight for our country, and nothing would deter him from his sense of obligation. The children were excited, not understanding the implications if he faced active duty overseas. I had to supress my fear in front of them and watched tensely while the recruits were lined up on different sides of the Painswick village street according to age. I was appalled at the flag waving excitement of the crowds that gathered. We learned that the younger men would be sent to fight overseas after the initial training period, whereas older men were considered only fit to fill jobs on the Home Front. Teddy was too old, and his pride suffered that morning. I saw it in the tightening of his jaw and his moody silence, but I was very relieved for my children and myself.

I answered, "No, he was lucky. As he was over thirty-five Teddy never saw active service. He served in the Royal Artillery and ended up as aide de camp to General Adair who was Commander in Chief Army Operations. His lasting claim to fame was that he learned to take jumps sitting back to front on his horse!"

"Ah! The mysteries of warfare!" she smiled.

Myriads of flies awoke and came out over the low marsh by the lake's edge. This special variety of lake fly, big with long transparent wings, was reputed not to bite, but something was biting me with troublesome persistency, so we turned back again ship wards. I noticed in the darkening sky what appeared to be tiny, bright spots flying round in pairs, unattached with no visible means of suspension. The little pairs darted away, returned, hovered, descended, and then repeated their performance. We watched transfixed; our bites forgotten. They flew like dragonflies with transparent iridescent wings, backwards as well as forwards, and that was indeed what they were.

All was quiet on deck on our return, the Army occupied out walking. Mr Wilkins produced wine glasses and showed us how he played tunes on them. I have heard musical notes made on fingerbowls or glass rings, but never had I heard such a bell-like melody in such an exotic setting. It was entrancing.

Later that night loading started in earnest, the winches running noisily until well after midnight. Sacks of hapogo and coffee lay about. It was impossible to sleep with all the noise and I tried to read Helen Simpson's 'Below Capricorn' lent by Miss Morris, but it was a losing battle. When we finally left port, the night was further wrecked by a crowd of young men camped below our deck. A local princeling, the Kabaka of Buganda, had just come into power owing to his father's death and had embarked to return with many attendants to his domain. I couldn't resist a quick peek at the crowd, but it was hard to detect which one the king was, as they all looked scruffy in the dull night lighting. They were enthusiastically celebrating the occasion with no sign of fatigue. The party extended into the early hours. Miss Morris finally went out on deck to find a ship's officer to go and remonstrate with them, and at last came peace and some sleep.

June 2 1943

Tea was brought early as we were coming into Entebbe, on the Equator. I dressed quickly and watched our arrival at this charming port. The tiny quay lay quiet. The ground sloped up through park-like green lands, with shady trees and part of a golf course visible. A fine residence crowned the hill behind it. Entebbe was the administration capital of the Uganda

Protectorate and looked wealthy from my view of it. Our stay was all too quiet and brief with no time to go ashore, or perhaps no permission to do so?

Then came Port Bell with its delightful jetty. Low green hills with woods at their feet, and the Sesse islands, only partly wooded, formed a most attractive setting. Here Miss Morris left us, and I waved goodbye as her friends came to carry her off. She had been a pleasant and reliable travelling companion, if not particularly stimulating.

I was leaning over the ship's balcony when to my delight the two District Officers joined me.

"Hello, I see you've been deserted!" Brian Roberts introduced himself and his friend Rupert Beech, "Are you hoping to have a look at Kampala? I'm sure it would be interesting."

"I did hope there'd be a chance, but it's six miles inland. I don't know how long we'll be staying. My name's Ethel Warmington Reed."

"Goodness, that's a mouthful!" seemed to escape from Rupert before he looked stricken.

I laughed, "I couldn't agree more, but it has a history! My husband Edward Thomas Reed had the misfortune to be called the same name as his father, Edward Reed. As a young man, still living at home, he was fed up with having his post opened by his father. The climax came when their attaché cases were mixed up and my future father-in-law arrived in church to play the organ for a wedding and found cricketing whites in his case! At the same time my husband, about to play in a local match, instead of white flannels, found organ music! 'Warmington' was his grandmother's maiden name and he decided to adopt it. It would be refreshing if I could ask you just to call me Elf." Even I surprised myself! I had decided that the chance to connect with interesting people was all too brief and felt unrestricted by this charismatic couple.

"Elf? How charming! Makerere College is only two miles outside Kampala, and I'd love to revisit that." enthused a relieved Rupert, "It's the university for the East Africans. One of only three in Africa!"

"What do they study?"

"The college covers scholastic studies and agriculture and a technical school nearby trains the future artisans. Most of the students are Christians and all hold scholarships."

Brian laughed "Don't get him started! He can become boring! He lived in Kampala as a child and is proud of it!"

"But I put you both down as English through and through?"

"There is none so English as those who have only been educated in England, don't you know?" Brian smiled widely and I had to agree.

Rupert continued, "Risking the boring tag, there is also Malago, the African's hospital where students receive medical, pharmaceutical, and nursing training. Most importantly they train reliable General Practitioners who can help their own people."

"I've heard they're often clever in research and especially in diagnostics." I was cut short by an outburst of cheering. The newly appointed king, thronged by his followers, went slightly shakily ashore. He wore a brightly coloured long coat to be greeted by a small crowd who had been waiting patiently. Nothing else distinguished him from his hungover friends but I imagined that this would be quickly rectified!

"We're wasting time. Let's grab a taxi. Are you with us, Elf?"

But finding a taxi was not so easy, as the king had beaten us to it. Telephoning from the boat failed to produce another one, so we contented ourselves with a walk. The road was excellent, and the luxuriance of greenery hedged it on each side, but it was extremely hot. Having thought I would be driven I carried my embarrassingly heavy handbag. Brian saw me struggling and helped me carry it. I am sure he must have cursed me! My companions pointed out the big Government prison we could glimpse through the trees on top of the hill. They showed me the cassava growing, tall stems with big spreading leaves; also pawpaws, bananas, and mangoes. We passed a little shop that had dried fish spread out on the ground outside, where we ran into one of the majors about to return to the ship as it was too hot. He told us the fish were dog fish, the smallest variety of shark, and that they lived in fresh water. Later Rupert told me that in fact these were catfish.

On the way back we encountered a local European who stopped us, keen to talk. He wore a white shirt with an emblem on it, green trousers, and a red belt. His hair had not been cut for many a year.

"Nice walk, Madam?"

"Delightful, thank you. It's lovely and quiet here." I answered.

"You wouldn't have said that last month. We had an American troop transport landing here at Fort Bell. I saw them myself, about a thousand troops. They were hanging about, stretching their legs, walking about. They were guarded too! Sentries all around with anti-aircraft guns!"

"I'm not sure you should be telling us this!" Brian cut in.

"Oh, there's no harm in mentioning it now! It was last month!"

"But still! I think it's important not to talk of these things." Brian continued

"Well. They weren't here long. Just enough time to refuel as they had a long trip still to go. They were on their way to China!" He stared at us to see our reaction. This last piece of information made me doubt his credibility!

The quay was littered with many cases of dried fish, ghee, cassava and some brown material, swathed in bundles that looked like bark. The breeze was freshening and before long the ship started again. By lunch there was quite a roll on the little steamer. I could hear soldiers on deck playing quoits lurching, laughing, and joking. I had retired to my cabin, but the motion of the boat upset me. The room felt oppressive.

I wished the South African Railways had been able to arrange a break in my journey, I would have liked to stay in Kampala for six peaceful days instead of going on in that heat from Kisumu to Nairobi, and back to Namasagali and Butiaba. This would have saved three nights in Nairobi, and another three on the train. When I had tried to arrange it in Cape Town, I was told the Army had taken over the hotels in Kampala, and South African Railways had been asked to send no more travellers there at present. There was also a difficulty over African drivers taking a solitary woman traveller on so long a run to Namasagali or Butiaba. When questioned about that last point, I had been met by evasions on the subject and a brick wall approach. There had been no arguing with them.

The departure of Miss Morris meant that I remained the only woman left on the ship. This might have bothered me had I been thirty years younger. I had only received courtesy and genuine interest from the British Army who I appeared to be travelling with. Did they view me as some mad grandmother, who I might well be if all had gone well with Ronny's pregnancy? At sixty-four I was hardly a honey trap! I hoped they saw me as a mature and interesting woman in her own right.

Another lurch of the ship took me out of my cabin as I tried to forget my queasiness in interesting talk with two officers, one of whom was Intelligence. They talked, and I mostly listened or asked questions trying to put a break of discretion on my interest. I lacked the skills of Mata Hari and the patience, so I learned little, but it was refreshing to meet progressively minded Army men.

I started shivering that evening which was concerning with malaria always present. The heat was still oppressive, so I was running both fans in my cabin. As we sailed along the fresh breeze had turned into a persistent wind and there were indications of rain arriving. The cabin was too hot, and the deck was too cool! I thought this contradiction reflected the country I was crossing. In many areas I had passed through, drought and failure of crops had produced famine and the relief being sent out would have to be kept up for some time. Superficially, untrained eyes like mine could detect no unusual signs, though the locals I passed were often very thin, and the children had the usual prominent tummies.

As I closed my cabin door for the night, I was tired, below par, and feeling alone.

June 3 1943

During the morning we reached Kisumu and across the little bay I saw the airport and watched the seaplanes alight and taxi around. We were now in Kenya, and I was told there were over three million indigenous people, fifty to sixty thousand Indians and about thirty thousand whites, roughly speaking, living here. Feeling stronger, I finished my packing and went ashore escorted by a young corporal who insisted on accompanying me on the long walk into Kisumu town. He and his mate oversaw the smart and disciplined local troops on board. He was worryingly pale as he was just recovering from malaria, and his side kick was now ill with it. The heat was oppressive, and our steps flagged in the lack of shade. My companion looked grey by the time we arrived. Having found a chemist, I left him there to rest while I wandered around but found little that interested me. We had been warned to be back on the ship punctually for lunch and then to secure our berths on the train to Nairobi. This train was stationary alongside the steamer on a siding, and we and our luggage were to board there before it drew into the station ahead.

The corporal, looking marginally refreshed, and I reached the ship again parched with thirst. We sat with his ill mate to order drinks, but not a drop of anything could be served until the lunch which eventually arrived just as we were giving up hope of survival. I was leaving the table when I ran into a breathless Brian and Rupert on deck.

"Are we too late? Has lunch been served?" panted Rupert

"Yes, they're finishing up now. Where've you been?"

Brian groaned, "We went on shore early and walked to a hotel Rupert knew of to get a drink. Quite a long trek! Great looking hotel but they wouldn't serve us a drink until lunch! We didn't dare wait for it, couldn't find a taxi, and had to walk back! And now we've missed lunch here! That's the last time I am following your advice Rup!"

"I'll wangle a drink for us at least." Rupert disappeared below.

I smiled recalling what an issue food was for my husband. Teddy was always concerned about where his next meal was coming from. It was a top priority for him, a security blanket! When as a newlywed I was pushing for us to live on our own I think he was alarmed that he wouldn't get fed if he left his mother's house. He knew my interest in food did not compare to his. I used to joke I would have to bury him with food, like the ancient Egyptians, to accompany him on his last journey. Mrs Reed obviously had the same concerns for her darling son and organised a village girl to come and cook for us once we had our own house.

Brian and I were distracted at that moment by the hair-raising sight of an apparition on the shore close to the steamer. A skeletal man, his face hideously painted, was making uncouth noises, and shuffling his feet in a sort of dance. The front of him was covered in dead white ash and the back of his head was reddened, his head fringed in a semi-circle of high gaudy feathers. Showing beneath grotesque tatters of clothing were coloured patches of skin.

"Is he a witch doctor?" I asked

"Yes, a medicine man. Most likely gone mad, by the look of him!"

As we watched the gyrating vision, Rupert returned armed with four bottles of ginger beer, and I suggested we repaired to my cabin where I shared with them the two pineapples, I had bought on the lake at Bukata.

My luggage was duly taken off to the railway siding. I had long since ignored the look of disbelief of porters seeing my pile of suitcases and my trunk. I was sorry to leave the lake, but I followed my luggage in the sizzling heat to board the train. Once again there was a problem with my coupe, as two people were already occupying it. Fortunately, Brian and Rupert had caught up with me and pulling their District Officer status, called over the assistant stationmaster who was again, a Sikh. Suddenly I had a coupe to myself for which I was most grateful. This excellent person, bearded and turbaned, smilingly refused cigarettes or money for his trouble. Relaxing, I watched while British soldiers, perspiring freely, trudged past shouldering their heavy kit. How I loved their Britishness, their good temper, and honest young faces. By now there were quite a few I recognised, and we exchanged smiles and greetings.

It seemed crazy to know that we were heading south again to Nairobi when instinct said we should have been heading north! The train started round the pretty bay beyond Kisumu, past the Vacuum Oil and A.P.O.C. wharves and past the fishermen in the water with their nets of skilfully constructed twigs. I had been told that it was well worth a walk to see these nets, but as always, time did not allow. I had to content myself with a highly interested glimpse at the stakes and netting rigged up in the water. How I wished to slow down this once in a lifetime journey.

Everywhere there was luxurious greenery, and I noticed a different variety of euphorbia tree, new to me. Much green maize was growing, fringed by cassava. The huge high plants were sisal, their stems in the centre of long branches and spiked leaves. Many mauve-pink flowers with deeply coloured centres, not unlike aloes, were in bloom and great trees were hung with canary-coloured blossoms. The colour combinations in Africa were so vibrant and could never have been found in England. There were many huts, one especially large one was tin roofed, others were smaller with thatch over the tin-roofing. All had neat high hedges surrounding them. Perhaps they were Government buildings, or some chief's domain. With all this lush, succulent turf around, it was no wonder that there were such numbers of grazing cattle, and sheep, with their small attendant herders. Not all the cattle were humped, and I remember in the Belgium Congo Madame told me that these were native breeds, now dying out, and being replaced by others more productive. We passed many Indian farms and a Government Experimental one.

As we crept up to Kibos station, a few yards in front of my window a grandly attired young man was sitting on a railing, his modern bicycle lying on the ground at his feet. Scarlet fez; scarlet tops to long pale khaki socks; bright blue knee-length coat; open, showing white shirt, the cuffs of which were neatly turned up over the coat; light khaki shorts; ebony legs below them; black shoes. A gay, gleaming eyed, devil-may-care lad! He was a fascinating picture, and I managed to get a photograph of him. He turned round to shout to somebody and showed a splash of white down his back, where the blue coat, so elegantly cut, had split. It may once have been a woman's coat as it had a row of buttons along each outside sleeve edge. Completely unselfconscious, he surveyed the scene before him with languid interest.

Women passed, walking easily and gracefully, some white striped material wound round head and body, and little naked boys, ran up and down. One walked more carefully, his thin scrap of a body almost floating along balancing an orange a soldier had given him, on his fuzzy little head. I was told the Kavirondo tribe, who live in these parts are very dark-skinned and usually naked. The women wear a little bunch of waving feathers, grasses, or fresh green leaves like a hanging fringe, attached to the base of the spine. To my disappointment none of these women could be seen from the train. Many villagers here wore bangles on their long, thin upper arms, so tight that the flesh stood up around them. They wore them on their ankles too. They were slim boned and the mens' and boys' legs were often terribly thin.

I was delighted to be joined in my coupe by Brian and Rupert who perched on the bed as I had claimed the one chair. Rupert told me that the tribal people here were hard workers in the corn and cotton industries and were peaceful and friendly. We passed several of their closely connected villages with euphorbia hedges surrounding them. As the train continued, on our left the horizon showed a long range of mountains capped with heavy clouds. Green scrub and long grass cut by several streams filled the land between the mountains and the train. The sky, heavy with rain, lowered over us.

We passed Minwani station. Minwani means spectacles which seemed bizarre and had nothing to do with sugar for which this area was best known. I saw many black and white kingfishers perched on the telephone wires, and towering anthills. It was intensely hot and so far, we were only about eight hundred feet above the Lake.

As we passed Kivigori station, with its high eucalyptus trees, the mountains were coming nearer, and it became a shade cooler.

"We're coming into skin country now." Brian said.

"Meaning?" I queried.

"The locals are expert at hunting and skinning in this region. I bought a fine leopard skin here for only a few pounds, a couple of years ago. It looks great in my house." I was not comfortable with the concept of hunting these glorious creatures and rapidly changed the subject.

"Whatever is that huge green crop on our left?" It stood like a solid vertical phalanx, the stalks tall and strong, growing close together.

"I've no idea. It looks as if you could walk for miles on the top of it." Brian replied.

Chemilil station came next, a pretty place whose trees sported very beautiful scarlet flowers, all facing skywards. My charming companions, despite knowing the country well, were disappointingly ignorant of flora and fauna names. We were now 4,039 feet up and it was growing distinctly cooler.

Mohoroni station in the Nyando Valley was our tea stop so, clutching my handbag, I hastened with Brian and Rupert across the tidy little station into the room allocated. A second sitting, if not three were obviously going to be necessary to accommodate everybody. Brian and Rupert, having missed lunch, wolfed down my share of sandwiches and cake, but I insisted on drinking the tea, and afterwards we strolled along the platform. Rupert told me the tribesmen here were Masai and Nandi, of Nilotic origin. I saw two of these tribesmen, thin as usual, wearing knee length sacking tied in a knot on the right shoulder. Each had a long stick in his hand and wore bangles. One of them sported a rather tall hat with a brim, something like that of an old English farmer. Girls, very dark with elaborately dressed hair, gaily arrayed in bright clothes and jewellery, chattered together strolling up and down to catch attention. Their ear lobes were pulled shoulder low with their heavy earrings. I found this an ugly custom, but

Brian, who was used to it, liked it! My interest in them was obvious and they returned it with friendly smiling faces. Rupert tells me the men too are good humoured and friendly, but they certainly look much scarier.

Leaving the station, luxuriously green open country surrounded us. Big white birds in flocks were feeding. A deadly looking tree was covered with a glow of purple thorns. Golden-flowered creepers with rounded leaves, were spreading their branches against the sunlight, casting dark shadows along the ground, spilling vividly in all directions. The mountains had fallen back towards the horizon. Weaverbirds' nests tasselled the trees in a patch of woodland. Majestic billows of cloud hung slumbering motionless in the blue sky, ominous and threatening a downpour. When the train stopped at Koru station, I hung out of the window to find the air was filled with the incessant shrill of crickets. Marvellously hedged in by frangipani and hibiscus, the station was filled with intoxicating perfume and colour. A moment of beauty never to be forgotten. The embroidery of shade and sun entranced me and in a moment of stillness even the sound of wind was quietened.

Later a heavy, black cloud built up to loom above us darkening the sky. At Fort Ternan the rain descended in a sheet. Brian and Rupert, clad in Mackintoshes splashed up and down the platform, revelling in its cool and playing like the children they were. I watched them with envy. Tempting as it was, I had no Mackintosh, and my hair style would suffer irretrievably, so I had to simply watch. How quickly rain scent filled the air, earth, trees, even clothes, and bodies adding to the rich potpourri. Knowing sun is ever near makes wallowing in the rain even more enjoyable. I was reminded of my daughters when they were children in Painswick. In the hot summers I had encouraged them to dance naked on the lawn in warm rain showers. Their bubbling uninhibited laughter continued as I wrapped them in rough towels afterwards. It was another, more innocent world.

Fort Ternan was the country of the Masai. Some of the locals in the station were huddled against walls, or under trees for shelter, looking wet and cold. They wore many necklaces and bands across their foreheads, and their ears were pulled down by earrings. The broad, light-coloured anklets on some of the men were apparently strips of inner tubes of tyres. I then noticed that many of the men's sandals, police included, were made from rubber tyres, each with two bands across the instep to hold them on. Water streamed everywhere, down, along, and up from the choked grating. Brian and Rupert returned to their coupe, and after a delay of half an hour the train was on the move through fine forested land.

We crossed a high, impressive viaduct, curving round a hill. I craned out of the window and looked over and down as much as I dared and shivered over the vastness around, and especially, immediately below me. There were immensely deep cuts in the rock which told me building this line must have been a colossal engineering feat. Still high in the mountains and in the growing dark, the train skirted a grand pass, then thumped and thundered over what appeared to be another immensely high bridge. My side was almost touching a very high rock wall, and I was tempted to lean out in the high wind and gather flowers growing up the cliff face. Sanity prevailed but, in my imagination, it would have been an exhilarating experience. A tiny halt announced 'Tunnel', whose five hundred yards of length or whose very existence I might have missed so easily in the deep twilight, had not somebody's lantern at the little halt met my eyes. Travelling slowly now I could see the smiling friendly faces of the workmen by the line, and we waved to each other in the last glimmer of daylight. All this was the lovely Molo country.

Loombwa station, where we were to have dinner in the station's refreshment room, was totally blacked out. I climbed down gingerly from the train into the darkness. Others were doing the same, and with care we groped our way along the platform till we finally approached a long, lighted room to grab the first seat available. A hungry throng gathered outside for the second sitting. Soup, meat, vegetables, banana and coffee, minus milk and sugar as usual, chased each other down at speed. The train hooted hurryingly, and we all sprang up, our hunger satisfied and hastened out into the pitch black to make way for others. It was with difficulty that I re-found my coupe after walking up and down the platform negotiating all sorts of unlit obstacles, so I was tired and ready to retire to my bed.

Suddenly my coupe was filled with commotion. The refreshment room steward and my bed boy arrived in a heated argument, each politely but insistently demanding from me, my bed and dinner ticket.

"Madam, your ticket for your dinner is to be handed to me. It's my responsibility, and you've omitted to deliver it at the end of your meal." The steward was superior but firm.

"Madam, I have to have the ticket, in order to show it to my boss." The bed boy insisted.

"Madam, once the train has left, I'd have no way to account for the dinners if I do not have the ticket. It is mine. Please hand it to me." The steward held out his hand expectantly.

"No! I need the ticket. It's part of my bed boy duties, and I will be expected to have it." The bed boy tried to elbow the other out of the way. Both seemed desperate.

Finally, I was allowed breathing space to insert my answer, "Neither of you can have it. The waiter who served me insisted on taking it at the end of the meal and promised, without fail, to tell you, bed boy." Both men were now glaring at me.

Brian and Rupert, strolling up the train to say 'goodnight' came to the rescue at that timely moment. Rupert disappeared to summon the waiter, while neither man was prepared to back down and the argument rumbled on between them. We were becoming the light entertainment for the carriage.

Brian suggested, "I've got the solution. The dining room people should keep the card, as they already have it. The bed boy can copy the number of the ticket onto his slip." When the waiter appeared producing the flimsy ticket from his pocket, the number was then copied, and all ended peacefully. Brian and Rupert bade me goodnight.

At last came signs and sounds of departure and I could settle for the night. What a terrible pity it was so dark! Before daylight, we should have passed through and missed seeing Mau, the highest peak of the Kenya uplands, and Molo itself and the lake stations of Nakuru, Elementaita and Lake Naivasha with its flamingos. My only consolation was that this irritating diversion to change trains at Nairobi, meant I should see some of these on my return journey before we branched off towards Mount Bulamati.

EIGHT

June 4 1943

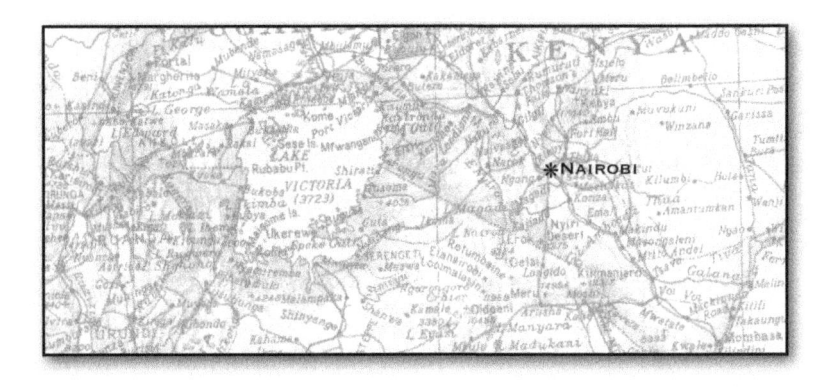

Rain had fallen in torrents during the night. Daylight showed dense forests with occasional clearings through which we were passing. Everything was saturated with moisture and the air was foggy. At that height we must have been on the edge of the Great Rift. I caught a vague glimpse through the mist of a high mountain top, shining clear in the sunrise. At nearly 7,400 feet up, we passed Escarpment station, manned by a few workmen, looking chilled, their garments forlornly lank with damp. The train had risen to 7,689 feet by the time we reached Upland's station. We were still buried in trees, giants of the forest, but fog shrouded everything. A great hill slope was entirely covered in mauve and beyond that sweep the red tinted earth was dotted with cattle and poultry. Limeru station was surrounded by wet rail sheds, wet everything and more fog obliterating the landscape as thoroughly as if it were night-time.

Finally, we started descending and at 7,029 feet we passed Mugug station. I spotted the usual incongruous blue advertisement of one-time British India Sailings to London, Marseilles, and Suez. Somebody's whisky was also advertised.

As we continued to descend, along the railway lay the familiar sight of stacks of wood. These trains burn a good deal, as well as the coal used specifically for some of these precipitous ascents. We passed through groves of black wattle trees from which they extract the juices for tanning purposes, but I understood that these trees were now viewed with concern as responsible for reducing catchment water yields. It was still cold, and piercingly damp, but fertile farmlands started appearing with cotton and maize abounding.

Desolate and empty Kikuyu station displayed a notice declaring 'Camping on Platform Forbidden'. Nothing could look less inviting than attempting to do so! The tribes belonging to these parts were called the Kikuyu, the largest ethnic group in Kenya. They had big reserves with fertile land, but in former days they were always fighting their neighbours and hereditary enemies, the Masai. All seemed peaceful now. How quickly I tired of so much rain. Still 6,210 feet up, we passed the station of Kabete where there was a great barren railway track, open and empty except for huddled shapes sitting in little groups round small fires. From their expressions they appeared half-perished, their sacking and clothes soaked. I shivered in sympathy.

As we approached the Nairobi suburbs, the gardens were full of shrubs and flowers looking even more colourful perhaps in the rain than in sunshine. I opened the window and a breeze blowing in gusts scattered the scent of blossom and tree leaves. In moments when the wind fell, a soft green odour of rain and earth stole through the air like a blessing falling. This was so different from the acrid dustiness I had experienced on much of my trip. I remembered the old Indian saying, 'The fragrance of a flower goes but with the wind, but the fragrance of holiness goes even against the wind'.

Nairobi station was heaving with bustle and colourful crowds, and the city noise was challenging. The rain continued to descend unrelentingly. After a tiresome wait outside the terminus, surrounded by my mountain of luggage, I gave up on the hotel bus that I had been assured would meet me. Abandoning my trunk and cases, I ran skirting wide puddles to the taxi rank and persuaded two of them to attend to me. Finally, the dripping luggage was piled in or tied on and we drove to the New Stanley Hotel.

In reception I was handed a most welcome packet of mail, including a cable from Teddy. The sight of it formed an instant knot in my stomach, but I read it immediately and to my relief, it was warm, surprised, and concerned for my welfare. Containing no sign of paternalistic recriminations, he appeared to be genuinely delighted.

My room would not be ready for half an hour, so I settled for a hearty breakfast despite being extremely tired and aware of the onset of a headache. To my disgust settling the bill created a problem, and I was asked to walk down the street to the offices of the Food Controller. Fortunately, there was a lull in the rain, but I still did so most unwillingly. There I was presented with a token for 'three units of food and one breakfast' to last me for the next few days. Having walked this far I decided it best to do whatever had to be done straightaway, which meant seeing the Superintendent of Railways to whom I had an introduction from Cape Town friends. Inevitably he was out at a meeting. The enforced march had been much longer than anticipated, in fact, practically back to the station. I was in a bullish mood, feeling rather sorry for myself, so I decided to visit the Stationmaster according to my itinerary instructions. He confirmed that all would be well for my continuing journey, so, my halo polished, a taxi took me back to the hotel where I most thankfully went up by lift to my room.

Too tired and dazed to do more than read my cables and bits of my letters, I lay down with these dear possessions in my hand and fell asleep. A gong raised me for lunch, which I decided to ignore and only rose later in the afternoon.

Teddy's cable had reawakened thoughts of him, and recollections of our past life together. It had not been a straightforward road. When we had first met, the physical attraction we had for each other had flared immediately on both sides, and when we discovered that we came from the same neck of the Cotswolds it seemed that our fate was sealed. We laughed that it was absurd that we had to travel the distance of Europe to find each other. There seemed so much that guaranteed us to be a snug fit, our mutual love of music and proficiency with the violin and piano, our enjoyment of playing tennis, our skill handling horses, and for dull days, bridge playing!

The heady romance continued back in Gloucestershire once our studies were over, and inevitably our families were drawn in. Teddy lived with his parents in The Rockery, a beautiful house next to the lucrative Reed's Mill in Painswick, and, being the oldest son, was destined to inherit the running of it when his father stepped down. My uncles considered Teddy a good match. Teddy's parents could not but be impressed with The Vale House, and my uncles' successful business of carpet making. In the haze that overtook us, we found ourselves the centre of family enthusiasm and were spectacularly wedded when I was twenty-four and Teddy was twenty-six, too young! I found myself living with my in-laws almost before we began to understand how different in character, we in fact were. It took time to learn who we had married! Compounding this, Joy was born to us a year later, and Ronny three years after that! Difficulties and misunderstandings, often in the shape of his mother, had to be overcome to make our marriage work. Teddy and I had now lived a lifetime together based on simple love, understanding, tolerance, respect, and liking. After forty years the physical side of our relationship was no longer significant, but I would have been stupid not to understand that the lure of forbidden fruit might be enticing to Teddy. I had no intention of allowing anyone to jeopardise our future together and could only pray that I was not too late.

Strolling leisurely round streets of this fine city, I purchased razor blades for Teddy, a native tray, salad servers made from wild boar tusks, an ivory cigarette holder, and elephant hair twisted into bangle shapes warranted to ward off bad luck. I found an interesting booklet on the Arab horse, and an intriguing one titled 'Crowded Life of a Hermit'! On my return to the hotel which proved to be a popular rendezvous, I met Brian and Rupert in the foyer.

Brian enthused, "We were hoping to catch you. Would you like to have dinner with us this evening at our hotel? The Norfolk."

Rupert continued, "I'm going to invite my boss's wife. The provincial Commissioner's away in England, and she could do with cheering up. Please say you'll come."

"Afterwards we thought we'd go to the cinema." Brian added.

"It's a great invitation, but I warn you, I may not be much company. I'll probably nod off once the film starts. What's showing?" I was dubious.

"Desert Victory! I've heard good reports of it. It's about the Allies' North Africa campaign against Field Marshall Rommel and the Afrika Korps."

"Oh! I've heard so much about that film. They use actual footage of Churchill, Alexander, Montgomery, and Hitler himself. I'd be fascinated to see it. I missed it at Cape Town." I perked up.

"That's a date then!" Rupert beamed.

I found a note had been pushed under my door. 'It is essential all food coupons be handed in at the reception office. You have not yet handed in your coupons.' Wearily I complied, aware that I was becoming disenchanted with my choice of hotel! My bedroom was good, complete with electric clock, telephone, and bathroom, the food was excellent, but I felt that the hotel officialdom was heavy handed and pedantic.

The evening meal at The Norfolk was fun and held a surprise! Rupert and Brian's guest was an eccentric lady with Eton cropped hair and not the pathetic abandoned wife I had anticipated. She was witty and energetic and taught me about a local Nairobi fly, identified by sections of red and blue on its body. To everyone's surprise, she produced a box containing a dead one and I caught Brian rolling his eyes! It was an attractive specimen, but she told me it was in fact a beetle and well known locally for its poison spray. If it lands on you and you brush it away, it sends out the spray that burns your skin. These burns can be very unpleasant and long lasting, especially if they touch the eye.

'Desert Victory' was a good vivid picture, with lots of live footage which I imagine was dangerous to film. We do not know the ending of this terrible war yet, but thousands are already dead, and how many more will be before the end? We must live with the firm belief of a positive outcome.

Rain was falling once again when we came out and no taxi was available, so Brian offered to walk me back under his umbrella, skipping puddles, to the hotel. We had a night cap before we parted, Brian to return through the rain, and I to my welcome bed.

June 5 1943

I slept until midday, and still felt exhausted. Nairobi, the capital of Kenya, was beckoning me to explore but lethargy and anxiety, kept me to my room. I felt as if I had been travelling for months, and I also felt very alone. The cables from my dear daughters, Joy and Felicity meant that they were safe and thinking of me, whilst the letters flown in from Cape Town, full of social events, left me feeling cut off from normality. I found myself in tears reading the letters, caught suspended between worlds and thoroughly miserable.

My worries about my girls, caught in London, so vulnerable to bombing, was no less than the fear of the blank wall of no information from the Philippines where Ronny and Pat were presumably captives of the Japanese. I could not think about the baby, my first and possibly my only grandchild. The energy generated to get this far disappeared in this Nairobi cocoon, and I had no idea from where I could muster the stamina for the next leg. The driving distance from Cape Town to Nairobi was approximately 3,272 miles, and 3,542 miles were yet to come to reach Haifa. How was I going to make it? How totally stupid I had been, not to understand the wear and tear on my person and how vulnerable I really was. Why hadn't I paced myself better instead of hurling myself against a timetable to take in climate, geography, and war conditions. I still had no idea whether I could complete this journey as there was no evidence that I would receive my precious Palestine Entry Visa. All this risk would be to no avail. I felt utterly despondent.

I wished Teddy was with me. He was intelligent, funny, never dull, infuriating, and irresponsible and I loved him. We had been together for forty years now. I remembered so well the day after the honeymoon when I moved in with my in-laws. I had not anticipated living with them, but Teddy had assured me that there was lots of room in the house, and it would work well! Charlotte Emma Reed, Teddy's mother, was an intimidating lady, big bosomed and bottomed. She towered over her husband both physically and verbally. The daughter of a Baptist minister, Thomas John Cole, she could hold forth, and it was her money, the family Cole money, that owned the house and grounds the mill stood on. Cleverly, she rented the property to the mill business. Teddy's father was just the manager. Teddy's much younger sister, Bertha still lived at home but of his two younger brothers, Bert had moved to London and Arthur, had died of appendicitis.

I found that Mrs Reed adored her oldest son and indulged his every whim! Once I was under her roof, relationships became difficult. It did not take long to realise that Mrs Reed resented me and disapproved of my 'tomboyish behaviour' and thought I was a bad influence on the teenage Bertha! Teddy, like his father, knew which side his bread was buttered, and Mrs Reed was indulged with her every whim, all to ensure peace in the household. I struggled to balance my comparatively new relationship with my husband with his long-standing one with his dominant mother. Initially I was no match, and it took hard learned guile to wrest him from her influence. Some of Teddy's traits, learned from childhood, always presented problems, but over the years we managed bleak times together. I had issues too of course and we provided a rock for each other when problems appeared insurmountable.

My pile of luggage lay stacked in a corner of the hotel room. I was totally responsible for this cavalier journey to make sure that my marriage remained secure. Could I have managed to do so in a different way? I had been so sure that this was what I had to do and was prepared to take the risk of the journey. Yes, I could have flown up, provided war restrictions allowed me. I could have tried to wangle a passage somehow, but that didn't feel like the answer. My flat and furnishings still in Cape Town would have given Teddy the message of a temporary reunion. He needed to know that I was home with him for good. I also carried with me, deep in my trunk Teddy's most treasured possession, the cause of much concern and joy over the years. An emblem of all that our marriage meant. My life in Cape Town had ended. My life with Teddy was to be resumed. If I had a dragon lady to outwit, I had to be on the spot. I would be like a crocodile! One of the facts that fascinated me about crocodiles was that they had a second jaw joint, enabling them to clamp down on their prey spreading the force so their jaws did not twist or lose grip during a struggle. That is what I needed. No one was going to take my husband from me. Teddy knew I was coming. If he had been foolish, he had time to put his house in order. I had been painfully aware of one or two secret liaisons he had conducted in the past and had subtly blocked them without dreaded confrontations. My husband was an attractive, charming man and I realised early on that there would never be a shortage of women interested in him.

My thoughts were interrupted by a knock on the door. A messenger relayed a phone call from Brian, an invitation to dine with them again that evening. Time spent with this charming couple was limited as they would stay in Nairobi where Rupert worked, and Brian was about to take up a position there. Long-time close friends, they had been holidaying together, and now were house hunting. I wanted to enjoy their company while I could. They had adopted me, without doubt, over the last few days. Heaven knew why they found my company so entertaining; I was certainly old enough to be their mother. Whatever their reasons, they had made me feel cushioned and I would miss them. I doubted we would meet again. However, that night my body was telling me that I needed time to myself, a relaxing bath, and an early night. They would be my guest on the following evening.

June 6 1943

Listening to the rain against my windows before I opened my eyes, I had to resist the desire to stay curled under the covers. In the night I had recalled my obligation to the Austrian manager of the Park Hotel in Tabora, to go to the Red Cross offices here, in search of news of his wife's mother. She was still in Vienna when last heard of and it was a vain hope, but I had made my promise to him. I treated myself to breakfast in my room before venturing out. Still feeling fragile, I took a taxi and was pleased to curl up in a corner and look at the wide rain strewn streets from comfort. We passed the impressive museum which was known for its excellent bird collection which I hoped to visit, after the Red Cross mission.

The morning passed in a long winded and exhausting way, being passed from pillar to post to no avail. The manager's mother-in-law could not be traced in occupied Austria, which was disappointing if not predictable. The Red Cross staff tried their best. They must have been inundated with similar requests in this terrible time. Certainly, their offices were piled with shambolic looking paperwork and files galore. It must have been difficult for them to keep up with the ever-changing war front and the endless flow of refugees.

I asked methodically for news of my family in the Philippines under the Japanese, as I have done many times before. This time, to my amazement, they did have news. After a couple of phone calls, the homely staff member was able to confirm that the name of Patrick Rynd, my son in law, was recorded as being interned in Santo Tomas prisoner of war camp in Manila.

I was so relieved I could have hugged her and stammered "Thank you so much for that. I was sure that was where they would have ended up, but it's good to have it confirmed. It was the most likely location for the family. Now I know for certain they're there I can relax a little. Given the circumstances they could have done a lot worse."

"Yes, as camps go, we're told it's well organised. Santo Tomas is the old university campus in the city and has all the city facilities. It's run by Japanese civilians, which is bound to be more humane than if it's run by their military."

"I can't tell you how relieved I am. Thank you so much." All those months of silence and worrying had dissipated in that untidy office. A burden had shifted, and my world was suddenly lighter. But…

"Mrs Warmington Reed. Patrick Rynd is the only Rynd mentioned in the register of internees. Could your daughter and the baby be elsewhere?"

"Are you sure? Please check again?" A cold fear gripped my heart.

"I assure you that your daughter's name is not on the list."

"But where else could she and the baby be?" I asked naïvely.

"Are you sure she would be in Manila? The Japanese invasion was very sudden?"

"The last time I heard from Ronny was before Christmas '41. She was about to go to the mountains at Baguio for a week's break. She was looking forward to the baby's arrival in March. Ronny must have returned to Manila to be with Pat. It must be a mistake."

I saw the sudden evasion in the woman's eyes, "If she was in a smaller camp she might not be registered. The Japanese don't feel bound by the Geneva convention, so our information is unreliable."

"Wouldn't you have a record of a British baby being born in a prisoner of war camp?" I couldn't face the lack of hope.

"In the bigger camps like Santo Tomas, yes, but I'm sorry to say not necessarily in the small ones."

I was near tears, "She must be in Santo Tomas. The camp houses men and women."

"Mrs Warmington Reed. I'm so sorry. I wish I could have given you other news. I promise you that I'll keep asking on your behalf."

I had to digest there was no record of Ronny and the baby. I had always assumed that they would be supporting each other, interned together. That morning the silence had been broken, but only for part of my family. My son in law had been traced but the whereabouts of Ronny and the baby were still in inky blackness. If anything, this lack of news was even worse than the images I had comforted myself with before. What had happened to Ronny? Where was she? Surely, as her mother, I would have somehow known if something too terrible to contemplate had happened to her?

Ronny, short for Veronica, had always been the most difficult of my daughters. She was born when Joy was 3, and we lived in the beautiful rented, Wickstreet House. Joy had been such a good child, quiet of nature and obedient. Teddy and I smugly thought she reflected our parenting skills, whereas it was soon apparent that Ronny was a law unto herself and turned our theories upside-down. She had inherited Teddy's reddish hair colouring and his temper! Our interlude of tranquillity was over. Of course, I loved her but confess to handing her over to her nanny's care more often than I did Joy. My second baby seemed to have a will of iron and had reduced me to tears on occasions. Teddy required instant obedience from children which Joy was happy to provide, but I started a lifetime of playing pig in the middle with him and the children. As Ronny grew up, life and relationships always seemed challenging to her. She confronted life head on and lacked the awareness that there were more subtle ways to achieve her aims. I had wanted my girls to grow up independent women and they were. I just hoped that if Ronny was now in trouble, this headstrong characteristic could help her when she needed it.

I left the Red Cross offices before I broke down. All I wanted was to shut out that whole morning. I wanted to be with people I loved, not halfway up Africa, thousands of miles from any comfort. I vowed not to pursue this enquiry again until I was in Haifa with Teddy at my side. I was in no mood to even contemplate examining the famous bird collection afterwards.

Back in my room, I forced myself to repack the smaller cases. The hotel had laundered all the dresses, blouses, slacks, and underwear I was travelling with as I had no idea when my next opportunity would be. Several handles and straps had gone from my luggage, so I begged string from reception and made sure all was secure. Writing letters to friends, I tried to sound positive and entertaining, but it was a struggle. I just wanted to leave Nairobi behind. It was charmless for me now. I had failed dismally to get a real flavour of this city. I had needed the time to recuperate from my exhaustion, and now I had been placed in an even more despairing place. I had been forced to stay in Nairobi by the travel arrangements made in Cape Town to accommodate South African Railways, and the Army requisitioning hotels. If it had been up to me, I would never have been in the Red Cross offices there. All I wanted was to get back to my old home as fast as I could. I was tired, weakened, and in need of all my strength to persevere with this journey.

An appointment at the hairdresser's filled numbed hours until Brian and Rupert, as my guests for my last evening in Nairobi, arrived promptly to distract me. Listening to their gay chatter, they appeared so young, so protected from life, that I could not cloud the evening with my dark mood. I was not able to share my emotions with this inexperienced couple, attentive as they were. The dining room gleamed with white tablecloths and silver cutlery, and the staff were immaculate in red uniforms. This was a world, far from war or other humanitarian crises, traditional and reputedly attentive to a traveller's needs. It was a cocoon, but I found it hard to relax.

Nothing felt right that evening. I was shocked to see how expensive drinks were and how quickly exhausted. It was embarrassing to see one of the staff going round carrying a large placard announcing 'No More Beer' only half an hour after service had begun. Of course, Brian and Rupert were happy to swap to soft drinks, as was I, but I felt I had short-changed them. Other hotel guests were not so obliging. A group of irate and vocal Army officers made a great show of leaving to seek bottled sustenance elsewhere. I did not want my friends to leave at the end of the evening. My solitary company, for once, was something I did not seek, and I detained them for as long as I could. Finally, they left promising to see me off at the train station next morning.

NINE

June 7 1943

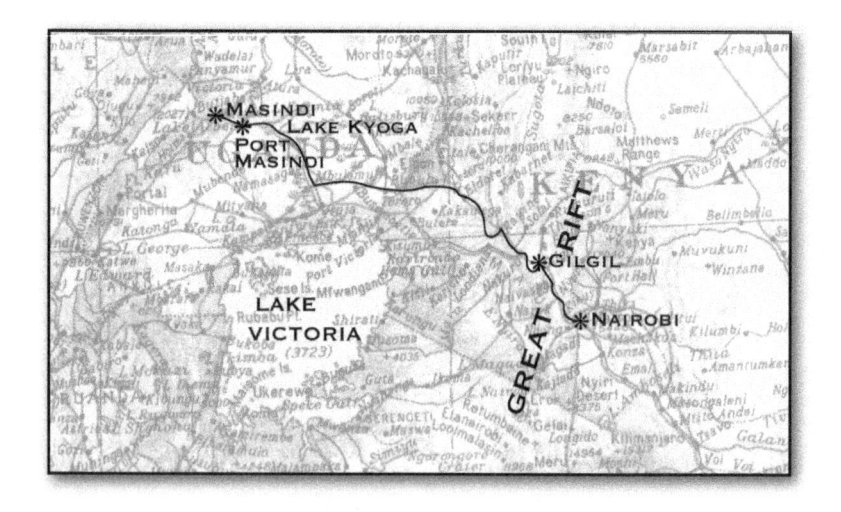

I was up early in a more determined mood, settled my account and had breakfast. Slipping out of the hotel, I bought a pound of ginger biscuits with the half unit that the restaurant had given me as an apology for the shortfall in beer last night. Again, it took two taxis to take me and the luggage to the station. Despite all my best intentions, I had accumulated more luggage, with all the tempting trifles that I was picking up en route. When my train compartment was found, it was a two-person coupe. Having been warned that every seat was taken on this packed train it was with difficulty and ingenuity that my luggage was stored in the corridor by the attendants. Brian and Rupert, as good as their word, came to see me settled in and wish me good fortune. Rupert was on the way to work at the Commission, and Brian had pressing chores so they didn't stay long, which avoided an extended goodbye I would have found difficult to manage. They had been a tower of strength for me, and I was genuinely bereft that I would have to journey on without them.

I was sitting on my berth when a very lame old lady with her officer son entered. He settled her comfortably, gave her a quick kiss and departed promptly. Her pale, lived-in face mapped with fine lines, seemed vaguely familiar to me. Obviously tired, she dropped promptly into a little nap, so I decided to give her quiet time before we started.

Stepping down onto the platform, I startled the son who was still standing outside.

He introduced himself as Major McInnes "I'm so pleased you're sharing your compartment with my mother. It's a weight off my mind."

"I'm happy to help. Where's she going?" I asked.

"To Jerusalem."

"Goodness! That's a long way for her! She's unaccompanied?"

"Yes. I'd be so grateful if you could keep an eye on her."

I was surprised and a little taken aback. Had he meant to speak to me before the departure, or was he leaving the care of his old mother to chance?

"I noticed how lame your mother is, bless her. Aren't you worried this will be too much of a handicap for her to make such a long journey?"

"Oh, she can manage sufficiently with that. Her problem is that she has a very bad memory." He spoke searching my face. I was becoming more alarmed by the minute.

"Do you mean she might forget her name?" I asked thinking that I should have to learn all sorts of information immediately if she was being handed into my care.

"Oh no", he said, "It's not as bad as that!"

"What about the heat? How does she cope?"

I was interrupted by the announcement that the train was leaving, and I scrambled back in without an answer. In truth, I was dumbfounded by this responsibility, dumped on my plate by a seemingly unprotective son.

Her eyes were open again when I re-entered the coupe.

"Mrs McInnes. Your son's on the platform. Wouldn't you like to go to the window to wave him goodbye?" I suggested.

She smiled vaguely "I hadn't realised he was there." The train was just beginning to move by inches, but I helped her to the window in time for her to give him a final wave.

That was the end of Nairobi. The rain had passed, and a pale sun shone on brilliant shrubs and trees as the suburbs were left behind. I had been told in clear weather Mount Kenya, far to the north-east, could be seen, but not on that day. The mountain was only a few miles south of the Equator and reached a height of over 17,000 feet. Somewhere at about 16,000 feet its snow slopes dropped to a little lake, which, despite being so close to the Equator, was covered with ice all the year round.

Mrs McInnes turned out to be an old acquaintance. This gentle lady was the widow of a former bishop in Jerusalem.

"I'm sure we've met before." Mrs McInnes's face furrowed in concentration. "What did you say your name was?"

"Mrs Warmington Reed. Your face also seems familiar."

She smiled, "Of course! I could never forget a name like that! Weren't we on some committee together many years ago? Would it have been in Jerusalem?"

"I rarely went to Jerusalem. My husband and I lived in Haifa!"

"Oh dear, how I wish I could remember better. I've been on so many committees. Part of being married to a bishop, my dear. Haifa? What would I have been doing in Haifa?" she pondered. "That's not a place that I would normally have gone to."

"I can understand that! Haifa opinion is that in Jerusalem, the Palestinians barely exist. No notice is taken of them whatsoever." Where did that come from!

"I've upset you! I'm so sorry. I didn't mean it in that way. I'm only too aware of the Jewish/Palestinian problem and fear it has only got worse over the years."

"No, I apologise. I'm just falling into familiar patterns. Let's think! If we were on a committee together, could it have been the Y.W.C.A.?"

"Of course. I was the Chairman for when it was being wound down in Haifa! That's why I was there. I believe you were a king pin in the organisation and that's where I met you!"

"Yes of course. That was it!"

Mrs McInnes told me that since her husband died, she had been living mostly in England and Nairobi. There was nothing wrong with her long-term memory, and she turned out to be informative and interesting.

The train returned the way I had come, through Kabete, which I learned was famous for its experimental farm and bacteriological research laboratory. A Nandi flame tree burst into sight in full bloom, a superb picture. On neighbouring cork trees little branches like red candles grew skyward. The train was travelling slowly, climbing all the time. Away south-west of the track lay the big Masai Reserve. These Masai, now settled peacefully, were once extremely warlike and gave a great deal of trouble to the surrounding country. We passed Kikuyu Station again and Kikuyu women from the large reserve were carrying loads on their backs, supported by broad bands across their foreheads. The men and boys of this tribe wore just a sack from knee to shoulder where it was tied. A swathe of blue forget-me-nots lit up a hill slope and reminded me of blue wild hyacinths in Sussex, and the blue thistles of Palestine.

Again, we came to Limuru Station at 7,341 feet. This time, with no fog impediment, I could see the bracken on the hills. I was told there was no malaria here. English fruit, tea and flowers grew well and there was horse breeding. Bamboo forests with feathery masses flourished, and wattle for tanning was a great source of revenue. Just before reaching the top of the ridge lay Uplands Station at 7,830 feet up. Vast cattle plains lay to our right with a view over it to distant wooded hills.

Then, suddenly we started descending the Great Rift Valley. I was beside myself with excitement. To cross the Great Rift Valley, that had fired my imagination since English school days, was a feat I never envisioned undertaking. The view was breath taking. High volcanic craters rose. Two of them, Suswa at 7,666 feet and Longonot at 9,111 feet rising out of grand forest scenery, arrested the eye. This time, when we reached Escarpment Station, instead of the dripping mist I saw there a few days ago, the forests were vibrant. A good scent of timber and sawdust pervaded the air. The Rift Valley was a contraction of the earth in its dim youth, an extraordinarily gigantic cleavage in the earth's surface, forty to sixty miles wide. It ran south to Beira and north from there to Lake Rudolph, and through Abyssinia, across the Red Sea and Sinai to the Jordon Valley and Taurus. The enormous valley below the Rift, which was once one of Africa's biggest inland seas, was itself 3,000 feet above sea level. A solitary break in the immense eastern cliff gave a view of the valley which could be seen stretching far into the distance. Along a narrow single platform ran the interwoven tracks of railway line and motor road.

We approached the huge fertile, flat-bottomed crater of Longonot. Locals on the edge of it were driving their cattle to graze there. Little ravines ran down the mountain sides worn out by rainstorms and lava. Kijabe Station, whose name appropriately means 'wind', was halfway down the Mau escarpment. Across the sky the wind chased the dark clouds and a flock of smaller ones; their ghostly shadows fled over the sunlit earth beneath. Far down the Rift Valley, on the plain stretching endlessly away below us, herds of big game could just be distinguished. The railway here skirted or bridged very sheer precipices and chasms and the immensity of construction involved was mind blowing. Longonot Station was like one drop hanging in an ocean of space, the sparkles of Naivasha Lake reflecting up to it. The lake was fresh water, very slightly alkaline, in which fish, wild fowl and hippo abound. Naivasha Station was the hub for European farms of cattle and sheep.

I saw grazing buck, light fawn spotted with black, lovely shapes and colouring on the vivid green grass.

"Do you see those ostriches?" Mrs McInnes pointed out some handsome black-and-white, plume waving birds, spectacular against the light coloured plain. "Those are males; the hen is grey."

"I can't see any females."

"That's because it takes six weeks to hatch their eggs, the cock sitting on them by night, and the hen by day. They're wonderfully camouflaged. I had a pet ostrich once. A man on the farm next door bred them but when the ostrich feather business fell out of the market, he gave the birds up. Couldn't be bothered with them and just turned them loose. One of them strolled into our farm and stayed. When my husband and I went on walks with the dogs, the ostrich came too. If the dogs became excited and barked, the ostrich would immediately come to us for protection! It was the funniest thing!"

"Is it true that that they have a booming note for speech? A bit like a lion's roar?" I asked her.

"There might be some resemblance, but I can't recall any sound they made. It's not ringing a bell in my memory." And she lapsed into silence.

We spotted zebra, numbers of them grazing by the lakeside shaded by pepper trees. Far away on the right I noticed a large camp of some kind and asked Mrs McInnes about it.

"That's the chief East African training camp. Wonderful position for it, isn't it? The plain in the front, the foothills to the side, and the mountains behind. Perfect!"

"Do you know what the mountains are called?"

"Yes, the Aberdare. That camp is where the First South African Division was trained before going into action in the Abyssinian campaign. General Smuts, himself, came up from the Union to address them."

I looked at Mrs McInnes with greater respect. "The Abyssinian Campaign? Wasn't that the campaign against the Italians in `41?"

"Yes, my dear, and very successful it was too!" This was fairly recent information and I wondered how my companion had recalled it.

We reached Gilgil Station at 6,582 feet, the highest point up the slopes of the Rift valley. The Melawa River running through there had excellent fishing, said to be the best in the country for rainbow trout. There were military groups on the platform, many uniforms, including the King's African Rifles, which I recognised. Obviously, the large camp we had passed was fully operational. There should have been information there on the state of the war, if only I could ask. Watching the uniformed men, so far from conflict, I wondered about my own sense of responsibility in the appalling war. Here in the heart of Africa there was no more I could do other than look after myself. In Cape Town I had chafed incessantly over the microscopic help I had been able to give to our lads. The heart-breaking pity of it all had been overwhelming.

At Eburru I learned that this was great bee country. I saw many rolls of matting in the trees, put up for the bees to swarm in.

"I had a friend who lived near here and two swarms of bees a day would pass regularly over her house looking for suitable homes." Mrs McInnes would drop these vignettes into the air and would then forget she had spoken. I was still trying to find a comfortable way to talk to her.

I spotted a small mountain-antelope resembling an oribi, with tufted knees and wished the train would slow down enough for me to have a good look. The lake, a peaceful stretch of water near Elementeita Station now lay east of us. To my delight zebra were grazing near the station, heads all in the same direction, like cows or sheep.

"Zebras have little stamina, but they do avoid horse illnesses like nagana."

"I'm sorry, what is nagana?" I asked

"It's a form of Trypanosoma in horses or cattle carried by tsetse fly. In humans a strand of it causes Sleeping Sickness. There's quite a bit of it around here."

"Isn't Sleeping Sickness fatal to humans? Don't you go to sleep forever once bitten?"

"My dear! Where did you get that idea? The name Sleeping Sickness comes from the insomnia that's one of many serious side effects. Certainly, it attacks the nervous system including the brain and without treatment it can often be fatal."

"I remember playing a game with my daughters when they were little. Smelling sweetly and dressed in their nighties, they'd pretend to have been bitten by a tsetse fly and had Sleeping Sickness. I had to march them up and down to try to stop them going to sleep. They loved that game in the safety of an English house. Now you tell me it had no basis of fact whatsoever!" It was a favourite bedtime diversion and I remembered Joy and Ronny collapsing with innocent laughter.

Mrs McInnes interrupted my thoughts "Zebras stand up badly to breaking in or captivity. They have no heart, poor things. If you try to train them, they just lie down and can die quite easily."

It was my turn to be distracted. I had been looking at the lake, the centre of beautiful grassland set against the mountain backdrop, when I saw what appeared to be a pink sunset cloud or rosy mist. They were flamingos! I had never seen such a sight before. Innumerably gathered along the shores of the blue lake, most of these birds were now fishing for their suppers, heads down, and feet doing their peculiar dancing tread along the lake's edge. Others were whirling and flying around. It was hard to tear my eyes away from such a vision. Was this the essence of Africa? I was delighted to have seen all this splendour, which had been cruelly kept from me by darkness on my original track to Nairobi.

It was sunset by the time we reached Sabatia station, passing east of Mau summit. The train moved between and through grand forested hills and past broken masses of rock bridged by slender arches. Everywhere lay magnificent views, the sky darkening over them, as the last light faded. I stared into these forests where death stalks, but not from war like ours; not humans killing humans.

There was just enough light from one solitary porter with a lamp to stop at a tiny empty halt labelled 'Equator' before we were plunged into a tunnel. We came out again to a similar brief halt, also called 'Equator'. And so, we crossed it at nearly 9,000 feet above the sea level of the far Indian Ocean.

Timboroa Station at 9,150 feet was the highest point in the line but it was too dark to see the magnificent scenery around, only visible to the imagination. Then rapidly we dropped down to 6,875 feet before coming to Eldoret, a healthy spot populated by white European farmers who originally came from South Africa. The Transvaalers still farm on the Uasin Gishu plateau which lay a little north of the Equator on a great plain with the Nardi Escarpment rising to the west. I knew Mount Elgon, with its twin peaks and amazing caves and cave dwellers, would be located to the northwest. Would it be better not to know these things, rather than knowing what you are missing? In the darkness we crossed the Nzira river at Broderick Falls before we came to Totova, the first station inside Uganda. The day had been long enough and with nothing to be seen, Mrs McInnes and I settled down to sleep.

June 8 1943

A difficult night! The heat in the coupe had been stifling and the bed had been so hard that I was surprised not to have found bruises on my body. My original extra mattress had long since vanished during my transfers. I had tried to conceal my restless night and to my amazement Mrs McInnes appeared to have had a good sleep. She must have been tougher than outward appearances would indicate. Our sleeping compartment was fitted with a washbasin and mirror, but the lavatory facilities struggled to accommodate an overcrowded train. Mrs McInnes was in need and the one nearest us was occupied with a man selfishly shaving! I was furious and gave him a piece of my mind.

In Budumba station, whilst sharing my breakfast table with Mrs McInnes, she disconcertingly started a conversation as if she was already in mid flow.

"I never met your husband, but I can vouch for you being a dynamo. I remember well how proactive you were on that committee. I seem to recall that you had written a very sound textbook on marriage when you were younger!"

"Goodness! I'm amazed you remember that!"

"Oh, I read it, but now can't recall its name!"

"'Women and Marriage' under the pseudonym of Margaret Stephens."

"Very good it was too, my dear."

Mrs McInnes smiled at me, sighed, and closed her eyes. I was used to these cat naps and the fact that she would have no memory of conversations when she woke.

I was left recollecting the early, pre children, days when I was living at Teddy's parents' house, The Rockery. He was always busy at the mill with his father, who was a gentleman of few words, and I didn't know what to do with myself. Everything I did felt disapproved of by Mrs Reed and sometimes even the servants. "Now, you don't want to do that, Mrs Teddy!" often rang in my ears. The family didn't own riding horses, but the Reed coachman let me ride the carriage horses when I became desperate for lack of stimulation. I tried to make friends with Bertha. She was a lonely child, timid and repressed by her mother. Hoping to extend her horizons, I borrowed a pony from a local stable and set out to teach Bertha to ride side-saddle. I firmly believed that all women should ride, but sadly Bertha had inherited the same large shape of her mother and was not a natural pupil. The pony, aptly named Dumpling, was lazy and only a slap on his fat rump would induce him to go forward. The lessons went smoothly until the fateful day when Bertha was thrown, right in the path of the Governess cart bringing the coachman and Mrs Reed home from an engagement. Bertha was none the worse for the tumble but my standing in the family reached an all-time low. Something had to be done and Teddy could no longer ignore my entreaties that we lived in a house of our own. His solution, with the help of an architect friend, was to design a house to be built on land abutting his parents' house and the mill. The location of the proposed house seemed to satisfy his mother, and when he rented a house nearby for us, it certainly satisfied me! The saga of building our own home dragged on endlessly while Teddy, obsessed by the Arts and Crafts movement, strove for perfection. Time and budget dictated it to be a battleground with the builders. My special delight were the beautiful painted tiles of birds that Teddy found to line our fireplace. They were of recycled tin glaze and were already over one hundred years old. They and the stone corbels of intricately carved nature and animals helped create exactly the house we dreamed of. We called it The Knapp, and in its two acres I started my small holding in '14 when war was declared.

We left Budumba station but not before I had bought a brightly coloured satchel from a colourful character who was hawking his wares along the platform. It looked very strongly made, was incredibly cheap and I thought I had a bargain.

That day we passed several pretty stations. At one there were large posters displayed of Churchill and Roosevelt and I wondered what possible sense the local population made of that. The brilliantly blossoming trees we passed were Nandi Flame or African Tulip trees. At Kabiro Station I saw paw-paw trees full of green clusters of fruit which I desperately hoped would be sold from the platform, but I was out of luck. We crossed a big marshy area called the Mpologama swamp. The railway had to have an earthen causeway, a mile long and a five-span bridge to carry it across the swamp. Frustratingly, every time we passed close to water my hunt for crocodile was thwarted.

Passing through maize fields, banana groves and ant hills, we stopped at tiny stations all presented with great local pride. Kaquali station even displayed roses growing in profusion and I was reminded of Teddy's passion for roses. One woman on the platform was selling a product that was balanced on her head wrapped in green banana leaves tied with bass. I was curious but made no headway communicating with her, so settled for buying a pineapple from a charming small boy with a smile that split his face. I could foresee a great future for him!

It came as a shock when we arrived at Mbulamuti Station where we were due to change trains. We were given no advance notice to gather our things together and I had to organise Mrs McInnes as well as myself. To my horror the ancient train on the other side of the tracks awaiting us, was rapidly overwhelmed by far too many passengers. The heat was now considerable and chaos, shouting, and frayed tempers were in evidence. I couldn't compete with this scramble especially with the responsibility of Mrs McInnes who surveyed the scene with quiet patience assuming that all would be well. Nervous about leaving my considerable luggage behind, I hung out of the open coupe door, and eventually caught the eye of porters.

The old lady and I followed behind the perspiring men and finally found ourselves squeezed into a tiny coupe that already housed another two women. The porters wanted to be rid of their burdens as quickly as possible and piled the luggage into the coupe, there being no room in the corridor. To my embarrassment it blocked most of the light through the window, and none of us could move around at all. It was hot and dusty, and the odour of too many closely packed bodies was unpleasant. Stories of train transports of prisoners or displaced persons came to mind. I could not believe that I had paid for this privilege, and it was considered an acceptable form of transport for anyone. I felt like a prisoner and Mrs McInnes felt like a ball and chain, through no fault of her own. She was obviously to be part of my burden and in these tight confines, she was a charge I did not appreciate. The two women who shared our coupe were as dismayed as we were, especially when they saw the number of paraphernalia I was bringing with me. They complained bitterly to a passing official. We were told that it would only be for an hour, so being English, we settled down to make the best of it.

Through a triangle of visibility out of the dirty window I managed to see the flat and wooded land we passed across. Great stacks of timber lined our route, as fencing and rail sleepers seemed to be a stalwart industry. Later I caught sight of a fresh and winding river, running parallel with us. It struck me as almost insignificant but I was informed it was the young Nile! It was fresh from its old mother Lake Victoria and its outburst at Jinja and the Ripon Falls and, streaking along, it was growing visibly with such a life story. How I wished I could study it in less uncomfortable surroundings.

The heat was exhausting and Namasagali Station arrived not a moment too soon. The two ladies were delighted to see the back of us. Mrs McInnes found movement without sticks almost impossible and needed someone to steady her, so we tumbled out of the train with relief and no dignity whatsoever. I secured several porters. With no knowledge of the number and location of her luggage, the old lady's cases just joined mine, and the responsibility was mine too. The number of porters we needed and the funding of them did not seem to occur to her. What was she doing wandering around Africa on her own like a babe in the woods? I totally understood her need to remain independent, but the reality was that unless someone, like me, chose to help, Mrs McInnes would have been lost. Dangerously so! The heat and tiredness were getting to me, and I needed to concentrate hard not to answer brusquely to her innocent chatter. Fortunately, the steamer at this small port was within an easy walk from the train, and I chose to do that rather than join the taxis that transferred the old lady and all our luggage. I needed the breathing space to myself.

On arriving on board, I asked for Captain Jack Muir. I had been given to understand that he was the captain of the steamer and an old friend of my Cape Town friend, Phyllis. Cape Town and fun with Phyllis was a distant memory, but I had given my word that I would deliver an introduction to him.

In the oppressive heat I was desperately thirsty by the time I collared an officer, the ship's head-steward who explained "I'm afraid that this isn't Captain Muir's ship."

I was stumped. "Oh no! I promised to deliver a letter to him!"

He pointed "That's his house, over there. It's an easy walk if you choose to go over, Madam. You've plenty of time before we depart."

"The first thing I need is a drink. What's available, please?"

"I'm sorry Madam" was the answer, "No drinks will be served until we serve lunch in a couple of hours." Why was I not surprised!

Captain Muir's house suddenly looked very attractive set up a steep slope above the lake's beach. I determined to go there immediately, to find a drink if nothing else. Starting out in the direction the officer indicated I could not see the path he had recommended. Drooping with heat I decided to take a direct climb up a high perpendicular bank and after much slithering, scrapes and puffing found myself in a pretty garden. The attractive roomy-looking bungalow was well wired against insects, and my unexpected arrival was spotted by a servant. A pleasant Mrs Muir appeared. Conscious of my beetroot colour, and dishevelled hair I produced my note and received a warm welcome. To my joy the captain and Mrs Muir offered me iced beer which I drank gratefully. I cannot recall wanting a drink so badly except in Kabala. Really absorbing thirst is a surprisingly painful condition.

The Muirs had just finished lunch, but we sat and talked in the cool of their bungalow. They showed me photographs of their son who was in the army, in France they thought. A good-looking young man, quite close in age to my youngest daughter Felicity. Flick had been our surprise child, our unintentional gift to ourselves, born thirteen years after our oldest daughter. She had it easier than either of her sisters as Teddy was older and was always charmed by her. She could do no wrong in his eyes. Born the year before the Great War ended, she was our symbol of hope of a new world. How infuriating and tragic it was that we were now struggling through another war. Not knowing how your children fare is painful no matter what age they are. Lunch was to be served shortly on the steamer so after a civilised hour Captain Muir took me back to the ship. Amused at my unconventional climb to his bungalow, he showed me the path much nearer the boat that I should have taken.

I found that my cabin had been changed from the one I had assumed I would share with Mrs McInnes. Suppressing my delight at my good fortune I relished the single berth at the back of the boat. From the little deck behind I could watch the lovely line of foam the churning paddles made. Mrs McInnes had been allocated a new cabin companion; a young, slender Polish girl called Miriam who was travelling along the same route.

***

The Victoria Nile finally reached Lake Kyoga and we started on the one hundred and six mile run along to Masindi Port. The coastline was brilliantly green. Here and there I saw large advertisements propped up in the most conspicuous way possible. Somebody's Brandy attracted my eye, and I thought it was a shame that the commercial world was intruding on this wild landscape. The afternoon was spent indolently, the heat of the day relieved by a light breeze rising from the lake. All was quiet after the constant hubbub of the train and I allowed my mind to drift over the water, bringing it firmly back to the present every time it strayed into dangerous emotional territory.

My new friend, the head steward had no pressing engagements and made an informative companion when we spent time together on deck.

"Lake Kyoga is more like a maze of waterways than one sheet of water." He explained. We stared at the landscape in companionable silence and watched it change as the water became host to islands of vegetation floating around us. "This swampy network is called sudd. I've been on this route for ten years now, and it's never the same. I guarantee you that in a hundred years' time there'll be no lake here."

"What do you mean?" I was surprised and studied the dense subaqueous growth as it floated by. Some islands were crowned by tall pampas rising as high as fifteen feet above the water.

"These islands are a growing mass of vegetation. They're

gradually winning as the water recedes. Sometimes sudd is quite a danger to these little steamers. At flood times big masses break away from the main marsh, colliding and piling up on each other." The officer enjoyed an audience.

"Do you mean that sudd behaves like pack ice? Breaking off and drifting on whatever current carries it. Even catching boats between blocks of it?" I asked.

"Yes, much the same. Often the waterway must be cleared to make steamer traffic possible. If the sudd remains in one place long enough it becomes root attached, although the force of water can tear it away. Floods are when it's at its most dangerous. It's totally unpredictable in that drifting state and can force other stretches to break away from the mother swamp too."

"How fascinating. I imagine that steering through those conditions must be a skilful job!"

"I can assure you that Captain Dix has been doing this route for a long time. He's Norwegian, and navigation is in his blood!" The head steward was swift to allay any fears. I had seen this hairy gentleman, hunched like a Nordic chessman and definitely unapproachable.

"How come Captain Dix ended up in Africa? What's his story?" I probed, but my friend was not to be drawn. He was equally reluctant to talk about himself and his decisions that led to this backwater of life.

Later, in my cabin before bed, I thought about his prediction that the lake would finally eat itself up. Why should the world we live in stay static? We were imposing so much on our world in the name of progress, and it was difficult to remember that the natural world would be sorting itself out in tandem with us.

June 9 1943

My little 'stern' deck was a delight. I was glued to the beautiful sunrise on land and water. The glorious colouring and swish of foaming track behind the ship made me wish I could capture that hesitation, before the day started, in paints. My camera was so limited. Perhaps the process of trying to catch the glow in oils would freeze this breath-taking sunrise in my mind. Sadly, my talent is in making music or poetry, not paintings.

Masindi Port was reached after breakfast, and I was sad to be moving on. Once again, I had to collect my luggage in the space of a hectic half hour. A battered posse of small buses destined for Masindi Town, about thirty miles away, awaited us and I allowed myself to be sandwiched into one of them. On the route I saw sisal drying beside the road for the first time. Fine, light silken swathes of gold were laid across raised lines for the purpose and it was a pretty sight.

It took all of two hours' travel to cover the distance in vehicles that were on their last legs. I was grateful to see the straggling hotel that greeted us in this small town. The bedrooms ran along an open balcony of the hotel, and Mrs McInnes was immediately escorted to a single room, before our group was attended to. No single bedroom awaited me!

"It seems that we're sharing this time, Miriam!" I had run out of energy to challenge these decisions when I had originally been assured I would never have to share on this journey.

"I'll just check with Mrs McInnes whether she wouldn't feel easier sharing with one of us." Miriam darted out of the room before I mustered the thought, but she was not gone long.

"She's happily ensconced and doesn't want to move!"

I caught Miriam's eye and started to laugh. It was so obvious that both of us had been angling for the single room, and Miriam joined me with an infectious guffaw totally out of keeping with her slender frame. We sank on our beds gasping for breath. The room was painted pale green, and I saw the fly blown notices on the wall warning us of several types of insects that were prevalent here. The mosquito nets were the most welcome sight.

An easy morning was spent getting to know each other. Miriam was a young Polish Jew, with impeccable English, embarked on travelling from Mozambique to Cairo.

"My father runs a jewellery business. He had a family business in Krakow, and our roots were in Kazimierz for several generations."

"Africa must seem a far cry from Poland. Are you here on your own?" I wondered if Miriam's story might be a difficult one. She was a lovely looking young woman, with a sweet smile that dimpled on one side. Her short black hair was cut in a modern style, and she moved with the ease of a lean athletic body.

"My mother and father are here in Lorenzo Marques. One of my brothers had already come over here in '40 as my father was expanding and starting branches in many capital cities. My father's a shrewd businessman." I wasn't surprised at this. Miriam's clothes and luggage indicated discrete wealth.

"Are you going to Cairo on holiday?" I asked.

"My younger brother lives there. I'm acting as my father's emissary. My father doesn't want him living in Egypt anymore. He doesn't think it's safe."

"Surely, it's less dangerous now that the Germans are retreating. But I can understand his concern. This isn't a safe world now. With your background in Poland, I imagine you experienced Hitler's threat at first hand." I was fascinated to hear her story, but I was still a stranger to her.

"It was my older brother in Milan who managed to get the family out. We owe him a lot." Miriam changed the subject pointedly.

A visit to the Police H.Q. was necessary and Miriam and I took Mrs McInnes's passport as well as our own to be stamped. Later we walked on along the flat, hot road to the little native shops. They were poor, but we had a good laugh at the grotesque hats of a bygone fashion in the window of one shop, even if we couldn't find anything to buy. Could I have ever worn such a narrow-brimmed enveloping basin? I seem to remember one such hat on a particularly romantic rendezvous with Teddy in Leipzig! There were unattractive dress lengths for sale in shanty shops, with men working sewing machines sitting outside. I bought Teddy some stamps for his collection and one stamped envelope which was said to be becoming rare.

Too soon the unrelenting heat and sparse shade drove us back to the hotel. I was concerned by how the constant heat was affecting my ankles which had become swollen and puffy over the last week. I had to take every chance to elevate them as the endless journeys in the seated position obviously did not suit them. I never had problems with my ankles when I was younger, and I hated this indication of age.

Later, in the peace of our hotel garden, our conversation resumed.

"Our life changed so much in Kazimierz. We couldn't really understand what was happening. I guess we had a pretty privileged life, lots of social fun." Miriam opened the topic again.

"Did you work in the business, or was it only for your brothers?"

"I'd always wanted to be a librarian, and that's what I did. My father was content for me to follow that path. My mother was the traditional one and would have been happier if I'd stayed at home and married the right boy that she found me."

"Did you find the right boy?"

"Ben was the right one for me. He was a trainee banker, and my dearest friend." She pulled out an emerald ring secured round her neck on a chain. "His family was perhaps not as kosher as my mother would have liked, but with all the uncertainty I think she was happy that someone would look after me."

"What happened Miriam?" I asked quietly

"My father woke up! My brother in Milan had been telling us that we had to get out for over a year, but my father thought he was panicking. Since `39 Jewish families were being deported out of Krakow, but my father had so many Aryan customers he thought we were safe. It was a long time before we began to believe the stories. It was only in `41 when the Nazis sealed off Podgorze, that he decided the family needed to escape."

"Podgorze? What is that?"

"It's an old area some distance from the heart of Krakow behind the Vistula River. The Nazis wanted Krakow to be totally cleared of Jews and Podgorze was constructed as a compulsory ghetto for all Jews. My father had shipped out all his business that had not been confiscated, and my brother had arranged the papers from Milan. My grandparents, my mother's parents wouldn't come. We had no choice but to leave them behind. I think we got out just in time. It was very frightening."

"I'm so sorry. Can I ask where Ben is?"

"He and his family were picked up for deportation about three months before we left. There was no warning, and we've no idea where they ended up." Miriam fell silent.

"When this is over, you'll find each other." I spoke with more confidence than I felt.

"It's hard to imagine what sort of Europe we could have in the future. I don't imagine it will be one we will recognise. Sometimes it's hard to keep positive."

"It can't go on much longer, I'm sure. We seem to have got the upper hand in Africa now. Ouch!" The sharp pain on my shin, made me cry out. I slapped my hand down to it in retaliation, but nothing was there. Whatever had bitten me had vanished and all I could do was rub the area. The pain didn't disappear so I went and put soda water on the bite in the hope that it would calm it.

It was growing dark when I returned to the garden and the cicadas had started loudly buzzing. Distinguished birds had chosen to roost in the tall trees opposite and I could see bands of white across black wings, long tails and crests on their heads curving back. I wondered if they could be hoopoes and regretted my lack of knowledge. Miriam was no help. The cicadas seemed to grow ever noisier, and we retreated to the shelter of the hotel as the night became thick with darkness. A great thunderstorm broke, with heavy rain and brilliant forked and sheet lightening. It was a reminder of what, in my imagination, it would be like to be in the centre of a battle scene. Such storms were a common occurrence around there, but to me the lightening was frighteningly impressive.

TEN

June 10 1943

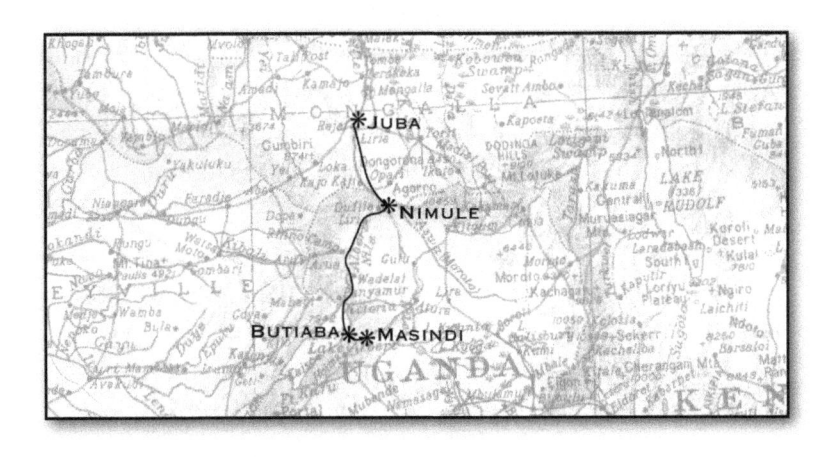

It was always a difficult job packing, settling the bill, and arranging for an early departure. My trunk was of particular concern to me. That morning the luggage was once again packed onto separate lorries, whilst we scrambled into our buses, one large single decker and one smaller. Over the course of the trip, I had noticed how many women stood back and allowed their men to take all the stress. I confess to having allowed men to gallantly organise me when it suited me, so I had a spark of envy for these women. Miriam and Mrs McInnes and I could only rely on paid masculine help, and our transfer problems were a continuing headache to navigate.

A forty-five-mile run lay ahead to Butiaba which was our destination to pick up the steamer to take us across Lake Albert. The drive was interesting and often lovely, through masses of greenery, high and low. Trees looking like curtained buttresses of some ancient castles were swathed and laden in the luxuriant, rampaging life of creepers and hanging foliage. We saw rubber growing with some of the tall trees obviously tapped, and much brick making. At one point a large Polish refugee camp lay half hidden, away to our right among rich agricultural country. We passed a bunch of shops under the trees on the roadside. Polish women were buzzing round them, fit looking, pleasant folk. I waved to one rosy cheeked girl, and she smiled and waved back after a long stare.

Miriam leaned over and shouted in my ear, "Their men are all out farming the land. Polish people make good farmers."

"It's wonderful that they've been given these plots. I imagine it's a healing place after the tragedies behind them."

"I'm sure they feel safe here." Miriam confirmed and I wondered if she was referring to herself too.

Our bus stopped first at Basingiris Forest station, a spot full of sun and deep green shade. We had diverted to deliver mail and while we waited, I could see the waving shadow across the road and foliage cast by a great tree, itself hidden. It was odd how our eyes could grasp the shadow but not the real thing. Perhaps it was one of the giant mahoganies? A hush fell on the entire bus as we waited, an angel passing over. I strove to feel empty of everything but receptiveness, trees, road, distant views, green luxuriance almost within my touch. Within the confines of a hot and dusty bus, I tried to be part of the scene.

As we passed, the people of the forest and glades waved in greeting. We welcomed the droning hum and good scent of busy sawmills, climbing steadily all the time, until finally, we came out to a vast, entrancing view. Some way off, far below us by the lake, its horizons slightly hidden by mist, we could see a tiny steamer alongside the little port. Ours probably.

Immediately below us stretched for a hundred miles, the great Budongo reserve, covering about 825 square kilometres of continuous, barely penetrable forest. This forest sits at the top of the Albertine Rift, part of the Great Rift Valley. Through this immensity the road to the lake had to pass. The enormity of it was hard to assimilate and I craned my neck, willing myself to remember every detail of the drive. In those secret, impenetrable depths roamed vast herds of rhino, giant hog, buffalo and especially elephant. My frustration bubbled at not being able to see any animal life. Even monkeys, said to abound there, hid from our noisy passing. We paused by a monument to Pearson, an early fearless pioneer who was killed here by elephant. At the foot of it was a relief of two elephants, fighting head on, a palm tree separating the actual collision. This great forest, Uganda's game reserve, had an unpleasant feature which only a hide inches thick can face, the tsetse fly.

As we descended, the view became even grander. I wished we could stop and absorb it all. I told myself again and again that, at last, I was crossing Africa's Great Rift. To the left of the lake, far across it, lay mountain ranges away in the Belgian Congo and somewhere due west would be Stanleyville. The dense forest below, on whose tree tops it seemed you could truly walk, showed only a few open spaces or glades. Mostly it looked impenetrable. We passed a small hotel, once a hunting lodge where the ex-Prince of Wales used to stay when on big-game expeditions. Descending to the plain below, I craned round to look behind us, trying to catch a glimpse of the famous Mountains of the

Moon, Ruwenzori. Unlike most African snow peaks, they were not volcanic, but stemmed from six separate glaciers. I had to be satisfied with the vaguest outline of a peak wrapped in cloud and snow. We drove steeply down the escarpment and towards our little steamer waiting by the lake side jetty.

On boarding the boat at Butiaba, still dazed, I found that Mrs McInnes and I were to share a pleasant but hot cabin in the bows. Any belief that this journey would follow the original schedule had vanished long ago. The old lady, exhausted by the coach journey fell asleep on her bed immediately we started. The cabin, although supposedly cooled by a fan for each of us, was too hot for me. The bite on my leg I had received in the garden at Masindi was still painful, and I sought some cool air on the deck.

A figure whom I recognised from the last steamer was leaning over the rail staring into the water. He had always been a solitary presence, despite his intelligent, attractive face and I decided to approach him.

"Most people seem to be sleeping. I imagine you also found it unbearably hot below decks."

He introduced himself as Mr Parry and was something in education at some mission at Juba. On our left bank was most luxuriant vegetation and on our right behind a strand of sand, impenetrable green jungle. "The heart of Africa!" he said, studying it, "Nothing could trek through such growth but four legged beasts with at least two-inch thick skin. No wonder they have it to themselves."

"It sounds as if you know the jungle well."

"I've lived here for a long time. We're just a handful of white folks in the school mission, and we all have fine bungalows. Mine has a lovely garden with flowers, vegetables, and fruit. But there's no meat and no milk to be had!"

"I can imagine that anything will grow well in this climate." I encouraged him.

"I grow pineapples, oranges, lemons, and grapefruit. Passion fruit, bananas and nuts also grow well. I'm trying to grow hazel which I think will thrive. I grow cashew nuts. Do you know about cashew nuts?"

"I've certainly eaten my fair share."

"The nuts are enclosed in delicious looking long gold-pink fruit. But what you don't hear about is that the fruit has a poisonous little dark knob at the end of it which causes blisters and skin rashes. There can be a lot of pain and misery for those who process the nuts."

"How interesting! I'd no idea!"

"It's a well-kept secret from the consumer. I provide my workmen with stout gloves to pick cashews, but I've heard of commercial companies who pay them a pittance and don't give them any protection."

"That's appalling. Mr Parry, you've certainly surprised me." In future I would show more respect for the familiar cashew.

Mr Parry's face was impenetrable. "The jungle's not an easy place to live. Every kind of insect, and every variety of disease lives here. Sleeping sickness, bilharzia, malaria. Insects are far more deadly here than animals!"

"They're certainly impossible to avoid." I was troubled by the bite which seemed to be gaining in strength and irritation. I hoped I wasn't going to have to find a doctor. The steamer was quietly chugging down the river, the sudden flutter of wings or a distant monkey's cry were the only intermittent sounds from the depths of the tropical vegetation. The colour and size of butterflies hovering on flowers or over the river in search of nectar was an astonishing feast for the eyes.

Mr Parry quietly continued, "The locals, immediately after

the first rains, know exactly when the flying ants will emerge from their ant hills. They make a hole in the ground in front of the exits of the ant hill, and then heat fire brands. As the ants come out, they catch them against their brands and burn off their wings and hundreds of them fall helpless into the prepared hole. Some ants miss the trap and are then snapped up by the dogs waiting round for their share. Even my cat waits for her share. The locals cook them and pound them into a nutritious mess."

I responded, "Ugh. That sounds unappealing!"

"I tasted them once. A little like white bait. I didn't like them!"

As we talked the river gradually narrowed until we appeared to be restricted in a cramped canal, then suddenly it widened again, the banks stretching away from us. We caught glimpses once or twice of little round hut villages. The sun in the endless blue sky penetrated even the shade and I could feel the sweat running down my back. I couldn't imagine how stifling it must be in the cabin where Mrs McInnes continued to lie on her bed.

A few native dug outs, truly dug out of tree trunks, lined up against our left bank while others, long and narrow were propelled through the water by standing fishermen. A strange stillness hung over the scene and even the steamer's engines seemed intimidated. We appeared to have left the river and now were on Lake Albert. Some of the larger villages of round mud huts, showed by their many dugouts that a viable fishing industry thrived here. The villagers often smoked their fish and smoke drifted slowly away over the jungle from nearby huts. At last, I saw my first crocodile. A long black crocodile stretched himself, mouth agape on the shore. I was delighted and once I had seen one, I saw others. I wondered if the only animals who preyed on crocodile were men, and presumably only then in self-defence. Over the low hills, we could still see the mountain tops of the Belgian Congo in the distance.

The rest of the day was spent in a strange, suspended animation as our boat glided through the water. Passengers took shifts leaning over the sides to pick up any breeze from the motion and in the heat, conversation lagged. Meals below deck were unappealing, and siestas in the supposedly fan cooled cabins were taken by many.

We often passed, floating in the water, little round lily weed flowers, opening in tiny white bunches, golden hearted and floating in clumps of roots and moss. These tufts must have been bits of sudd I imagined. I would have loved to present these lily daisy bouquets to my daughters. I felt remote from the world and those I loved in this backwater of the world. No matter how companionable the fellow travellers were, they were not family, and I felt alone in this experience.

As I lay on my bunk that night, my leg was becoming increasingly painful. It throbbed, and a red rash was starting to spread from the original bite. Applications of soda water did nothing to alleviate the insistent throbbing. Listening to the sounds of the humid night I queried my sanity. I still did not know if I had the required permission to cross into Palestine. My insignificance overwhelmed me and in this primeval jungle I knew I was as important as a flower's petal. And as useful. In the safety of South Africa, my work in Cape Town assisting the troops travelling to and from the conflict had felt important to me, but the reality was that I was cushioned. The whole world was in a state of war and there was possibly as much danger in dear old England as there was in Europe, in Asia, and the Philippines. Here the war was remote. Most of Africa was untouched by this man-made imposed savagery, its own version being centuries older.

That evening I was gripped with the certainty that I should have stayed where I was. What madness had induced me to take on such a journey? I had been playing childish games, overestimating my capabilities, and placing the importance of my marriage on an inflated pedestal. I wondered if the North African arena was as clear of conflict as I would like to believe. Would I become increasingly a nuisance to our Allies? Did my desire to reclaim my husband justify any of this? Would my daughters view this as responsible behaviour? What was I doing here? In this landscape the purpose of this trip had become irrelevant. Silent, self-reproachful tears slid down my cheeks before my exhausted sleep.

June 11 1943

The vast dome of the sky was infinite, the heat oppressive, relieved by a little, green-scented breeze playing around us, while white clouds moved in billows on the horizon. Mr Parry was again my companion for most of the day. He was interesting company and distracted me from last night's despair and my leg, which was giving me increasing discomfort.

"We produce great quantities of honey. We send ours to Khartoum in four-gallon tins. It's a good business." Mr Parry's small holding was his chief topic of conversation.

"We used to buy honey straight from the bees in Palestine."

"It's been slow work teaching the Africans new ideas. Some of my locals still kill swarms when collecting honey. It's a bad custom. In some places the killings have reached such proportions that it's too late. Areas are denuded of bees, so the locals have begun to see their short sightedness."

"What do you use to encourage the bees?" I was genuinely interested.

"On my plot we use old pipe lengths of matting placed horizontally in a tree. A swarm finds it and settles down. I like to think I have very happy bees."

I was watching a shoal of birds flying low like small swallows. They appeared to be black with white on their wings, and touches of white on the under body. Mr Parry had binoculars and we took it in turns to watch. The little swallows did not alight but kept swiftly swooping down and up, skimming the water, chasing insects.

"How fast they are! I recall someone telling me they can reach a hundred miles an hour!"

"And high too! Airmen have reported them as high as 5,000 feet!" I wondered at these statistics as the birds looked so fine and fragile, as if they would disintegrate under that sort of pressure. My biggest thrill that morning was in spotting several elephants.

We were joined on deck by Mrs McInnes, who was stretching her swollen legs with some difficulty. It appeared that Mr Parry and Mrs McInnes already knew each other.

"Mr Parry is a Derbyshire man, you know. His people live outside Abergelly now. They had an estate but unluckily sold it to some lord, who developed quarries on it!" The old lady seemed unaware of the embarrassment of the poor man having his fortunes explained and encapsulated in a nutshell. I rapidly changed the subject.

"I've been told about a violet leaf tea that grows here. It's been recommended for pains of all sorts. I thought I would try it for my bite. Have you heard of it?" I asked.

"It's especially good for cancer I believe." Mrs McInnes confirmed.

Mr Parry was in his own world, "Have you heard of koso leaves? They're from a mimosa like tree growing in Abyssinia and are used by my locals to prevent or cure worm. They eat a lot of raw meat. About once a month the servants doctor themselves with these leaves. It makes them feel ill and no work is done for two or three days." I wondered what that had to do with pain killing.

Mrs McInnes rose to the competition and launched into an account of a friend of hers. "My friend's son, aged sixteen, developed a lump on his arm after tree climbing in Kampala. The Nairobi doctors diagnosed a malignant sarcoma and thought the lump should be removed at once. The boy was on holiday from Denmark, and the specialists advised that he be flown there immediately for an operation. My friend, his Danish mother, wouldn't be panicked and insisted that the boy travelled home by water without stress. Once there the doctors x-rayed the arm, and some curious nerve condition was diagnosed, but they weren't at all sure what was the trouble. However, the treatment given resulted in a total cure. Later the Kampala doctors were amazed to see the boy back in perfect health. It had never been a sarcoma!" She smiled triumphantly at the three of us. The conversation died, my question unanswered, as we all contemplated the vagaries of nature.

The Nile was navigable as far as Nimule before the rapids began. Floating islands frequently passed us, some quite large, or bumped against our sides with the current, at times turning us completely off course. We watched one huge island of sudd on its slow voyage. It appeared to be grimly fighting to keep us company against the strong current. It twisted and turned, piled bits of itself upon itself, broke off other fragments, and hit the bank. But the fight was unequal and our last glimpse of it was a sudden, swift pull away, as it disappeared into the maws of the rapids in the direction of Juba.

The day advanced slowly, much as the day before had done.

I took care to keep distracted by talking to fellow passengers rather than revisit the depression and uncertainty of the previous evening. It was a curious existence, travelling with strangers whose lives were interwoven so briefly like a dance, before spiralling away like sudd islands, never to be thought of again. Lots of passengers from Sudan were on board, many returning on leave. They appeared to be nice folk, but their conversation was mostly about people they knew or knew of, which was dull talk for those not involved.

We pulled up that evening at the port of Loropi. Many of my fellow travellers went for a walk just to stretch their legs and I would have liked to join them but the bite on my shin had become poisoned. It was very evidently swollen and much too painful for me to move unless necessary. Mrs McInnes, Mr Parry, and I stayed on board and watched the great piles of wood being loaded onto the steamer. The smell of the disturbed wood was pleasant, and the waves of unceasing workmen's talk as they were loading, was amusing. Excitement exploded out at the smallest provocation. I wished I could understand their dialect, and even Mr Parry was no help and warned me this work of moving timber would be going on all night!

As the sky darkened to an accompaniment of melodious frogs' belches and gurgles, the twinkling of countless fireflies began flashing in and out of the rushes below us. We had been assured that the mosquitoes were not a pest here in June, but later in the evening they discovered us, and we had to retreat to the protection of our nets, earlier than usual. I was grateful that the night was cooler and with the fan on, despite my painful bite, I slept better.

June 12 1943

The dancing light and the sound of chattering awoke me from a deep sleep, and it felt as if this was a continuation of the same activity I went to sleep to. I had lost consciousness in Loropi and awakened in the harbour at Nimule having missed all the intervening scenery. From one of the barges attached to our side, empty aviation fuel barrels were being unloaded, and in another, a charming green vegetable garden flourished apparently destined for a distant island. That morning we unloaded sugar and wooden cases of tea. The slight fresh scent in the air, a product of rain last night, belied the growing heat of the day. We lay by peaceful, low banks on this wide part of the Nile, and I would have liked to remain there indefinitely.

My wretched poisoned bite was frightening me. It was now badly swollen on my right shin, the puffiness running round to the left side. The ankle too was enflamed, very red and shining. Two large swollen spots on the thigh on the same side and two more just below the knee, now showed. Miriam had helped me look for medical advice, but none was to be found among my fellow passengers. I could only continue to apply soda, cold compresses, and Milton to the areas. Many advised me to stop and rest in the nearest town but that was impossible. I could not afford to lose my reservations on to Haifa as I had been warned that the route was totally booked up till December. Go on I must, and hope there was little standing required of me.

The relentless schedule again demanded that Mrs McInnes and I be packed and ready to disembark to drive on to Juba, about 126 miles north. The old lady's luggage and mine were removed to the quay where I could see it all piled up, including my trunk which had created so many headaches at every step of this journey. No straps were left and few handles, but the locks were holding. Mr Parry and I parted company at Nimule, which saddened me. He had been an uncomplicated support and I genuinely hoped that he found the companionship he was looking for in his life.

Our four-hour drive from the port was on a long straight red road over tediously level country. Ant hills, scrub and grass dotted with trees were relieved by occasional distant views of the famous Imatong mountains on one side and Ugandan mountains on the other. It started off as a dull drive. I was sitting behind Mrs McInnes and the chauffeur, next to an irritating man who, though he said he knew the road, knew nothing. Natural life just rolled off him like water off a duck. He knew neither of the names of the two rivers we crossed by stalwart bridges, nor the trees or anything that interested me. He probably had one of those intricate, engine driving types of minds about which I know nothing. I knew that I ought to be elevating my swollen leg but there was no way I could do that without laying it on the tiresome man's lap. A prospect neither of us would even consider!

Our five cars of people and luggage stopped after two hours, and we stretched our legs in rare woodland shade while the chauffeurs rested and smoked. I saw no flowers beyond convolvulus and a small daisy, prickly-thorn and what might have been a wild trailing blackberry. We were warned about snakes, but I saw no animals and few birds. There must have been plenty of life hiding in that open woodland, but even if my painful leg had allowed, there was no time to get far enough away by myself to listen. A recurring complaint of mine!

Moving on, we passed a large army lorry, turned turtle at the side of the road.

"That's not an unusual sight." Mrs McInnes informed me. "There's a fault of balance with that type of car." I stared at this ever-surprising woman. There certainly appeared to be nothing rough or lopsided about the road to have caused the accident. Nearing Juba, we had recently passed a little village named Salaria, consisting of a tiny group of huts, when the front car brought us all to a halt, to talk to a large, flamboyantly dressed white man by the roadside.

"Oh, it's Baron Potzen! He's a well-known character!" Mrs McInnes declared, and my irritating companion also seemed to know him. Baron Potzen had a young chimpanzee in his arms, tightly clutching him round the shoulders, turning itself away from us like a scared child. "He once owned an estate near Trieste until the Italians took it. Then he came here and was something in Government. Elephant control, I think it was."

The man added, "I heard that he was forced to retire due to the war and his Austrian nationality and now lives on a small pension. I wonder what he's doing here?" We drove on none the wiser, anxious to reach Juba.

A further obstacle awaited us, and the convoy came to another abrupt halt. The recently built bridge, which we were about to cross, had been partly washed away and was totally unusable. Pandemonium ensued as the chauffeurs gathered to discuss strategy lengthily over many cigarettes, while we passengers watched, wilting with heat. Men and women reacted according to their natures, some trying to organise the drivers, and some sunk in despair as we awaited our fate.

"It's a disgrace. This bridge cost thirty thousand pounds. It seems high flood levels hadn't been considered." My companion growled, before leaving the car to add his weight to the confusion. I stared after him. Flooding? Weren't we supposed to be suffering from low river levels in this season? I wondered if the bridge's demise was down to another, more man-made cause? I could see that the river water looked brown and swollen, confirming the sudden storm theory, but the destruction of the bridge did not look as if it had just happened. Red tape partitioned it off, and it was obvious that restorative work was already under way, although there was not a workman to be seen in the relentless glare.

"Is this the Nile again? I do hope so!" I suggested brightly.

"Yes, this crossing's famous." Mrs McInnes smiled back at me. "This is where Gordon, regardless of crocodile danger, swam across the river holding a rifle high above his head. The Africans admired him greatly!"

I had heard that Juba had a large quota of army barracks, so it was no surprise when a jeep pulled up and the good old British army took charge. Apparently, a short walk down river, there was a wooden raft attached by pulleys to each bank for temporary use. However, the chauffeurs were in doubt, endlessly expressed, as to whether the cars could make it. They were pronounced too heavy for such a makeshift contraption, piled high with luggage as they were. The chauffeurs wouldn't chance it. Flies buzzed and Mrs McInnes took the opportunity for an impromptu doze. I envied her! Miriam, who had been travelling in the last car came up to join us. She had no qualms about letting me elevate my leg onto her lap and had a much-appreciated bottle of warm water with her.

Finally, the army resolved the issues. We passengers were instructed to go down the bank on foot to be helped onto the raft and taken across, to await our cars on the far side. Miriam and a soldier supported Mrs McInnes, and, invalid that I now was, I too had to be supported down the treacherous slope by a young army sergeant. He was very attentive, and his help was much needed as I felt extraordinarily vulnerable. With Mrs McInnes's comment about crocodiles in mind, I kept a wary eye on the banks.

Suitcases were put on the raft on which the old lady and I could thankfully rest. We waited while, with military efficiency, the ropes were tightened, and the swaying platform moved slowly from the near bank. The force of the water was considerable, and I was thankful for the seat, as I was surrounded by standing passengers striving to keep their balance on the shifting water. It surprised me how hard and bumpy the river felt.

Dragging the raft across was no picnic, even for the army. Impressively I was still dry when I was helped, slowly and unsteadily up the other bank. Sitting in the dappled shade we watched our army boys in action, driving the lightest of vehicles in a luggage bearing relay over on the raft. The chauffeurs had happily relinquished their cars and came over on foot. I noticed that local villagers had silently joined us, drifting out of the vegetation, to watch the entertainment. Soon most of the luggage was on our side, my much cursed over trunk included.

Our drinking water was finished, and I knew I was in trouble. My vision had started swimming, my head hurt, and my leg was throbbing. I was worried that I might faint. The attentive sergeant produced a white handkerchief dipped in water to wrap round my neck and muttered gruff encouragement. My leg was giving rise to real concern from everyone who saw it, and I confess that I was secretly frightened too. Stories of amputations sprang to mind and couldn't be pushed away. What kind of fool was I to have ended up in this situation?

At last, we were reunited with our cars which had traversed the river without mishap due entirely to our disciplined and good-natured military. Thankfully, our ill-matched fellow traveller was only too happy to swap places with Miriam.

The further few miles left to drive were littered with acres and acres of huts, many of them superior erections of brick and corrugated iron. We never saw the real town of Juba, just this huge area of army camps. Thankfully, at the port our vessel, the Nassir, was waiting.

Desperate to find my cabin and lie down, we first had the wearisome task of showing and changing money, passport inspection, and customs inspection. My luggage lay dumped on the quay as I queued behind the lightly travelling Miriam, who was helping Mrs McInnes ahead of me. A young, immaculate, shiny-faced officer with his junior appeared to be in charge, and he had something to prove. Mrs McInnes had already told a porter to take her typewriter on board, but the officer wanted to see it. He seemed to expect Mrs McInnes to fetch it for him. Miriam explained that it was as old as the hills and nearly in pieces, which it was, and after much show of authority, he finally agreed to let it pass.

He turned to me. "Is all this yours? Just luggage?" He eyed it dubiously,

"Yes."

"But what is it all?" he asked raising his eyebrows.

It did look rather a dishevelled crowd. I tried to smile, "Only personal effects, clothes, shoes, riding boots, books, frocks, possessions. I've been away from home for two years. It might be easier to tell you what I haven't got."

I couldn't imagine unpacking any of these tightly wedged suitcases, let alone trying to force their contents back in again. My trunk particularly worried me. It contained, deeply hidden in clothes, something that I didn't want examined even by the most careful of individuals.

I continued rapidly. "I haven't any firearms, swords, telescopes, field glasses, microscopes, cutlery, spirits, scents except one open half bottle. I haven't any cigars or cigarettes except one open box of fifty. Is there anything else I shouldn't perhaps have?"

He smiled broadly and I relaxed. A mistake because after a pause he told me that the paperwork showing what money I had on me was missing. He demanded that I had to collect a form from the little ship's office and return it completed to him. I stared at him, beyond protesting. Defeated I pulled myself up the gang plank to be handed the form and told to return to the quay to fill it in. The blinding sun made the white form dance before my eyes as I struggled to overcome nausea. Were two Egyptian pounds, six English, two travellers' cheques for ten pounds and five pounds respectively and odd change, of any importance? I returned to my officer who looked at my paper closely before marking my luggage with his red crosses. Thanking him through gritted teeth, we bade each other a pleasant good evening.

I had spoken truly. As far as I knew I had nothing declarable. I knew it could have been worse when I saw a heavy, crammed case of books belonging to another couple, being turned out and rummaged through for inspection.

Finally, I summoned porters to carry my luggage on board the Nassir. My well-appointed cabin to myself was clean if small, with a cubby-hole lavatory and basin, lights in the right places and a thermos jug. A wire was waiting for me from Teddy. He had just got my letter to him from Tabara and had been relieved to receive it. I immediately wrote a quick cable back saying 'Reached Juba, cheers' with no mention, of course, of my now alarmingly sized painful leg and ankle. Any hoped-for medical help on this steamer was dashed when I was told they had no medical provisions on board.

We were still in port when I received an extraordinarily kind, possibly lifesaving, gesture from the British army. I was preparing for an early night, having skipped dinner because I felt so unwell, when there was a knock on the door and a package was delivered to me. Someone from the army group, my young sergeant possibly, had taken the trouble to contact the army medics. They had bothered to send over sulfa pills and powders for my leg. I burst into tears when I saw it. I was overwhelmed. All the pent-up fears of the last few days spewed out and in the privacy of my cabin I had a good howl. Now, I stood a chance of getting better.

ELEVEN

June 13 1943

A bottomless sleep was followed by a breakfast of stewed prunes, fish, bacon and eggs, marmalade, toast, and coffee! The food was a miracle on this boat! The eggs were small with tiny yolks and sugar was rationed as usual to two lumps per person despite the plentiful sugar cane. I was not complaining! Possibly psychological, but I was already feeling more hopeful.

We had been joined by several Sudan Railways men

who tended to bag the best seats, but Mrs McInnes and I commandeered good ones on the upper deck. I was able to elevate my leg on another chair and sat as happy as a Pharaoh on his Nile. That morning we swept past meadow-like land and swamps punctured by millions of broad stalks looking like an army of spears. The Nassir kept negotiating difficult bends of the now narrow river and we bumped into the bank several times due to a big, camouflaged barge attached to our right side, which doubtless hampered the steering.

That morning I heard crew members talking Arabic and my ears pricked up at the once familiar sound. It wasn't as melodious as Swahili with its liquid sounding vowels, but I loved it. I dug out my small forgotten Arabic vocabulary with the intention of a little revision. Mrs McInnes told me that many of the white robed, turbaned men were of Abyssinian blood, not pukka Arab at all. She was about to say more, but her chin dropped, her eyes closed, and she was gone! It was indeed a peaceful scene. Big horned cows were on the right, and several quiet elephants, lazily flapping immense ears like colossal leaves were on the left. Two hours of this sightseeing was all I could manage before claiming my bed once more.

Most of the afternoon was lost to me in sleep but I rose in time to witness a strange scene when we put into Mongalla. Several times lately we have stopped a distance from the banks, and I put this down to river currents and changes of depth. At Mongalla we stayed about three yards from the bank and the Africans on board started bargaining noisily with others on land who had tall bundles of sugar cane to sell. Police on the bank were trying to contain the latter. These locals were the Num tribe, I learned, and the odd reddish-brown colour of their hair, and whatever clothes a few of them wear, was obtained from mud mixed with cow manure. Some had their skins whitened by wood-ash. I found the result most unattractive visually as well as to the nose. Local men also held up leopard and cow skins for sale, very roughly dressed, hard and stiff, with little expectation of buyers.

Shouts erupted as one man had parted with his sugar cane before he got his money from the buyer on board. Shedding first his one garment, a stringy bit of leather round his waist, he slipped into the water, reached the ship, grabbed payment, and scrambled back again on to the sloping bank clutching some coin. His ebony smooth body was slippery and shining. Others, who had parted prematurely with their cane bundles were not so lucky, and an angry altercation went on between them and those on board. I felt sorry for the sellers and ashamed of my fellow passengers. The boat finally moved on, leaving behind a justifiably angry group.

My battered body needed the long hours of sleep I was able to give it that day. I slept as soon as my head hit the pillow, despite the temperature. I certainly did not want to return to my husband an invalid. My darkest hours struggling with thoughts of hospitalisation in some unknown African outpost at best, and amputation at worst were now behind me. I had turned a corner and had hope again. Getting back to Teddy was once again my primary aim, and the need for renewed health was all important. That day I had little interest in the world outside my hot cocoon of a cabin.

June 14 1943

After another heavy night's sleep and restorative breakfast, I felt I had turned a corner. My leg was noticeably less swollen and some of my vitality was creeping back. I had missed so many sights, never to be repeated, yesterday and wanted to make sure that I took in as much as I could. Just before lunch the vessel called in at Terakola. I wanted to go ashore and persuaded Miriam to accompany me. She was on the hunt to buy some native beads, called 'sook sook' so was happy to be an escort on a limited expedition. Sadly, the small established shops we hoped to visit were shut between noon and 2 pm on Government orders, by which time the boat would have left.

However, we spent our time with the village group on the shore bargaining for fruit. All around us naked, or all but naked, men and boys were as curious about us, as we were about them. Tall people, their skins painted, and their scant garments dyed the prevailing reddish-brown, which might account for their strange smell. Some carried bows and arrows in carriers of hide. They gave me permission to photograph them. The girls were clothed but often had rings and ornaments through one nostril. One girl even had a watch threaded through hers! They had friendly faces, smiling at once if you smiled at them.

A good deal of squabbling went on over the sale of fruit. Sellers seemed much less anxious to sell, than buyers to shop. Miriam and I bought four little oranges, and two pineapples very cheaply. They were poor quality but still fruit. It was amazing how little fruit and salads came into catering in ships and trains. Even hotels often grudged themselves and there was nothing I missed more. The sun beat down relentlessly, and my excursion had knocked the stuffing out of me, so I retired to my cabin for another deep sleep.

In the afternoon Mrs McInnes and I took up our thrones on the top deck again and watched many white birds, egrets of two or three varieties, some with very long necks. I saw an extraordinary stork wading in the rushes and asked its name. Apart from being very large it was extremely ugly with black, cloak like wings and long skinny white legs. There was a white hair like tuft on its bald skinny head.

"That's a Marabou stork! It's also called the Undertaker Bird for obvious reasons!" Mrs McInnes laughed. "They say it's wingspan is eleven feet across, although it has the reputation of spending most of its time just standing around."

"It's certainly no oil painting, poor thing."

"It does have two curious habits that make it unusual. It's drawn to grass fires. That's when they fly! Just ahead of the flames and swoop down on smaller animals that are fleeing the blaze."

"I didn't realise they were carnivorous! I assumed that little fish or frogs were the most they would tackle." I queried.

"Oh, they aren't fussy. They also feast on animal carcasses. They're known to compete with vultures and hyena for scraps." At that moment, the sinister stork produced a sharp clacking sound by clapping its bills together, and then a croaking noise using its throat pouch.

"They don't have a voice box!" said Mrs McInnes "I must tell you that they also have one very unsavoury habit. They squirt excrement on to their legs to cool down, hence the white appearance!"

I stared in fascination at the bird and at the old lady! She really had a wealth of knowledge in her, despite its distinct cut-off point. Her short-term memory was extremely poor, and she repeated herself endlessly, but often produced fascinating nuggets of information. All around was flatland. We were told to expect two or three days of it and after that 'just sudd'. We were also told to expect increased heat. It was so hot now, that this news was barely believable.

Later in the afternoon Miriam and I tried shopping again when the boat stopped at the little port of Bor, one hundred and nine miles from Juba. This time we were in luck as there was a little village street with basic shops. We bought strings of red, white, blue, and pink native beads and Miriam promised to show me how to thread them into attractive necklaces.

Endless papyrus swamps now clothed the banks, and the river channel was a deep muddy brown. The steamer ran on diesel engines which were very hard to slow up quickly, hence our constant bank bumps. I had thought it was wood that we are burning due to the many stacks of it piled up at every hamlet, but it was oil we used! We carried oil and aviation spirit and two big army lorries on one of our two side barges.

I must have been on the mend as I was once again anxious to hear war news. We heard so little of it despite heading straight towards the arena of the North Africa conflict. I had been assured by the travel office in Cape Town that the major fighting there had been resolved, except for some 'mopping up', whatever that could mean.

Most of the Africa I had travelled through seemed totally timeless and self-absorbed and the war that was crippling Europe and the Far East felt as if it could have been played out on a different planet. I had only been reminded of the conflict occasionally by the presence of the British Army. Fighting on African soil could still be going on, and I could be heading straight for it, but I had to rely on Teddy warning me if there was danger. He would have access to far more news than I have had these last few weeks. It was the news of Europe I needed, the news of dear old London, news of Joy and Felicity, and news of Ronny.

June 15 1943

Shambe, 223 miles from Juba and 856 miles from here to Khartoum, had little to show except for a few huts. The boys, very thin, were excited by our presence but no one else took any notice. Nobody got on or off. The lounging men were tall and attractive, the women were wearing long robes and as usual carrying anything they required on their heads. Again, I marvelled at their neck muscles! They looked regal. African women carried their burdens on their heads, an outward display of their status and their difficulties, and I thought of how I carried all the burdens of my life internally. Of course, my physical existence could not be compared to the hardships that were part of their daily life, and I would be ashamed to complain of my lot compared to these courageous women.

I pondered how I had carried emotional turbulence throughout my life of a kind that would not occur to these village people. Children appeared to be accepted as a communal responsibility in African villages, so why should I have been so shocked when I learned that my sisters and I had been removed from a parent who was considered an unsuitable father? I was sure it was done all the time in these communities. The admission by my uncles that they had removed us from our father and life in Durham, had created in me a storm of emotion on the very eve of my wedding. I was devastated. Illogically, in shock, I forgot all the care and nurturing these dear men had given me. I was wretched and angry at my father, and my uncles, and tried to block them out of my life. I juggled so many questions. Had my father been relieved to be rid of his wife and three demanding daughters? Had he tried to keep in contact with us only to be met by a wall built by my mother's family? Poor Teddy. Instead of the glowing bride he knew and loved, he was faced with an unhappy, angry young woman who was a bit of a mess. He was amazingly supportive and patient as I endlessly talked the shock out of my system. He dealt with my tearful desire to find and confront my father one minute, followed by my icy cold rejection of him the next. At the same time Teddy was defending me, without giving explanations, to his parents who doubtlessly wondered who they had agreed to harbour. It was not the greatest start to our marriage but gradually, together we worked through it. Marrying Teddy was the best thing I had done in my life. Of course, we were very different people. Teddy had a quick temper, an impatience with stupidity and a need to control his environment with fastidiousness. He was also a spendthrift and an irresponsible lover of beauty. I had emotional control issues, was impetuous, thirsty for life, and a hard worker. Possibly irresponsible too! We loved each other and reached our understanding a long time ago and it was time we lived as a couple again.

I was feeling much better and was thankful that I had enjoyed those few days on the Nassir in which to recover. I had demolished several books lent to me by fellow passengers. 'Cold Comfort Farm' by Stella Gibbons and 'The Two Saplings' by Mazo de la Roche, were particularly diverting. My favourite 'go to' book was still the one giving me information about crocodiles. Mrs McInnes tried to lend me 'Letters of Paul to the Hebrews', but I declined the offer on the grounds I was not in the right frame of mind to do it justice. In the quiet times Miriam and I enjoyed bead-stringing which resulted in pretty necklaces, and I got to know her better. I believed the trauma she experienced having to get out of Krakow because of the Nazi threat, was a very tough one. I wanted the chance to learn from this fine young woman if she would let me.

"Miriam, please tell me what your life's been like here in Africa." I started.

"Very different of course! My parents aren't in good health, and it's been an extremely hard time for them. My mother is particularly distraught as she hasn't heard from my grandparents for over a year now."

"Have you felt that it's your responsibility to look after them?"

"Of course. Who else? This trip's been something of a holiday for me."

"Yes, I can understand that. Personally, I think of this time as a lull between two lives."

"You see! I'm not the only one who's having a deliberate pause from worrying about family and events I can do nothing about! You're going through a similar experience. I don't see you talking about your life much."

"Touché. What are your expectations for getting your brother to re-join the family? Do you think you can persuade him?"

"I imagine Maurice has a well-established life of his own. I know he believes the war is on the turn. Egypt is the principal Allied base in the Middle East, so, as a Jew, I'm sure he feels more secure there. My part in trying to persuade him to re-join the family, is a selfish one. I'd love to share the burden."

"Burden? Is it that bad?"

"My father had a stroke back in February. We were lucky and he's almost OK again, but it's certainly knocked his confidence. He and my mother have become very anxious."

"What about your other brother in Milan? The one who organised your escape route."

"We've heard nothing from Theo for several months now. He was relatively secure in Milan while the Italians were in charge, but we know the threat of German occupation of Northern Italy was alarming him. He was making plans to flee. Switzerland is so close to Milan, so it was the obvious place for him to go. But we've heard nothing for months. It's hard not to assume the worst."

"I'm so sorry. As you say, all we can do is hope."

"And you? Do you have brothers or sisters? You say little about your family, but you look a little displaced too."

"I was the oldest of three girls. Grace was two years younger than me, and she was sweet and gentle and needed my support. Sadly, she died last year. I hadn't been able to see her since `24 when we came overseas. She was married to James Moraes and had two daughters to bring up, the same age as my girls. When she was widowed, I tried to persuade Grace to come over for a holiday, but she was always timid by nature, so I feel that I lost touch with her a long time ago."

"And your other sister?"

"Maude is exactly the opposite to Grace. She's very impulsive, more like me I suppose. She's gutsy and highly intelligent, and I think men find her a bit intimidating. When she didn't go down the normal route of a suitable marriage, she decided to try the adventure of going to India. I'm sure my uncles disapproved. I think she thought she would find a husband there, but instead ended up working as a governess." I remembered this conversation with Maude so clearly. Her piercing blue eyes twinkling as she described how she would have all potential bachelors lined up so she could take her pick. But it hadn't happened. Perhaps she was already considered too old, and she ended up working for Indian Army Colonel Rynd as the governess to the little motherless Patrick. It was Maude who was instrumental in persuading the Colonel that Pat should come to England when he was seven and needed to start his education. We invited him to live with our family and he fitted in well, eventually marrying Ronny a few years ago.

I continued, "Maude lives on the south coast of England, and has adopted a daughter who has special needs. Again, it's been many years since I saw her, and I couldn't persuade her to visit us either in Romania or Haifa. Sadly, we're a split-up family, although my daughters keep an eye on her for me."

"Where are your daughters?"

"I know where two are, London! Not the best place to be based but they're strong characters and wouldn't be anywhere else."

"I imagine most of the people travelling with us have a story to tell. Why aren't we all in our natural habitat, which is unlikely to be Africa! How come you're here? I know you're travelling to re-join your husband after a couple of years but how did you find yourself in this continent in the first place?" She hesitated, "Am I being intrusive?"

"No. I ask myself the same question sometimes, although it's an experience I'm pleased to have had. I was happily ensconced in rural England, Gloucestershire, which was the background to most of my life. Cheltenham and Painswick, which won't mean a thing to you my dear, but it's very beautiful. My husband Teddy managed a family mill, and we all lived an idyllic family life. I'm not sure Teddy was ever suited to running a business and it all went wrong financially. He finally left the company in '24 and took up a position as Staff Manager with the Daccia Romano Oil Company in Poesti, Romania. My oldest daughters were already living their own lives, and the youngest was only seven, so she came with us. It was a big move for us."

"Romania has always seemed a romantic place to me. Was it a good life?"

"It was! But it had its moments! One of the Company's oil wells caught fire while we were there, and it took several years and every known trick to put it out."

"How would you do that?"

"Even copious amounts of water couldn't quench it, and then we tried a gas turbine that blasted a fine mist at the base of the fire, but that didn't work. Dry chemicals failed too. Finally, they succeeded by using dynamite to blow out the fire by forcing the fuel and oxygen away from the fuel source. I loved Romania but after five years, Teddy was offered a similar post with the Iraq Petroleum Company at Haifa in Palestine, for a lot more money. That's how we got there."

"And you enjoyed Palestine?"

"We had a wonderful life there before the war. Obviously, the older girls visited us for holidays and Felicity finally grew up and fled the nest for London." How impossible it was to explain more than the surface of the life I had led. I was thirty-eight when I had Flick and her childhood had been one of privilege in comparison to the other two girls. I sometimes thought that everything had been a little too easy for my youngest and she lacked the realism that the other two had acquired.

"Do you think you'll return to England one day?" Miriam cut in on my thoughts.

"Well, that all depends on the war. I could ask you the same about Poland."

"I doubt that we will ever return. I suspect there are stories that we'll only learn after this war is over, and it will never be the same for us Jews. Luckily, we're resilient." We both fell into a reflective mood. It felt as if there were too many unanswerable questions. My first job was to make sure my marriage was secure and then all the other decisions could be made jointly, as we had always done. I was not going to discuss my marriage with a girl thirty years my junior, no matter how much I liked her. Miriam had experienced trauma in Poland that I could not imagine, so how could I give her the support she needed. She had lost her grandparents, her fiancé, her home and possibly her brother. The supportive silence was all we could offer each other.

The great banging and scrunching noises were as sudden as they were terrifying. I was resting on my bed with my leg elevated and I could not understand what had happened. Had we hit a sand bar and were in danger of capsizing? Had the barrels of water become unhitched on the top deck and were now rolling back and forth? Nothing made sense. I stumbled out of my cabin into the glare of the sun and joined the throng of passengers hanging over the ship's railing. There was little to see and no explanation. The engine was stilled but the noises continued, with weakening ferocity.

Finally, when the sound had petered out, word passed down the line of onlookers that a crocodile had become caught and churned up in the paddles. The awful crunching noise had been due to the creature's teeth biting at the paddles in a vain attempt to save itself. I knew too much about crocodiles not to be affected. They had extraordinarily sensitive mouths, and the pain that had been inflicted on it must have been appalling. Once the crocodile had engaged with the paddle it didn't stand a chance. Its unique second jaw joint, that was so useful giving it the power to secure its prey from twisting free, had been its downfall. The crocodile must have been in agony. I found I was trembling at the savagery our boat's paddles had been responsible for. This legendary creature who had an unthreatened life into old age ahead of it, had been chewed up by a convenience of man. A convenience for me. My query about whether crocodiles had any natural foe was answered and it was a lesson too close for comfort.

With surprising speed villagers appeared in little boats, with long poles and set about the task of fishing out bits of crocodile to free the paddles once again. I couldn't watch. I imagine the locals benefitted from crocodile on their menu that night and we, untroubled, were free to continue our way.

I was anxious to hear war news but the wireless on board rarely helped. I never seemed able to be close enough to hear it on the rare occasions when the buzz of static lifted to make it decipherable. That evening was an exception. We heard that the Syrian-Turkish frontier had been closed by the British. I wondered what the implications would be. It was a reminder, if we needed it, that we were drawing ever closer to fields of war.

TWELVE

June 16 1943

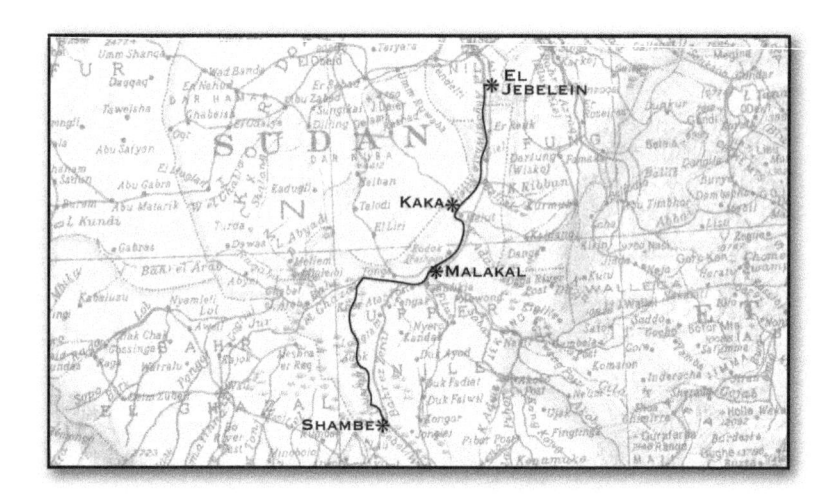

We stopped at the wharf of a tiny irrigation post, Thar Jath. Not a usual port of call but the villagers were being worried by a dangerous water snake and had begged the skipper to shoot it for them. Our skipper was apparently ill, which was news to us passengers, but the second in command, the engineer, stepped up to the task.

It was a glorious morning. From the stern of the ship, I could see huts lying back from the water's edge and a pond, totally smothered by beautiful creamy-white water lilies, growing in profusion. I hoped to see lily trotters, Jacanas, or Jesus birds as they are sometimes called, with their long toes and claws which enable them to walk on the pond vegetation. A fact special to these birds is that the males can sweep up their young and carry them under their wings. Sadly, none showed themselves. A young man, naked and crowned with the weird ruddy dyed hair so fashionable here, and two or three others also barely clothed, had come up to the boat and a lot of pantomime was going on. Two or three hundred yards away at the entrance of one hut, stood a tall woman with a baby in her arms. She was standing so gracefully, one knee bent, like a slim Greek statue in dark ivory. A sack, very short and loose, hung from one shoulder where it was knotted.

Mrs McInnes had joined me and was able to answer my questions.

"Do you know the name of this tribe? They're fine looking."

"Yes, they're Shilluk. They're one of the largest ethnic groups in Southern Sudan."

"Are they always this tall?"

"Yes, they're said to be some of the tallest people in the world, along with the Dinkas. They've mostly converted to Christianity here, which might surprise you."

There were a few boats tethered to the bank, which appeared to be made of rushes.

I asked, "I assume they live by fishing and farming? I see that hillock of potatoes by the pond."

"That's cassava, not potatoes. The Shilluk are considered more intelligent than the Dinkas and agriculture is important to them. Like most Nilotic groups, cattle raising forms the largest part of their economy. They're a lovely peaceful people."

We were distracted by much laughing and gesticulating as the engineer was shown where the snake was lurking. The excitement was so noisy that I imagined no self-respecting snake would be hanging around. We watched and waited, until the sound of the loud shot echoed over the water, startling the birds. Our engineer had found his mark with one bullet as witnessed by the quick disturbance down where the dense high reeds and rushes met the surface of the water. There was rustling and splashing, and then the alarming sight of the brown limbs of intrepid villagers wading into the water in pursuit. I caught a glimpse of the successfully killed black and grey snake, about two inches or more in diameter held aloft and doubtless headed for the cooking pot. The engineer accepted bruising pats on the back. The excitement over we continued our journey down the Nile.

We called at an established hamlet but for navigational reasons stayed on the other side of the river whilst sending a small boat over. There were fine huts there, crops and cows at pasture and four or five donkeys, the first I had seen for some time. Men and boys, naked, were attending to the boats or seated in groups on the edge of the tiny wharf. Others were clothed only in a row of beads around the waist and brass bracelets round their arms. Several girls near the quay were clothed slightly. I cursed my decision not to bring binoculars, having been advised in Cape Town not to take them for fear of being confiscated. Many passengers had them on board, despite the customs checks and I had excluded myself from so many sights. I regretted that enormously. Despite the lack of trees, huge stacks of wood stood on the shore and an ancient looking ship near the bank was also loaded with timber.

My leg was healing, but I was pacing myself and taking extended resting periods on my bed. It was good to know that if my ankles were swollen at the end of the day, it was my age and the endless heat that was doing it and not poison from a vicious bite.

After the intense sunshine of the day, the evening was mercifully cooler and intermittently cloudy, the full moon only visible in patches. I was sleepy and retired early which was just as well as the night proved far from relaxing.

I was awoken in the dead of night by two swift blasts of Nassir's whistle. It spoke of urgency, and I was so deeply asleep that I doubted my ears and settled down again. However, sleep was not to return and, unsettled, I pulled myself upright in a state of alarm. All was deathly quiet, the engines had stilled, and my enquiring mind would not allow me to rest. Grabbing my robe, I left the cabin and stepped into the clear light of the moon to see what was happening. I was met with a scene of calm and control as a skeleton crew manipulated the boat up to a tiny wharf in the middle of nowhere. To my surprise, I was the only person galvanised by the whistle blasts, so wrapping my robe closer around me I leaned over the deck rail to observe. I waited alone.

A group of eight men were on the quay, hanging around quietly in the bright moonlight. Some were smoking cigarettes, and all were wearing camouflage fatigues. I imagined they were about to board, but they gave no indication of preparing themselves. Examining them I noticed they were not carrying rucksacks or any specific equipment. The scene had a surreal quality as the light and shade put the men into high relief. They appeared to be white soldiers, but I couldn't recognise any specific uniform worn. The only sound was the gentle turnover of the ship's engines and silence prevailed as I waited for something to happen. Finally, tiny twin beams of light flickered from a distance inland, and I watched a vehicle slowly wending its way over the landscape. The car's sound increased as it approached, and it was obvious that this slow approach was what we were waiting for. After a circuitous route the camouflaged vehicle drew up next to the boat and unloaded two men dressed in civilian clothes. They carried travel bags and wore hats that cast their faces into deep shadow. Not a word was spoken as they scrambled aboard the Nassir and disappeared below decks. I was intrigued, but what surprised me most was the attitude of the men on the quay. They behaved with total indifference to the little scene played out. They continued to be patiently waiting for something as the boat moved slowly on again through the night.

It was only when I was back in my cabin that I queried what I had seen. Naïvely I had immediately assumed that this was a British or American group on some undercover assignment, but we were now approaching North Africa and there must be groups of Axis undercover fighters too, dispersed over the countryside. The two gentlemen could have been of any nationality, as could have been the soldiers. I resolved to find out what I could about them at breakfast. It was with great difficulty that I lulled myself back to sleep again.

June 17 1943

Flat meadowland stretched on both sides when I woke. Herds of cattle surrounded the many small villages comprising of round huts whose straw walls reached to the ground. This was the kingdom of the Shilluck tribe, and we saw many of the tall men with fishing rods walking by the shore. Rows of trees stood out against a sky sprinkled with swirling flocks of teal, making a peaceful pastoral scene. My disturbed night felt like a dream and there was no evidence at breakfast that we had been joined by the two secretive passengers. I was told that we had passed the little port of Tonga in the night, but I was met with blank stares when I suggested that men had embarked there.

The steamer was travelling faster now and there was another stretch of water, parallel to ours, with brown and green land between. Curious about finding out exactly where we were I turned to the engineer, of the snake shooting fame. He told me that we were on the Bahr el Jebel river and that the adjacent stretch was called the Bahr ez Zeval river. It was such a confusing network of waterways and names. I was told that we had been joined by the Bahr el Ghazat river from the west in the night, so he reassured me that we were now on the White Nile. The kind man, evidently with time on his hands, showed me a map of the Nile and I had never seen more confusing tributaries, resembling a giant sponge. No wonder the explorers had problems! I mentioned my midnight adventure to the engineer, but apart from a direct enquiring gaze, he fobbed me off with information that they were picking up and delivering people and products all the time. He suggested firmly that I did not concern myself about it.

After the river Sobat joined us, the tempo subtly changed. The waterway became busier. A few old 'covered wagons' of boats, full of timber and a few palms, nestled by the shore and in the distance gleamed the sails of felucca. Black and white geese were flying in V formation, and a multitude of that wonderful bird, the white ibis. Herons and many species of egrets were to be seen, looking beautiful especially when flying.

A commotion further down the deck attracted my attention,

and I followed the pointing hand of a man who appeared enormously excited. An ibis stood alone on the shore. It had a long slender down-curved red beak and red legs. Its face was white with a touch of red on the crown, and lustrous olive-green plumage.

"In all my travels, I've never seen one so far north before! This is a very rare bird here." The man told anyone who was within earshot.

"What is it?" I asked, elbowing myself to his side.

"The southern bald ibis. Normally it has a restricted home range in the mountains of South Africa. They're cliff nesters and usually only migrate short distances. This is an unusual sighting."

"It's not the prettiest of birds!" I eyed it dubiously.

"That head is skin, not feathers. It's Latin name 'Geronticus calvus' means 'bald old man'. It's usually only found in colonies, so I've no idea what's happened to this one."

We watched it until the bend in the river obstructed our view and only then did I realise that I had made no effort to catch it on camera. Cormorants and darters were numerous, busily diving especially where other waters met ours. My favourites, pelicans, were few. I was always surprised by what huge birds they are, their flight curious and cumbersome.

We passed a graceful felucca with a 'covered wagon' thatched boat attached, in which it was evident a large family with many children lived. They waved excitedly at us.

At the tiny town of Malakal, Miriam and I went ashore to purchase more native beads. The interested villagers surrounded us. Most of the men and women were decorated with the strings of the beads we wished to purchase, and many had rings through their nostrils. They were tall people, gentle and friendly. Again,

I was aware that we white people had a completely different natural perfume to us. I wondered what we smelled like to them! Probably not attractive! I was fascinated by their skin decoration done by inserting melon seeds under the skin in decorative patterns on the chest, shoulders, face and especially in a projecting line across the forehead. They generously allowed me to look at the decorations up close. I found these markings strangely attractive behind their dark skin, but Miriam shuddered. I did decline the offer from one cheeky fellow to perform the process on my arm, but I was sure that it was in jest! I believe there were serious coming of age rituals that attended those tribal markings. I wished I had the time and the language to get to know them better.

There was quite a good grocery shop and to my amazement the man spoke a form of English. I came back on board with more beads, fifteen skeins of different coloured silks, six tablets of Oxo, and eighteen grapefruit for Mrs McInnes and myself.

The Ibis enthusiast had a name. It was Colonel Ruch of Intelligence, and he joined me for gin and tonics on deck.

"I'm with the South African forces, although I'm born and bred English." He clarified with a curious crooked smile.

"I imagine we're all nomads really. I was born in the north of England but raised in Gloucestershire. Now Africa will always be in my blood I imagine." I countered.

"Ah, but there's Africa and Africa. I could do without a lot of it. I spent considerable time in Abyssinia, and I found that the most fascinating place."

"Abyssinia? Were you involved in the East African campaign? You certainly sorted out the Italians! If it wasn't for the Allied victory, our success in Egypt would've been far tougher to achieve." I tailed off realising my mistake as he clearly was not going to be drawn.

He ignored my question. "I've recently spent time in Madagascar. Now, that's a lovely island. Such a beautiful place. What a climate! So inexpensive and convenient. I would love to live in Antanarivo. A nice little flat, three rooms with kitchen and bathroom can be hired for five pounds a month. A small estate, house and all, can be bought for five hundred pounds. A chauffeur costs about two pounds a month, a house servant one or two pounds. Labourer's wages are seven or eight francs plus a small bag of cassava flour or its equivalent a day." Colonel Ruch showed no signs of stopping for breath.

I cut in "It sounds amazing. I wonder why it's not more popular."

"It would be popular if it wasn't for the French."

"The French? I don't understand."

"They are extremely difficult to work with, not dependable at all. Only a small percentage of the Frenchmen are good and likeable. French men often marry Madagascar women, then the women's family work cheaply for them! In my opinion, only ten or fifteen per cent of the French there, are pro Allies. It was very difficult to keep the peace."

"I suppose, being an island, Madagascar must feel removed from the war."

"Many Frenchmen would rather quarrel with one another than a German."

I like the French and rapidly changed the subject. "Am I allowed to ask where you're heading now?"

"I'm off to Cairo. They'll be redrafting me, and I hope to goodness that it's to Europe this time. I think it's high time I went there."

"I do hope you get your wish." I finished the conversation lamely. Despite our mutual interest in birds, I couldn't warm to

Colonel Rush. He reminded me of a man Teddy had to work with in Romania, who had turned out to be devious and not averse to taking bribes. He had created all sorts of difficulties for my husband as the locals expected all the management to operate in the same way. It had depressed and angered Teddy persistently for all the five years and ended with him losing his temper in a spectacular way. He was forced to quit his job. We were desperate and fundamentally homeless for a while as he drifted seeking work. When he landed the staff manager job for the Iraq Petroleum Company in Haifa, with a hefty pay rise, I was desperate to make sure that we had some stability. It had turned out well until the war.

An aerodrome, busy with sea planes alighting and taking off, so precisely and confidently one after another, was fun to watch in passing. I wondered at their purpose. I imagined the larger planes would all be based at Juba. A substantial Shell station stood on the shore opposite to service the aviation. I was curious to see the modern in such proximity to the traditional. Many huts on the banks had rush matting screens round them, often with little petticoat layers of straw in their circular thatch, finished with a neat top knot. Often the huts looked like miniature haystacks, some of bright straw, obviously newly built. We passed cattle and, increasingly, big herds of donkeys.

Two picturesque, long-shaped, canoe-type boats were being pulled across the river in front of us, forcing us to slow. The three locals were wearing their red brown garments with their hair dyed a striking warm, copper red brown to match. Palm trees were becoming more common, their lower leaves dead and long stretches of sand lay between cultivation and the river. The boat was still negotiating stray little clumps of sudd here and there.

I was sitting alone on the upper deck, totally absorbed in writing notes to myself about the landscape when I became aware that the pleasant breeze had increased considerably. My notes rustled and I frowned trying to ignore them. Suddenly, with little warning, my scribblings were whipped from my hand and scattered irretrievably. I tried to scrabble for the dancing notes as the wind increased making my task impossible. The sky had darkened ominously, and I felt chilled. The engineer materialised shouting a warning to beat a hasty retreat into the ship's interior. Sadly, it was too late. The heavy rain fell on us before I could negotiate the steps and we had to fight our way down against the treacherous wind. I was no longer confident on slippery surfaces and a fall resulting in an injury would have been a disaster. The storm growled over our heads. Torrential rain descended and splashed in every direction. It seemed to fall in icy sheets from the sky. The noise was considerable.

Soaked to the skin I made my way to my cabin, cursing my stupidity, only to find I had left the window open, and the rain was pouring in. My bed was soaked and struggle as I did, I was unable to close the window fully. Something outside was blocking it, so still unchanged I dripped out into the corridor to seek help. An unfortunate underling was sent on to the rain-whipped deck to clear the blockage, which thankfully he did. The ship had been swiftly anchored to see the storm out, and thunder and spectacular lightning joined the downpour. Now my room was secure, and my bedding removed to dry somewhere, I enjoyed the drama of the storm that had cost me that day's notes.

Having changed and towel dried my hair, I joined the passengers in the lounge.

"We could be delayed reaching El Jebelein." A frown darkened Miriam's face.

"Why are you concerned?" I asked. "Once my bed's dry again, I'm happy for this excitement. It's an adventure after the endless smooth scenery."

"Yes, I agree it can get monotonous! But while you were on deck, we were told the authorities are changing the train on our next leg. Instead of catching it at Kosti, which it's scheduled to do, we'll be picking it up at the new station at El Jebelein."

"Oh, I think that's about fifty miles this side of Kosti! I wonder why they've made the change."

"They announced it was because of the low level of the Nile!"

Counting the spaces between the thunder and lightning against the background roar of rain, I wondered if there could be another reason for our change of timings. There had been no sign of the two mysterious passengers we had picked up in the dead of night. Perhaps transferring at El Jebelein rather than Kosti was fulfilling their schedule rather than ours, or perhaps I was becoming paranoid! I told myself not to be so imaginative, and sensibly kept my theory to myself.

June 18 1943

I woke to a fine, cloudy morning, the air fresh and cool after the storm. Feeling the sensation of the steamer stopping, I dressed hastily. We had reached the little port of Kaka, among the Shilluk villages. The village men waiting to greet us were clothed, some in white robes and others with the usual sack tied on one shoulder leaving the arm bare. Nicely rounded water pots were set out for sale and native angareb. These light moveable bed steads, consisting of a wooden framework with a base of woven rope or animal hide, could also be used as sofas and I found them attractive. In any other circumstance I would have been tempted.

My helpful engineer was leaning over the rail beside me "Each village has its special craft, and those beds are obviously theirs!"

"I love those angareb. If only they were packable!" I sighed. I noticed two Europeans on the shore, who seemed very much in charge of the locals. Following my gaze my befriender clarified.

"They're Greek. We see them every time. One used to be a grocery assistant and now is a very wealthy man. They're apparently under a two-year contract with the army to supply it with amtatch and are making a stash of money."

"Amtatch? What's that?"

"That's what I've heard it called but I don't have the official name. It's the lightweight wood used in pith helmets, lifebuoys, ceilings, and such like. The amtatch bushes and trees grow in the water here and they have a good business going." One of the Greeks had already ferried himself across to the boat and organised a sale. The vast stack of wood on the shore was obviously going to be shipped. On a call from my companion, the Greek handed me up a sample, and it was a surprising feather weight.

The experience of travelling on the Nile reminded me constantly of ancient times. I knew of no other river that had the same effect. It took little imagination to put the clock back to the days of Cleopatra and even further back than that. It was awe-inspiring. Miriam and I were watching crocodiles lying on the banks.

"They're timeless. Leonardo da Vinci wrote a paper on them. Crocodiles eat anything that moves and are highly intelligent. They're called ambush predators, as they just lie in wait for others to make a mistake before they strike. They can camouflage themselves with twigs to help them catch birds!" I broke the silence. One of the crocodiles had a young one with her, about a third of her size.

"It's hard to imagine these horrid looking creatures being motherly or childlike!" Miriam mused.

"I've got a wonderful book that says that the crocodile can carry its hatchlings in her mouth without crushing them. They're caring parents. The crocodile's jaw is terribly sensitive. It has more nerve endings than a human's fingertip. It can easily distinguish between food and debris in its mouth."

"I thought they were distantly related to dinosaurs. They lay their eggs, like turtles, don't they?"

"They lay ten to sixty eggs at a time in the sand, and it takes about one hundred days for them to hatch. The mother crocodile is fiercely protective of her buried eggs and has extraordinary hearing. They can hear their babies from inside the eggs when they're ready to emerge. Only about ten percent hatch out and of those, most are eaten by predators when they're little."

"A tough start!"

"Their size and life span depends on the species. These Nile crocodiles are very big and can live up to one hundred years!"

"Well, they don't have enemies, do they? Nothing would take on those jaws!" Miriam was watching them repelled. "How come you are so obsessed with them Elf?"

"I promise you I wasn't until I read about them. I imagine it's that sensitive mouth that can be so lethal that fascinates me. When I was training and breaking in horses, it was the sensitivity of the horse's mouth that made it possible. With crocodiles I find it hard to marry that with the locking jaw that means any captive in that mouth will never be released."

"You know a lot about them! I'm not sure I want to!" Miriam shuddered.

I was now an enthusiast but wise enough not to continue the topic. The herds of cattle and flocks of sheep and goats grazing nearby would have surprised me, but I had learned that crocodiles only ate about once a week. I watched another one, crawling up the riverbank, dripping and darkly shining. Its back ridges were standing out clearly. I knew that with a lightening flick of its great muscular tail it could switch an unwary beast or native off the bank into its clutches.

It was no good, I couldn't resist carrying on, "Crocodiles stash surplus kill food in dry bunkers in the banks approached by underwater entrances. The carcases rot down which makes it more easily digestible for them. Their teeth aren't designed for chewing, so they gulp down their prey in large chunks, hooves, and all."

Miriam was not impressed "Hooves? How can they digest those?"

"Their digestive system is more than a match for anything." Seeing her face, I laughed, "My last word I promise you!"

I had now seen my twenty-seventh crocodile.

Behind the trees inland was park-like grass, rather like an English scene except for the ant hills and the tick birds in attendance on the cattle, and the lurking dangers of the shallow riverbank half covered in long grass and shrub. A fish eagle flew weightily by, white in front and at tail tip, black winged with chestnut underbody. A handsome bird with a wild cry. Four large pelicans stood on the bank, white shirt fronted. Below the pouched immense beaks, I could see their long pink legs.

Suddenly I saw something big and redly cavernous quite near and found I was looking into a hippo's wide-open mouth. The great head followed it, clear of the water. Another emerged showing cheeks of pink and dark skin. Heavy colossal shoulders came up and then sank back again. They all seemed to be watching us. Miriam and I counted five nearby and there were probably more about. Mostly they were dark grey, and their mouths were frequently wide open. One younger mother was paler coloured and had a mini hippo alongside.

The meadow land was hedged in shining reeds of most lovely

shades of green. Cattle lounged in the shade of grand trees which Miriam told me were of a very hard wood called 'sont' and was used for building.

Dozing off my lunch in my usual place on the upper deck, I was suddenly awoken by the piercing bark of a single shot. Shocked I opened my eyes to see the engineer standing close by, his attention focused on the riverbank, a gun to his shoulder. My brain took a few seconds to understand the significance and my instinctive emotions leaped into action.

"Got the croc in one!" The engineer turned with a smile of satisfaction.

"No! Please, NO!" The words were out of my mouth as I stared at him in horror. "How dare you! How dare you do that."

His look faltered at this unexpected reaction. "I'm sorry. I'd no idea you were asleep. I do apologise, Madam. I'd no idea that you weren't awake."

Tears had sprung to my eyes as I stared at him. "You've shot a crocodile! Is that sport? Does that make you feel better? Does that make you feel bigger?"

The engineer was now in as much shock as I was. "I can only apologise for startling you, Mrs Warmington Reed. Please forgive me."

"You've no idea, have you? You've killed it! What right had you to kill it? What had it done to you? Had it threatened you? Did you need to eat it?" My voice had become strident, and I became aware of all eyes on me. I didn't care.

He stared at me, his face flushed, then dropped his eyes. "The villagers will benefit Madam. They can live for a month on that one crocodile. We kill them occasionally for the villagers as a goodwill gesture."

I felt miserably betrayed by the friendly engineer. The deed was done and there was nothing I could do. Tears still wet on my cheeks, I stumbled to my feet and brushed past him shakily, muttering "Don't talk to me." as I sought the solace of my cabin.

The crocodile was dead. I had lost my dignity and accomplished nothing. Once I had calmed down, I saw how confusing my reaction had been to the man. When he had shot the snake, I had congratulated him heartily. What was the difference? I feared my fascination with crocodiles had become obsessional over the last ten days. My behaviour was contradictory. With embarrassment I remembered early in my journey, admiring Rupert's made-to-measure sandals, made beautifully from crocodile skin. I had considered purchasing some for myself. He had also owned a small, soft suitcase showing the ridges and squares of a crocodile, shot by a friend of his. He told me he had paid for the tanning and the making up of it with a zip fastener and I had honestly admired it. I alone had changed in my attitude and realised that my reaction had been patently discriminate.

I sat on my bunk now tired of this endless cruise down the Nile. I was tired of seeing the same faces. I was tired of eating the same food. I was desperate for this journey to end and my mission to be accomplished.

An event highlighted the last evening at dinner on board the Nassir. There was some excitement when the steamer, with much shouting and reversing of engines, was forced to come to a halt to allow a ship to overtake us. As it passed Colonel Ruch pointed out to me that it bore a high red light on its mast.

"That means danger." he said, "If one of two passing ships display that light, the other must halt and allow it to pass. I remember going through the Suez Canal, in December '39, our ship stopping to allow another, displaying that light, coming up to pass."

"I remember going through the Canal. The rule for the Suez is that the descending ship stops." Mrs McInnes clarified.

"But the ship that passed us was an unforgettable sight. It was a ghostly, unlit ship with hardly a soul to be seen on it. Just one man and a dog. I've never forgotten it." finished the colonel.

As we left dinner the boat stopped at the tiny port of Brank. The quay was in total darkness, with only the light of the full moon to throw the scene into strong shadows. Miriam and I hung over the rail watching but nobody appeared to be landing or embarking. We waited there for a long time until our interest waned, and attention was diverted back to the last night gin and tonics. Only later in my cabin, did I ponder about who might have left or joined the steamer under cover of night.

THIRTEEN

June 19 1943

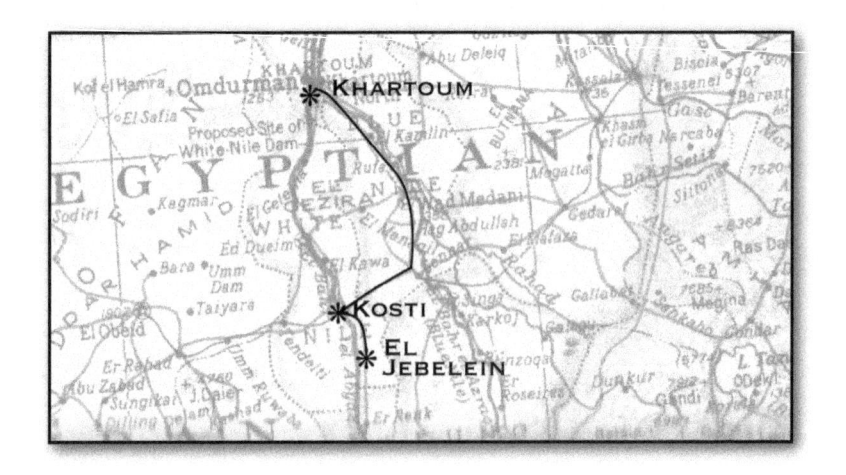

Our boat was late coming into El Jebelain and the pressure to transfer all the luggage across to the waiting train was immediate. The noise and tension of this undertaking never lessened as porters could not be found or were harassingly fighting for attention. There seemed no happy medium. Miriam and I took responsibility as usual for Mrs McInnes and her luggage, so it was with some exhaustion that I finally found my own reserved single compartment. Our panic in case we kept the train waiting did not appear to worry the staff who insisted that lunch was to be served before the train started.

The setting through the restaurant car window was a picture. I could see five granite peaks, rising to about six hundred feet, which rose inland of us. Sadly no one could tell me about them. During the serving of lunch, I was distracted by a flock of little waxbills alighting on the ground like a flutter of blue butterflies. These captivating birds with their round dark eyes were feeding round a heap of Dom palm nuts, which looked like brown potatoes.

"Vegetable ivory, it's called down Victoria Falls way." informed Mrs McInnes. "They make pearl buttons out of the white kernel in those nuts."

Young lads with strong white teeth were seated nearby nibbling them too. The sight was utterly charming, but the birds took fright when two clothed men, each carrying a tall carved spear walked along the sloping, tree shaded bank.

The train finally started for Kosti and we pulled out past a large army camp surrounded by stacked up piles of amtatch. I expected to see more of the Allied army and the requisite supplies it needed, the nearer we got to the desert. The soil here had an appearance, light grey in colour, like the scrub above it. What lifted the scene was the multitude of birds we saw from dainty ones like oyster catchers, white under body or at the base of wing, to small egrets. One large egret alighted on a thin twig; its fan-shaped spread wing blown by the wind into a lovely curve. I saw other ibis, black headed and tailed with white bodies. A stranger sight was what appeared to be a long line of black and white geese walking with fixed purpose all in the same direction. My peaceful contemplation of this landscape was shaken by the restaurant car attendant barging into my coupe with barely a knock.

"Madam, your lunch ticket did not cover your lunch. I must ask you to settle this."

"I assure you that my lunch ticket was pre-paid and covers all that I had."

"I need the extra money Madam. I must account for it."

"I do not carry extra money as I have paid for these meal tickets." My voice was raised as I was determined not to pay any additional money and we appeared to have reached a stand-off.

"Are you having problems? I couldn't help but overhear. Can I help?" A tall figure had arrived at the door of my coupe, and I recognised him as the gentleman in the next cabin. He introduced himself as Mr Darvell, one of the Railway's chiefs. Within minutes the dispute was settled, and the nice man apologised for the attendant's mistake. He, with great charm, invited me to have coffee with him in the restaurant car and I could not refuse.

It had started to rain, steadily and persistently, and enough to make me nervous. After so many days of enforced slow travel on water, when indolence made decision making impossible, I now felt the change of pace. My leg on the mend, once again I was travelling with purpose and needed to adjust myself to what lay ahead. I was nearing the last stage of my journey, and after the lull of the steamer I needed to rekindle my wits for the final section. Things could still go awfully wrong, and this downpour was one of them.

"I'm concerned about the rain! Do you think it'll last?" I asked Mr Darvell.

"Your guess is as good as mine, Mrs Warmington Reed. Do you have concerns about it?"

"I was warned that this stretch of track can be washed away at the slightest of provocations. I have a schedule that's tight."

"The line was only opened six months ago or less and they did a good job of work, but yes, there could be problems."

"If it really rains, I hear we could be held up for days."

"I must be honest with you; this stretch could be perilous. The trouble was that the constructors were put under pressure to complete the work at great speed. I suspect it was a War Office decision."

"Mr Darvell, are you confirming that if the rain continues, the track is at risk?"

"I'm afraid I am!" The big man looked embarrassed. "We're probably going to have to pull it up again. Not only is it not secure, but the powers that be appear to think we have no need for it now."

I was aghast "What a waste of effort! What a waste of funds!"

"I have to warn you that the same problem awaits you between Kosti and Khartoum." Mr Darvell concluded. If I was delayed, I could miss days, and the carefully timed connections would be useless. Suddenly the security of the previous steamer looked belatedly appealing and inviting.

I changed the subject. "I hear that Wavell is to be the new Viceroy of India."

"Yes, Auchinleck has been appointed Commander in Chief of the Indian army. I'm surprised as I thought that Churchill didn't like him."

"Yes, I wonder if that's true. I admire Auchinleck. As Commander in Chief of the Eighth Army, he did brilliantly in the defence of El Alamein. I never understood why Churchill and Sir Alan Brooke replaced him with General Alexander. I'm glad he's been acknowledged again. I think he'll do well in India." I had hoped for a war conversation with this attractive civilian, after the limitations of talking to the military, but this was short lived. He was patently not particularly interested.

Mr Darvell surprised me. "This is a lengthy and uncomfortable journey you're making, Mrs Warmington Reed. What's the reason for it?"

"Oh, I'm travelling to re-join my husband now that fighting in North Africa's almost over."

"I think that may be premature. What's your real reason?"

I stared at him. During all these weeks of travelling I had spoken to no one of the emotional side of the decision to re-join my husband. Phyllis in Cape Town was the last person I had shared my fear with. I saw compassion and a lively interest in the man's brown eyes.

"My husband's someone who enjoys company very much, and I've been away two years. I've heard that someone is trying to usurp my place by his side. I thought it was time to re-join him." I surprised myself!

"Are you concerned as to what you'll find?"

"Of course, I am!" I burst out "My husband is a charming, attractive man not overly concerned with the seriousness of life."

"And his wife is obviously an attractive, intelligent woman!"

"Thank you. I'm certainly intelligent enough to know it's time I was by his side."

Thankfully Mr Darvell did not attempt to probe deeper. The train was passing through dull, monotonous, and flat countryside. We called into little halts which usually comprised of two or three white tents and a few brightly thatched mud huts. I saw my first train of camels, and an unusual sight of a round straw cover attached to a camel's saddle to shade the man driving it. The glimpses of the now wide Nile showed that there was little evidence of sudd now.

We passed through Kabak station in the evening and over the first bridge across the Nile since it passed Jimja in the days of its youth. Mr Darvell and I walked along the narrow platform and bought some melons from the locals who squatted endlessly, hoping for custom. The light was poor, and it was only later that I saw that the melons were over ripe and most had to be discarded. I took my leave of Mr Darvell as I was beginning to feel unwell with the disturbing niggle of tooth ache. I retired early to bed, so missed seeing the small but growing capital of Blue Nile Province, Wadi Medina, which is only eighty-five miles southeast of Khartoum. Kosti and Kawa were also passed in the night.

June 20 1943

The blaze of the sunrise over the flat desert sand was almost unbearably painful to my eyes. I had survived a poor night and had eagerly awaited that moment only to be forced to look away. A full moon still shone wanly on our left. In the night it was becoming evident that my tooth pain could be more serious than I wanted to admit.

Masih was another insignificant little station with small pointed-domed white buildings, a few locals and two or three donkeys. There was still about thirty-five miles to go to Khartoum. The train travelled so slowly, continuously feeling its way along the young track which required such gentle treatment. Mr Darvell had told me that these broad carriages were on a narrow gauge, as it was throughout Africa, except in Egypt, and that they must be kept from 'swinging' and thus causing a serious derailment. Desert was on either side, flat, and endless. Having travelled through a good cotton producing soil, rich with nutrition, I could see only a little scrub which managed to provide a livelihood here.

Khartoum, where the two Niles meet was the seat of the Anglo-Egyptian Sudan government. I said a hasty goodbye to the charming Mr Darvell who rushed off late for an engagement. The station was every bit as chaotic as lesser stopovers I had needed to negotiate. Mountains of luggage had been turned out of the carrying car and left to the passenger to sort out on their own. Miriam and Mrs McInnes were, of course, travelling considerably lighter than I was, and left me to it. We agreed to meet at The Grand Hotel. It took a frustrating half hour to organise my trunk and heavier luggage to be collected by truck before I could depart in a taxi with lighter possessions.

The big central lounge of the hotel was heaving with activity, mostly army, so I sat in the early sunshine in a pleasant garden, waiting for my luggage to catch up. I waited a long time trying to ignore my growing tooth distress. Finally, a truck turned up, carrying a pile of cases that had nothing to do with me! It was quickly claimed. Gripped with fear that somebody had laid claim to my possessions, particularly my trunk, and tired of waiting I astounded the truck driver by insisting on climbing up into the passenger seat to return to the station. Thankfully my luggage awaited me there in solitary splendour, and I quickly recovered all of it.

My room was pleasant and spacious, with my own bathroom, so a very hot bath followed by breakfast revived my spirits. Aspirin lulled my toothache and stimulated my sense of adventure. Miriam and I had promised ourselves a trip to Omdurman on the west bank of the Nile, so no time was lost, and we set off by taxi. We crossed a great bridge of seven spans where the White and Blue Nile meet to enter this big old native town. It was a picturesque mixture of colour and mud. Many tribes met and mingled in its streets. There was an interesting covered market with squatting women selling their baskets, beads, food stuffs, bright calicoes, and shoes. Men displayed brass-work pots and pans. Little boys ran about offering to show you where to buy anything from elephant hair-and-ivory switches, to chewing gum and childrens' coloured toys. We found two good stores where curios of all kinds were sold including beautifully worked daggers. Gay native wraps, jewellery, and good leatherwork of all kinds were displayed, and there they were wise enough not to bother people to buy! In the Suq Kibeer, or big market, I was particularly taken by a delicate little dagger, silver handled, with antelope and crocodile strips. My recent heightened awareness of crocodiles made me hesitate.

Down narrow streets we found the museum in an old, low building that Mrs McInnes had asked us to look at. The heat was by then appalling but Miriam and I felt obliged to honour her wish. A horse's war-protection mask fascinated me, but we were on a mission. The top of the Mahdi's tomb piece was our goal, presented by Mrs McInnes after she had had it for safe keeping for twenty-nine years in her hall! We needed to report back that it was well presented. Nearby, in a small, enclosed space, was the Mahdi's tomb, in a dilapidated condition, its arches falling. We were saddened but a vision distracted us. Against this light, sandy coloured background stood a stately company, a bodyguard of five, very blue and grey guinea fowl. Poor things amid such desiccated surroundings! No greenery or water was visible although they must have had some somewhere.

"I think it's cruel to keep them here with so little water." Miriam was concerned.

"I imagine different birds have different drinking habits! I used to wonder at Sea Point how my cormorants managed with apparently no fresh water, beyond erratic trickles down the shore."

"I've seen swallows drink during their swooping flights over water."

"I remember a dark blue variety of swallow drinking soapy

water puddles on my veranda in Haifa. I used to watch them. They were probably migrating and desperately thirsty."

"I think you'll take any water if you have to."

"Earlier in this trip, I was waiting for a boat on the quayside at Albertville and there was absolutely nothing to drink. It felt like hours, and I was desperate. Apart from feeling lifeless my brain seemed to disengage too. I've never experienced thirst like it. I would've drunk anything!" I smiled at the recollection. Like the swallows, I was migrating too!

After lunch at the hotel and fortified by aspirin, I decided to return alone to the fascinating Omdurman. I chose to return by train, a long, hot ride but interesting. Being Sunday many tribes people, mostly dressed in white, were going to town. Black robed women contrasted against brilliantly attired ones and crowded their own 'women only' department of the train. The exotic musky smell of perfumed bodies was overwhelming. I was lucky I spotted the carriage and fitted myself in there, as I would certainly have insulted the men and exposed myself to hostile behaviour by my ignorance. It cost four piastres for the return ticket, and I was excited to be having a mini adventure on my own. Unluckily I didn't know where to alight, so went on much too far and had to wait for a crowded returning train. I had been thinking about the silver handled dagger, and sheepishly decided to overlook the crocodile decoration and buy it if it was still there. It was, and then on a roll, I bought a little coffee pot and mat, a big leather bag like a young suitcase and an elephant ivory necklace. I should have had Miriam there to contain my spending spree! By the time I was back in Khartoum my feet were screaming. White dust covered me, and I was parched. Crawling into the bar of the hotel I downed a superb gin and tonic.

That night my toothache erupted, shooting pains up into my ear. I staggered down to reception in pursuit of anything that would dull the sensation and allow me the rescue of sleep. I thought it was unmanned at first but spotted a sleeping employee on a mat behind the desk. Both of us were embarrassed. I imagined that the man's life must be tough and he was probably grateful for the job. He spoke excellent English and offered me enough aspirin to finish me off! I did finally sleep.

June 21 1943

After breakfast Mrs McInnes went to stay at the Clergy House. She was excited at this preferential treatment being the widow of a bishop and told me that Bishop Gelsthorpe would be there. The significance of the bishop and his presence escaped me as my mission was to find a dentist, an overriding focus if I was to survive the day.

I was lucky. Mr Alainak, who had trained in Beirut, removed the molar tooth, and treated the abscess and I felt immediate relief. It only cost me sixty-five piastres and I would have paid double that for his service. Life would be bearable again.

Entering the hotel lobby, I was surprised to find Mr Darvell sitting waiting for me. We had made no arrangement, but I was happy to be swept into his car to be taken for lunch at his house. His wife was away in Cairo, but he was offering a salad, which sounded perfect. The house lay off a quiet avenue and his spacious peaceful garden was laid to lawn with beds of gay flowers and shrubs, obviously benefitting from the richness of the Nile soil. Small bulbuls were flying around very timorously, smaller than our Palestine variety which has a conspicuous yellow rump. There were fine high trees and far away I saw storks flying, and kites hovering and floating on the warm breeze currents. In such a garden time stood still.

Following lunch and a couple of gin and tonics Mr Darvell continued the unsettling conversation of two days ago. "Does your husband know that you're coming, or will it be a surprise?"

"I wired him, about ten days ago. He was amazed and concerned but said he was looking forward to seeing me. He knows I'm home for good because I'm bringing everything with me."

"Will you stay in Palestine when the war is over?"

"I like your positivity, Mr Darvell! I know there's been talk about a posting to Bermuda, but I'm sure we'll return to England eventually. Two of my three daughters are working in London."

"Our daughter is in London, so I know how you feel. You must worry about them a lot."

"Yes, I do." I paused "But, my middle one, Ronny, is my biggest concern. She's in the Philippines, a prisoner of the Japs, I imagine. She was pregnant the last time I heard from her which was before Christmas '41."

He leaned closer. "I'm sorry. It must be hard not to be sharing your anxiety with your husband. I know how supportive my wife is."

"I think I've always been the most stalwart of the two of us. Teddy's been the one who has been away from home the most, while I looked after the house and the children, and tried to make a living on the side. Teddy was away a lot in the war, and later, on business in London. He was in New York for two months, on two occasions, but he always came back. That makes me sound like a poor little 'house frau', which I'm not! I've had my adventures too!" Mr Darvell had the most extraordinary way of listening which drew words from my mouth I never intended to say. Was he flirting with me? It felt as if it had been a long time since someone had flirted with me.

"I don't doubt that for one moment and I don't imagine 'house frau' fits the bill." He answered. Yes, he was most definitely flirting!

I smiled, seduced, "Teddy has always spent his money before he got it. He was indulged by his mother who gave him outrageously expensive gifts on a whim." One of those indulgences was at that moment securely wrapped in my trunk and caused me many a headache in case it was damaged. "Overspending's a pattern that has repeated itself throughout my husband's life. I wasn't aware of it until later in our marriage when it fell on me to try and balance the books. Teddy would always treat himself to whatever he wanted with no forethought of what the real emotional price was." I was aware that I was being indiscreet, but I couldn't stop. "It never ended, it was the most up to date camera, the stylish jacket, the rare book. It was always a bargain and his charmed delight in his purchase was contagious. I found it hard not to forgive him, although the novelty of his surprises wore off over the years."

"You had to balance the books? Do I take it you had to supplement his income during your marriage?"

"It was a difficult act. It was important to Teddy that his family and social group weren't aware we were struggling financially. He took as much as he could from the mill business, but it was never enough. I wrote a book under a pseudonym, which fortunately sold well. I even gave some semi-professional piano concerts. Teddy and an architect friend built a house for us near his parent's house and the mill, and it had a bit of land. During the Great War, when he was away, I ran a chicken farm from home and sent the eggs to London. I also bred ducks. I bought unbroken ponies and turned them into reliable ride or drive animals. All this was put down to my eccentricity, but it was keeping us afloat."

"What a remarkable achievement. I'm sure your husband values you."

There was no stopping me now. "My youngest sister, Maud, was working as a governess in India and between us we arranged for the seven-year-old boy Pat, whose mother had died, to join our family when he wasn't in boarding school. His father Colonel Rynd paid well. Everyone assumed it was just from the goodness of our hearts. Little did we know that Pat would eventually marry my daughter Ronny." I stopped, embarrassed now.

"What a struggle that all must have been."

"Looking back, I can see we went to stupid lengths to keep up appearances. The one thing that I insisted upon was a good education for the three girls. That was vital to me, and they went to Cheltenham Ladies' College, as I had done. When Teddy finally resigned from the mill in `24 and took up the job offer in Romania, it couldn't have worked better for us. The older girls were independent and could enjoy holidays out there and we had a clean slate."

"I think your husband is a very lucky man! Does he deserve you?" Mr Darvell looked into my eyes and touched my hand. I knew we had strayed into dangerous territory. He had made it very clear that he found me attractive, as I did him. The bees hummed in the shrubbery and the afternoon lay clear to do with what we chose. No one need ever know. Didn't I deserve a brief interlude of 'no strings attached' pleasure which would reinforce my long-waned perception of myself as a desirable woman? I like to think I hardly hesitated before my answer came.

"We made lifetime vows, and we've shared our lives. Our marriage is worth fighting for. You're a kind and generous listener, Mr Darvell. I've said far too much but thank you for listening."

He acknowledged the moment was past with a nod and

a sad little smile. I knew that he would not make me feel uncomfortable and that I had made the right decision. I stayed with my supportive host until the shadows lengthened, talking of many matters. He had his story to tell, and I mine. It was a restorative and memorable day.

It was only later, after he had dropped me back at the hotel, that I really understood what had happened. Mr Darvell had been a listening ear, just at my moment of need. He was an exceptional man and I had been extremely fortunate that day. To be able to tell a stranger I would never meet again my intimate thoughts was a relief and a kindness. He could discard that information without complications, and I could move forwards, my burden lightened briefly by being heard. As for the unspoken invitation, I knew that the decision not to indulge an enticing whim was mine. Teddy might have made a different decision in the circumstances but acting as my husband might would gain me nothing but disappointment with myself in the long run.

I turned down an invitation awaiting me at the hotel to dine with the famous Bishop Gelsthorpe and Mrs McInnes at the Clergy House and sought the company of my bed. I threw open the windows and shutters as the room was stifling and basked in the glimpses through the vegetation of the cool moving Nile, its surface rippling and shimmering in the night. No nets were needed to cover the bed in this hotel as there were neither mosquitoes nor sandfly threatening. The stars shone brilliantly, and I hoped I would soon be in my own home. This journey had gone on too long and I felt infinitely weary. Both my mouth and my shin bite were playing up and reminding me of my vulnerability. It had been a long and eventful day and sleep was thankfully beckoning.

FOURTEEN

June 22 1943

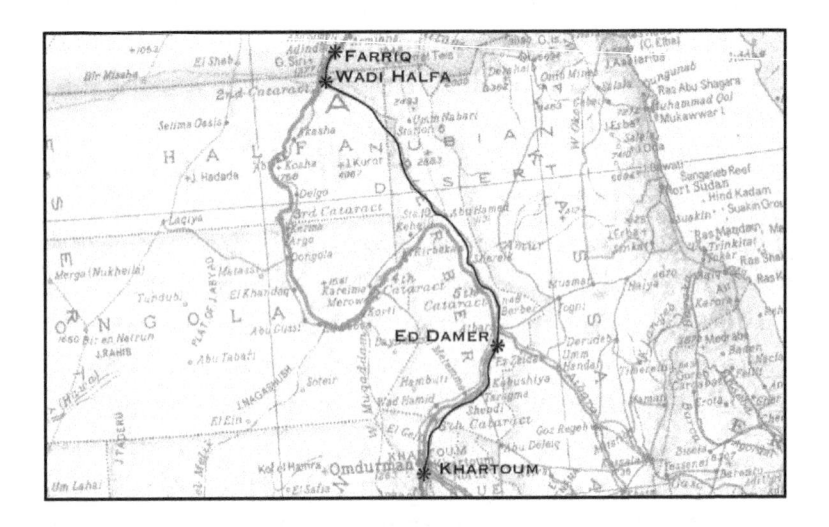

The hotel housekeeper was a tall, handsome woman, who hailed from Austria. She was charming, as were so many of the expatriots from that cruelly dominated country. Always strikingly dressed, uniform by day and evening frocks at night, she looked a young fifty but was in fact nearing my age. In a former life she was a sculptress, she told me. I wondered about the story that bought her to North Africa and tried to draw her out, but she became evasive at my interest. Surrounded as I was by secretive goings on, I put her on my list of suspect characters who might not be who we assumed they were. Was this inevitable with the war constantly shadowing our thoughts or was this a product of being a passive traveller with too much time on my hands? Certainly, nobody was quite who they seemed on limited acquaintance. The stream of interesting folk I had met since the start of my odyssey presented a frustration. There were so many people I would have loved to keep contact with. I knew we would exchange cards and promises but the reality was that meeting again would be highly unlikely.

When I sent Teddy a cable all I could say was that all was well, and I was looking forward to seeing him.

Mrs McInnes, Miriam and I left the hotel just as a convoy entered, and the lounge was swamped with people and paraphernalia. It was approaching midday; the relentless sun bore down, and I was detained at the station with a problem with my luggage. The station master demanded extra payment for it, and I knew I had paid its way up to Shellal. My shin was once again painful, and I had a headache, so instead of meekly complying, I stood firm and made a big fuss. To my surprise no lesser person than the Superintendent of Railways emerged from the back office. He was a nice Scot who put things right immediately. We found the extra demanded was the difference on to Cairo, but not to be paid from this station. From Shellal my luggage would be in the hands of the Anglo-American Nile and Tourist people. The train had been standing for some time and the crescendo of heat when I reached my coupe, was unbearable. The windows had been closed because of the dust particles that intruded everywhere and turning the fan full on made little difference. I was desperate for relief by the time the train started and gained momentum for the next stage in my journey.

We had just passed El Geili and its cemetery when, to my amazement, I saw a vivid mirage of the Nile and trees and their reflections on the right. Even knowing that this startling vision was totally false and caused by the heat haze, I found it some sort of miracle. The view was distorted, and it vibrated as I looked. The Nile and the trees looked so appealing, set against the flat, baked brown desert that excitedly I reached for my camera to try to capture the moment. Sadly, before I had the chance it disappeared as rapidly as it had arrived. I checked later but neither Mrs McInnes nor Miriam, in their nearby coupes, had seen it.

Six or seven miles out of Khartoum the train passed a spot by a hill with a large sign announcing it to be Kerreri. This was where the battle of Omdurman was fought in 1898, when the British Commander in Chief, Kitchener, finally broke the tyranny of the Islamic Mahdi. It was said that 35,000 – 50,000 Sudanese tribesmen under the Mahdi attacked the British and were defeated by highly disciplined soldiers and their modern artillery. Kitchener was also seeking revenge for the death of General Gordon, killed when a Mahdist army had captured Khartoum thirteen years earlier. After the battle British and Egyptian troops drove straight on into Omdurman to stop the remaining Mahdist forces withdrawing there. I thought it was strange to know that our prime minister Winston Churchill, as a young lieutenant, commanded a troop of twenty-five lancers in that fight.

The scenery was of little interest with endlessly flat desert and scrub with horizontally topped, stunted trees. I closed my eyes and reflected on my conversation with Mr Darvell the previous day. It struck me I had painted a picture of Teddy that was jaded and unfair. I had left out his intelligence, his sense of fun and the spark between us that had always been there since I met him in Leipzig a lifetime ago.

Teddy and I used to ride together after college on horses hired from a local stable. There was a large wide bank running round the town on which was a riding track. The Austrian stable master had a particularly noteworthy lady client who wanted to purchase a certain ex-racehorse and he asked me to ride it on the bank to see that it was safe. All went well until Teddy decided to pass me, without the usual warning 'Achtung'. What followed was madness. The ex-racehorse responded by taking off, thinking that it was another race. Teddy then compounded it by gallantly trying to catch my horse's bridle, but only made matters worse and the horse then really bolted. Do what I could, there was no stopping it. I remember my horror as I came thundering toward a level crossing on the track where both sets of gates were closed. All I could do was hang on and pray. The horse jumped them both! I finally managed to pull him up in a side street and was joined by an ashen faced Teddy who was convinced he had been responsible for my demise.

Other exploits gained me a reputation as an intrepid rider, but Teddy, who was equally proficient on a horse, was thankfully not involved and never learned about my adventures. We were happy. We had so much in common. Our romance had been intoxicating and before we knew it, we were married, too young to understand the gravity of that commitment. Later we shared the upbringing of our three daughters, and I liked to think that we had made it work.

Miriam and I were excited by the view of the Meroe Pyramids in the late afternoon. She had some knowledge about them.

"Around the seventh century BC, in Ethiopia 'proper', this was the Kingdom of Meroe. The capitol Napata was a place of note even down to Roman times."

"What sustained it? There seems little here."

"It was a rich trading, mining, and agricultural centre. A huge kingdom that stretched as far south as the modern Khartoum and east to the Abyssinian highlands. The first Ethiopian king to subdue and dominate Egypt was a Nubian king called Piankhi, round about 750BC. These Pyramids of Meroe show that there was Egyptian influence here before the eighth century."

We could see the pyramids clearly from the train, more than seven in a row, lying back from the railway up on a terrace. I would have loved to pause and have a good look, but instead we stopped at a village station where local women were selling caps and crude painted bowls. This universal selling from the tracks through the train windows must eventually have paid off or they would not have done it. As a passenger I learned that opening a train window was a big mistake as the dust penetrated even with the window shut. It did not encourage me to shop from my coupe; the price in dust was too high.

We were interrupted by a Mr Armstrong of Sudan Railways who had popped in to check that all was well. An amusing fellow, I suspected that this was the favourite part of his job. I commented that I had been surprised to see so many camel bones lying about near the tracks.

"Ah, camels!" He twinkled knowingly. "The army has a lot to learn about camels!"

"Meaning?"

"The British army were taken for a ride when they bought camels from the locals. They should have insisted on hiring them with their drivers instead of stupidly buying them outright."

"You mean they didn't recognise a good camel when they saw it?"

"Oh, they recognised a good camel, in fact they recognised the first forty very good beasts when they saw them and paid fourteen pounds each for them. Then the same forty were bought round for inspection again and were happily passed. The same forty did such duty again and again and were accepted, the army buyer never noticing the old, old trick. They never saw the rest of the herd making up the proper number! Those were the camels who were extremely poor and died off soon after being driven into Khartoum!" Mr Armstrong had doubtless told this story many times and could still chortle at it.

We covered large tracks of Nubian desert, dotted only with the occasional thorn bush, and a few picturesque buildings with rounded bases and high domes with a tiny cap on top. Once I saw a girl standing completely alone in the miles and miles of sand and widely separated bits of shrub. She was carrying a load of wood on her head. What a life!

The sunset was breath-taking. Each neat little walled hovel looked superb when tinged with gold and pink against the rapidly darkening sky. This must have been the best possible time to view such an utterly dry, dusty waste of a country. Black goats and odd camels strolled about grazing or stood lost in thought or sleep.

Sunsets depart so suddenly in Africa and at Zeidab station I got down onto the platform to give myself a little exercise. Immediately I was besieged by women who were falling over each other to secure a sale. They had no concept of giving prospective purchasers space and were intimidating as they pushed their wares into my face for my attention. For peace I agreed to buy four small, coloured raffia mats for next to nothing, and beat a hasty retreat onto the train. Discomforted I could not remember such aggressive marketing earlier in my trip and wondered why I found this here. With the war zones ever closer, perhaps the desperate vendors might have had to suffer greater hardship and had become more aggressive? Alternatively, having been exposed to ample soldiers and personnel in transit, the pushy quick sell had been learned the hard way? I noticed the picturesque huts were made of the same raffia as my mats were.

We passed Ed Damer station, which was a substantial town, the capital of the Berber Province, and then later Atbara which was the headquarters of Sudan Railways. There was a fine iron bridge over the Atbara River, which was a Nile tributary from Abyssinia. The most memorable aspect of the area was a peculiar smell attached to it, which no one seemed able to account for. The heat and the dust were pitiless as the train trundled through unending desert throughout the night, without even scrub to lift the monotony. For once I was happy about the obliterating dark.

June 23 1943

Waking to a cabin covered in a thick layer of dust, I rang for tea and a man with a duster. I stayed firmly in my berth eyeing the gentleman in question as he ineffectually swept up a storm of dust. So, cursing my stupidity, I asked him to return when I would not be present. The Sudan Railways provided a splendid breakfast. We had melon, fish, omelette and sausages with toast, marmalade, jam and two lumps of sugar with the tea. Many repair gangs were busy on that part of the line, so the train had to crawl along, and I breakfasted accompanied by the train's rolls and jolts. A low dull line of hills broke the flat monotony, and I noticed a sprinkling of lava on the sand. The train arrived at 'Station 6', and this was the first evidence I had of war preparations affecting an African railway station. Set against the endless blue of the sky and the usual red earthen buildings, there was a big round camouflaged water tower and by it a fleet of lorries. There was also a military looking aerodrome.

Mr Armstrong, who had taken to popping in, identified a Belgian Army contingent from the Belgian Congo. "They're on their way to join up with the main body who've already gone ahead. Those lorries have fallen behind, so I imagine they're probably being mended and regrouped."

"They seem to be rather far from anywhere. I wouldn't have expected to see any action in the middle of the Nubian Desert!"

"Ah, you never know! A new trail is being blazed, via Kordofan, which was once thought to be impossible."

I looked carefully at Mr Armstrong. He was enjoying this war. I had been told the only action now in North Africa would be of the mopping up variety. The Anglo-American landings in North-West Africa were supposed to have finally paid off last month, in May. Several hundred thousand German and Italian personnel in northern Tunisia were forced to surrender if I was to believe the news. That was only a month ago! Of course, our defeat of the Germans was not set in stone. Mr Armstrong could have said anything and in my ignorance, I would have believed him.

Dark hills still bordered our sight, while pale, biscuit coloured sand swept down over their feet and all around. To my delight we now enjoyed more frequent mirages as the sun heated up. Civilisation promised as telegraph poles now accompanied us, all under the dome of blue sky, like an inverted bowl. I noted that the windows were gently tinted to soften the glare, a sign of the intelligence of The Sudan Railway.

My shin, from the bite at Massindi, was still causing me pain. I tried to rest and sleep after lunch, but despite my tiredness I found the stuffiness of the coupe in the heat of mid-day made that impossible. The dust had got everywhere, into my luggage and into my hair. My skin under my underclothes even felt gritty with it. I longed to be back on the Nile again and was celebrating the approach of Wadi Halfa where we would once more be transferring to a steamer for the next leg. Waving palms either side of the tracks announced the proximity of this big town, when Miriam dropped in.

"I'm sorry Elf, you don't have to gather your things. The plan's changed. We won't be catching the steamer here."

"Why ever not? I'm sure we're just coming to Wadi Halfa."

"Mr Armstrong's just warned us. The Nile's considered too low now for the steamer to tackle it."

"Oh no! I was looking forward to being on the water again."

"Yes, it's a shame. He says we've got to stick to this train as far as Farriq. Another forty or fifty miles to go before we get our reward."

We reached the obviously brand-new station of Farriq in the late afternoon after an appalling journey of heat and dust, and this under the best Sudan Railway conditions possible. Once again, I was forced to wait in the direct sun by the train while the porters squabbled over my luggage. It took three of them to organise themselves and then they set off in a different direction to that of the steamer. Apparently, my porters were taking me via the customs official, despite Mr Armstrong previously telling me that I could go straight across and on to the boat. I noticed that this was exactly what Mrs McInnes was doing, but my porters took no notice of my directions. My head was pounding; I was tired, and my shin was hurting.

The custom's official was an ignorant young man with a chip

on his shoulder. "Madam, I must ask you to open your luggage for inspection."

"That will not be necessary. I've been travelling all the way from Cape Town, and it has not been required at any time."

"Madam, please do as you are asked. I must examine your luggage at this point."

"Why have you chosen me? My companions have gone directly to the steamer. I've been informed that it's not necessary to inspect my luggage here."

"Unlock this trunk for me please."

I looked at my tired looking trunk on the customs bench. My heart contracted and I stared at him. "You are exceeding your responsibility. I will not be opening my baggage to you, and I will be making a complaint to your superiors."

"I suggest that you don't impede my work Madam, or you'll be sorry."

Some of the passengers had gathered round to witness this standoff, sympathetic but helpless. I felt singled out and smarted at the injustice of it. The sun bore down relentlessly on my head, while the customs official and my porters lounged with all the time in the world. I was determined not to open the trunk, unless forced to, so tried my previously successful ploy of listing what I was not carrying in my possessions. It had worked before, but the young man cut me off angrily. "You're wasting my time. You'll either unlock your luggage immediately, or I'll be asking you to accompany me to the customs offices in town."

"You've no right to detain me this way!" The little steamer was waiting for me now. Once I would have reluctantly been shamed into obeying the official but now, as a matter of principle, I was rigidly determined that this man was not going to have that satisfaction.

"This is my post, and I can do what I like. You're obstructing me." He indicated to the porters that they were to take up their burdens again, and I had no idea as to how this would end. If I missed my connection, all these weeks of careful timings would be lost. There were only a few days travelling ahead of me, and this stupid man could jeopardise the entire plan. Anger overcame prudence.

"Don't even think of detaining me!" My voice had risen to penetrate his thick skull. "I have witnesses here that this has been discrimination. I'll make sure that you lose your job if you don't let me go immediately."

He was turning his back on me to direct my porters, when a clear voice cut across the group. "Is there some reason for this delay?" My rescuing angel turned out to be the passport official who had been on the train. He and Mrs McInnes had recognised each other. When she and her husband had lived in Cairo long ago, he had been one of her church lads. Now, caught in the act of rushing past, he asked why I was waiting.

The fuming official explained, but my angel waved him aside angrily, marked all my things and ordered them to be taken on board at once. My audience cheered and I could have kissed him!

So, at last I walked over and down the bank onto the odd little steamer that was lying there puffing and blowing. Glancing back past the amused passenger group I spotted my customs official heartily engaged in hitting and kicking one of the porters!

My cabin was a not-too-bad single one, for which I was very grateful. Totally drained from the unpleasantness of the afternoon I retired to bed without dinner. Standing naked in front of my wash basin I gave myself a thorough strip wash. I shook out my hair relieving it of a sandstorm of dust and washed and re platted it. I stared at the image of a sixty-four-year-old woman in the tiny mirror. I could ignore the fact no longer. The Elf who had started this journey had been a fitter one than the one who ended it. I had totally underestimated the wear and tear this travelling had inflicted on me. I only had to look at my luggage with its broken catches, scraped hide, and missing handles to see that I should not have imagined that I could have got away injury free.

June 24 1943

Rising through the pre-awake state when you are ageless, painless, and guiltless I awoke to Miriam bringing me an iced soda and checking if I needed anything. Lulled into an early sleep last night, I had missed all the excitement of leaving port, and was met with a strange sight on awakening, the door having swung open. I was sleepily shocked to see something strange across the narrow deck. At first, I thought it was the black headgear, beard, and white robe of an indigenous person, but to my surprise, found it was a black muzzled white-faced sheep! Miriam explained that this was one of many crammed on a big two-decked barge we were now attached to, simply loaded with sheep on top and cattle below.

"This is nothing compared to what's on our side!" Miriam smiled at me. "You're quiet here but we have a similar barge strapped to our side full to overflowing with travelling Africans! The noise and the cooking smells are bad, especially the noise!"

Pulling a wrap around me, and grabbing some left-over biscuits for sustenance, I left my cabin to examine my travel companions and immediately became concerned. The animals, although rather smelly according to the wayward breezes, were unnaturally silent. They were stupefied with misery as movement was all but impossible for them. They must have been suffering from thirst as they had no drinking arrangements as far as I could see. The great horns of the lower deck cattle locked themselves with others now and then resulting in some plunging, but overall, they were strangely dumb. Poor things.

"I can't see any drink containers for them. Is there anything we can do?"

Miriam replied, "I've already asked the second in command what the arrangements are for them and was told that it was none of their business."

"How long have they been there? How far are we towing them? We can only hope that it's a short leg of their journey."

"You've been dead to the world! They were strapped on late last night at the same time as the person carrier barge on the other side. The noise hasn't stopped all night!"

"Poor you. I didn't hear a thing. We shouldn't be on this steamer; it's a poor excuse for one."

"It's certainly not as big as the Britain, that we're supposed to be on. I imagine this boat is just a temporary stand in because of the water level. They're just doing their usual transportation, and we're the exception to their normal cargo."

"That would explain a lot."

I couldn't bear to ignore the misery in front of me and Miriam and I spent the next hour trying to give the sheep and cattle canisters of water to lap up. It wasn't very successful and just made us more aware of our limitations. Realistically there was nothing we could do to change the situation, and probably our interference could only have helped a few. I noticed that we were viewed with amusement by the staff and fellow passengers, and finally I retreated to bed again nursing a throbbing head.

I was nearing the last days of the journey and started to think seriously about what would confront me when I reached Haifa. Miriam and I sat on the uppermost deck, as far away from the animal and human cargo as possible. We strayed into difficult emotional pastures.

"I'm sure letters from Joy and Felicity will be waiting for me. I'm so proud of my daughters."

"My parents are proud of me, even though I became a librarian instead of marrying."

"I deliberately brought my girls up to be competent, independent women. I had some opposition as, with my background, this was not necessarily encouraged in young ladies."

"It sounds as if we were both a bit before our times?"

"I did it because I'd learned my lesson. Grace, Maud, and I were well educated but it was only to be marriageable young women. No one could say that studying the piano at the Conservatoire was aimed at providing me with a career."

"You must be a good musician."

"Adequate for small concerts. Not outstanding! It was only my experience of being married to Teddy that showed me how useless my education had been when confronted with trying to bring money into the family. Interestingly, Bertha, Teddy's young sister insisted on being trained as a chemist, which was unusual. The training was wasted as she immediately married a chemist and never practised again. I imagine as the youngest child, you're more likely to get your way with your parents. It's certainly been the case for my youngest daughter!"

"Did you learn how to bend the rules? I know I did!"

"Teddy's parents raised their eyebrows at me to begin with. I didn't fit in with convention. But later, where would he have been without me? It was hard for him to accept that I could bring money into the family. It was against all that he had been raised to believe. Luckily this overseas lifestyle suits us both well."

"With my parents it was always religion. They wanted me to marry to continue the Jewish line and observances."

"That's hard for you, although I'm sure they believed they

were looking after you that way. To be Jewish at this time in Europe must be frightening and they wanted to protect you. I remember when Joy wanted to get engaged and Teddy didn't approve of her choice of fiancé. I always felt guilty that I had not stood up for her when she was so deeply in love with Michael. He was a decent enough man, it was only Teddy who had taken against him, saying that at twelve years older than Joy, he was not a suitable match. He really thought the man wasn't good enough for his oldest daughter. Joy succumbed to Teddy's will too easily. With hindsight I should have encouraged her to defy her father. You'll find, when you're a mother, that guilt comes with the job. Balancing the needs of your husband with the needs of your children starts as soon as they are born, and never ends!"

"Ah, hindsight! I think your middle daughter married?"

"Yes, Ronny, finally married Pat who'd lived in the family since he was a boy. She'd been engaged twice, first to Harry, and then to Bonzo. Neither worked out. I'm very fond of Pat, but I think she settled for him when she thought she'd run out of options."

"Too many young men are dying."

"Yes, our world will never be the same."

The silence settled between us.

The night was blessedly cooler and once again I enjoyed a canopy of stars. I sat on the uppermost deck and felt less ill. I had barely eaten that day but ended it with a cup of Horlicks and biscuits. Our twin barges seemed to have settled for the night and it was time for me to descend to my stifling cabin. In two days, I would be by Teddy's side again. I would fight whatever battles I needed to and would pick up my old life. The fan only worked intermittently, so I pulled a blanket over myself and sleep finally came.

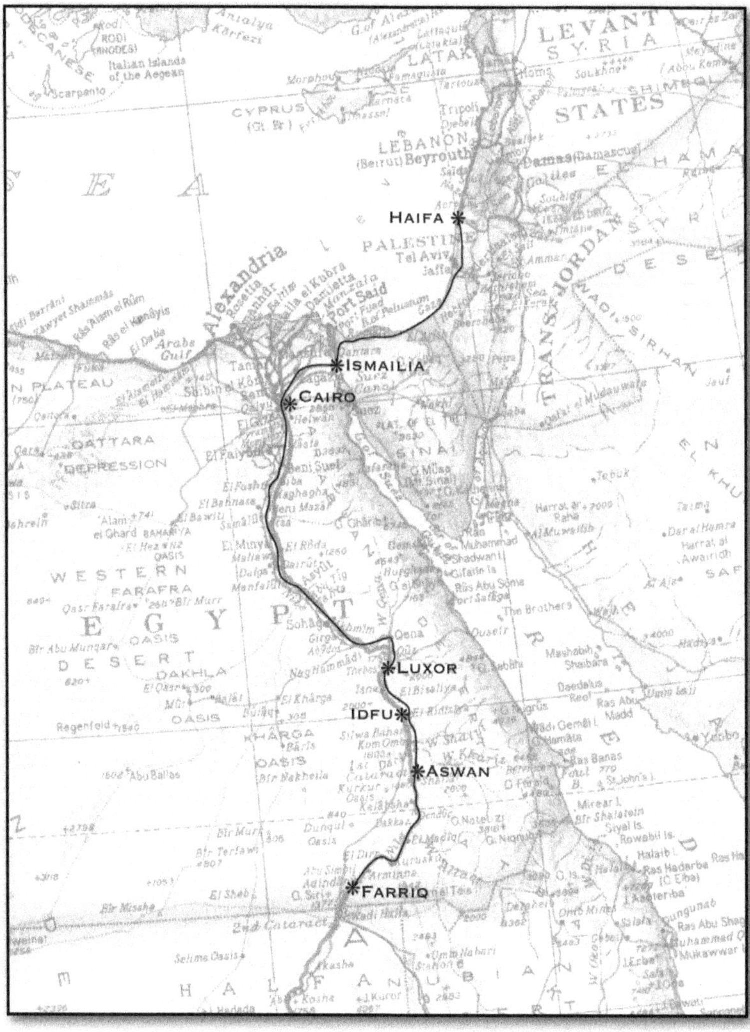
HAIFA
ISMAILIA
CAIRO
LUXOR
IDFU
ASWAN
FARRIQ

FIFTEEN

June 25 1943

I was up, dressed and out on deck for tea in the cool of early morning. The boat twisted and turned and jolted following the current, and I was amazed to see that we had gained yet another small barge attached on the far side of the people's transport barge. It appeared to be full of British army personnel who must have roped themselves on sometime in the night. Our original barge attachments had made manoeuvring a major trial, so this addition was mind blowing! The morning could have been pleasant in other circumstances, with the typical Nile scenery. On the left was real desert with flat dark rocks and sand hillocks falling and rising in lovely curves like sleeping waves. On the right was mud in layers, with green rice-growing terraces of such a vivid fresh colour. Away back were low hills breaking the faint horizon. One or two small steamers and a couple of feluccas shared our water under the cloudless sky.

The crew on this boat always appeared to be in a state of alarm, and the shouting and gesticulating reached an unprecedented level as we came across a steamer stuck on the river bottom near the bank. Instead of giving it a wide berth which seemed the logical thing to do, bearing in mind how encumbered we were, we steered closer to proffer aid! I could not imagine what the thinking was because, of course, we nearly got stuck ourselves.

We hovered ineffectually for a time. The small boat full of army personnel could wait no longer and decided to release their tenuous link to our steamer and made their way on ahead with the greatest of ease. It made me wonder what they were doing there in the first place. Our boat was such a third-rate little ship, just a makeshift one.

Eventually, another much more powerful boat managed to pull the stuck steamer off the bank, and having helped not one whit, our crew decided it was time to move on again.

Miriam had made her way over to me and had some salacious news to pass on. "You know the nursing sister or radiologist who's accompanying the patient?"

"You mean the one we first saw in the Khartoum hotel? The flirty one?"

"Exactly, her. I've been told she's a Belgian spy!" The nurse was an attractive but hard-faced young woman who had been leading on all and sundry in the officer line.

"Miriam! I thought you were suspicious of that other woman, who looked so nervous and shy. Make up your mind!"

"No, I decided she didn't fit the bill. I have it on good authority that it's the flirty one. Apparently, she's travelling, unconsciously 'under observation'!"

I retorted, "In which case she's not doing a very good job of it! You are funny Miriam."

Although 'spot the spy' had been a game between us, there had been enough strange unresolved encounters on this journey to prove there was far more going on behind the scenes than appeared on the surface. I was reminded of my man with the poisoned heel way back at Victoria Falls, and the sinister, middle of the night men, who embarked when we had reached the White Nile, never to be seen or acknowledged again. Strangers I had met on this journey could present themselves in any way they wanted, so who knows who I had spoken to. This trip may have felt like travelling across a back water, but it was war time, and I would never be the wiser.

We turned about again, our barges bumping and suddenly we were aground. Orders were shouted, panic reigned, engines strained but despite all these efforts, there we remained. If anything, we became further stuck the longer we struggled.

"This could be serious Elf!" Miriam was anxious. "We'll miss the bigger ship waiting to take us on to Shellal."

Her worry was infectious. "We could miss our Cairo connection!"

"We could be stuck here for days. The Nile's only going to become shallower!"

"If we're going to be stuck, there are nicer steamers to be marooned in." I caught the eye of a wide-eyed bovine.

The solution the crew came up with, after heated discussions, was that we would jettison our additional cargos. The barge overflowing with African travellers was the first to be released, and for the first time the occupants were stilled into a surprised silence as they floated off helplessly, drifting shoreward on their own. It seemed such a cavalier decision, and ethically, I could not help but be shocked at the crew's action. Was the luggage we carried more important than their lives? If a choice had to be made, surely it was our possessions that should have been jettisoned first! I watched anxiously and was relieved to see the barge ended up close enough to shore for its occupants to wade to safety. The chatter started up again as local villagers greeted them, but I had no idea how they were supposed to reach their destination.

This load lightening was not enough to release us, so it

was the turn of the poor cattle barge. I watched the barge float away on its own with as much concern as I had for the humans. When would these animals get a drink or use their limbs again? The current propelled it out into the mainstream away from the bank, and the lowing gradually faded as it retreated away from us. I was relieved to see two or three villagers in their boats push off from the banks to follow them and could only hope that it was in their interests to secure the cattle undamaged. I also saw my last dark crocodile gently submerge and head in the same direction. With our sides unfettered, our engines with much juddering shook us free and gradually we started to creep away.

We had lost a couple of hours from the schedule already, so it was with genuine hunger that we passengers sat down meekly in the dining room to an almost inedible lunch. The only thing to drink was soda water and I could not be tempted by anything on my plate. I retired to my cabin to prepare myself for the next transfer.

"The Britain is here! They waited for us!" The voice sang out outside my window shouting the relief that all of us felt. Our bigger steamer was the one we should have been travelling on and it was waiting for us mid-stream. We were to be transferred immediately, over water. Mrs McInnes, Miriam, and I decided that it was wisest not to watch the progress of our luggage, so we allowed ourselves to be helped from the one vessel to the better one via a little boat. I could not allow my anxiety about my cases and in particular my trunk, to mar my relief at the transfer. Queuing up under the direct sun, the wait while cabins were reshuffled seemed endless. The whole process took an age, but a small but decent lunch was served to those who had not had one, which I was happy to claim. Astonishingly, we found that the army personnel whose barge had deserted us were already well ensconced on board!

At Shellal our river spread itself into a lake with large grotesquely shaped rocks round its sides, and the Britain anchored. We had swung round and stopped opposite the Islet of Philae with its perfect little temple, columns, and pylons, all wonderfully preserved. What luck to see it all but uncovered by water instead of deeply submerged as it usually was. Its ancient beauty was still visible.

The famous Aswan Dam was there. Though hiding some of Philae's beauty when the waters rise, this first great cataract, heightened for the second time in 1934 was a triumphant scheme for regulating, irrigating, and directing the flow of water. It was a modern work of immense skill and a blessing to Egypt. It must have been at least a mile long, an impressive spectacle, and from now on the master of the great Nile and the best friend of the North Africans.

My fare from Cairo to Haifa had to be paid. This had been unobtainable in Cape Town owing to the long hold-up receiving permission, not only to leave South Africa but also to enter Iraq or Palestine. There had been no time for the South African Railways to arrange this and I still wasn't sure I would get permission to enter Palestine directly. I was becoming increasingly anxious and frustrated with authorities, which did not assist my mood. In the dining room the young, representative of the A.A. Transit Corp turned out to be a pain. My only way of paying my fare was by Travellers' Cheques without parting with my limited supply of ready cash, but the tiresome man refused to take these. He had to keep referring to his company offices to verify my arguments. As I stood waiting, I watched soldiers from the Britain floating in a little boat between the pillars of the beautiful temple. This picture of the balance of history past and present left me with an indelible memory. The official persevered but I refused to take the ticket he had ready for me for cash, preferring to take my chances in Cairo. I stared a little longer at the peaceful scene of Philae and her stunning surroundings under the vast cloudless sky. The official, perhaps accepting I was a lost cause, finally accepted the cheques.

After clearing customs without further trouble, I took a barge to the quay with Mrs McInnes. The poor lady was struggling, first with her balance on the crossing and then walking in the deep, soft sand. To our horror, when the delayed train came in, it stopped some distance along the track. The heat was merciless, the train was impossibly distant, but we had no option but to cover the ground. A long plodding scramble over the shifting sand would be necessary. I got Mrs McInnes started off with one porter to support her and two for her luggage, who went on ahead. My trunk and cases were still in a scattered disconsolate heap on the riverbank, and I wondered how they would be transported.

Two porters, chattering volubly descended on me and started strapping my suitcases together when their strap broke. I lent them my one remaining one off another suitcase, only to find that broke too. There was much head scratching and shrugging of shoulders and the journey to the train looked like an impossibility until I spotted a nearby donkey-drawn luggage cart. I insisted it should be taken on. In that awful heat the porters and I started organising the cart when a perspiring officer overtook us and suggested adding his luggage to the cart. I was doubtful on behalf of the poor donkey, but we loaded up and the officer offered to carry my heavy camera bag which I never allowed porters to touch. I reloaded myself with all the leftovers: hat on head as the sun was so powerful, heavy coat, sunshade, bag with thermos, Horlicks, biscuits and other oddments, a weighty handbag containing all my documents, and a light hatbox. The tiny cart started, the donkey pulling, the two porters pushing, and the officer walking alongside with a restraining hand on the wobbling luggage. A veritable demon was in the load, first one suitcase then another slid down and across and had to be hoisted back and secured. I simply couldn't keep up. My heart was pounding in my chest, and I was struggling to breathe. My legs were screaming, and perspiration was running down my back.

Trudging along at my own pace I spotted three smallish suitcases lying by the track in the sand. They looked familiar and studying the labels I saw Mrs McInnes's name on each! I shouted to the officer who stopped the cavalcade. The boys returned, collected the three cases, and piled them on to our cart. Determination was the only thing that started me again. The donkey cart vanished speedily ahead, while I struggled behind. I had come so far but that walk nearly defeated me, and I wondered how Teddy was going to learn that I had died of a heart attack on the sands of Shellal.

After two brief halts to catch my breath and give myself a stern talking to, I reached the train at last. Thankfully I caught up with my trunk and cases. The officer had abandoned my camera case with the luggage and vanished. I found my coupe and saw my possessions safely stashed. Mrs McInnes in the next carriage, already comfortably settled in, hadn't even missed her discarded cases!

The train took us through enchanting country. That side of Egypt was interesting, full of picturesque scenes which the train hurried through too quickly to be fully absorbed. Across a green field, a long diagonal line of women clothed in black and red, with light coloured earthen water pots carried at precisely the same angle on each head, provided an image I will never forget. Lovely, green land by the riverbanks, growing maize sprouting from thousands and thousands of irrigated oblongs of earth. The Nile was blue with great masts and swelling sails of various kinds of boats above it and I tried to impress all this into my mental picture gallery.

Passing Idfu I strove to see its temple's twin towers but was disappointed. However, the sunset light flooding across Egyptian scenery was ample compensation. Hundreds of fantastically haloed palm trees stood out against a crimson-orange sky, filled with fleeting shades of opal. A Nile sail looked like a great white bird's wing! I had never realised Egyptian scenery illuminated by sunset could be so lovely to watch.

As we passed a village I saw a commotion, a celebrating crowd filling its street, a procession of camels with richly attired riders at its centre. Yellow, red, and blue long robes added brilliant colour to the scene. The rider of one camel was robed in purple and pink, and the procession surrounding him marched, and ran, cheering, and shouting. Only the riders looked calm and dignified. The heat was unrelenting, even into the evening. On our left was the flat desert with a village here and there tucked away against the hills. As the sun set desert, village, and hills all became the same colour as the lands awaited the rising of the Nile to bring it to life again. We passed a big temple or church with dome and towers on our left, Coptic probably. On our right was a large notice 'Phosphate Mines'.

It was not until after dark that we came to Sabahi Station and Luxor. Not a thing could be seen from the train, and I could have wept. I walked up and down the station just to hug the thought that this was Luxor ground. This was the site of ancient Thebes, the pharaohs' capital at the height of their power, and the two huge temples still stood, graceful Luxor and Karnak Temple, "Plied by the hands of giants, for god-like kings of old."

In my lifetime I would almost certainly never be this close again to fulfilling my dream of seeing this ancient and sacred ground. After Luxor we went through the Arabian Desert, Assyat on our left, Beni Suef on our right. We would pass a spot where the Nile curved east in a little loop by Kena and from there about sixty miles away at Quseir, lay the Red Sea. Beyond that still directly east, Saudi Arabia lay. All lost to us in the cloak of darkness.

Twice in the night, without warning, Egyptian Railways staff entered the cabin and 'flitted' it for insects, without asking permission. They were so quick and efficient that I was impressed by their thoroughness and not awake enough to think of objecting.

June 26 1943

The train arrived in Cairo Station two hours late! No train breakfast had been served, only an early cup of tea. It was here that Miriam's journey ended, and she would be reconnected with her brother. She was sure he would be on the platform to meet her and her experience of him dictated that he would be waiting impatiently constrained by a schedule. She was happy that we said our farewells long before we were cramped for time. Miriam had been a reliable and agreeable companion on this second part of my journey. There were boundaries that we never crossed because of our insurmountable different experiences of life. I would never know what it was to be Jewish, to belong to such an identifiable group of people, no matter how experienced I thought I was. I did not share my personal tragedies and victories with her, but we had made good travelling companions. I would lose Mrs McInnes too. She was to be collected by Cairo's Christian community to stay with them for a night before changing trains on to Jerusalem. I wondered what would have happened to the old lady if Miriam and I had not taken her under our wings on route. I believed that the welcome committee would have been left standing, as Mrs McInnes would never have managed to complete the journey. It had been a challenging experience, but she had provided me with a welter of interesting and stimulating anecdotes that helped pass my time. I said a sad goodbye to them both before we arrived, knowing that I would never run into them again.

Cairo was a shock. The noise, activity and confusion were overwhelming. Cape Town had been the last major rail junction of that size, and now I had to steel myself to join the throng on Cairo's platforms. I had visited this city before on trips from Palestine but had never seen it so teeming with our Allied men. Groups of soldiers, either fresh faced from home, or battle wearied, were everywhere you looked. Despite playing host to thousands of British troops following the outbreak of the conflict, as treaty-bound to do, Egypt had remained formally neutral, and this led to a strange atmosphere. I was fascinated to see many people of unaccountable allegiances mixing in the station theatre.

My first task was to organise porters to take care of my luggage until my later train. Two gentlemen with big smiles and skin as dark and polished as Namibians caught my eye and I decided to leave my precious trunk and suitcases in their care. Teddy would have been shocked at the risks I had taken. I decided, the trunk, having survived so much rough handling, would survive Cairo station. I was not going to become paranoid now; I had a date with myself to attend to, an assignation with my stomach at Shepheard's Hotel, Cairo.

Hailing a taxi, first to the Thomas Cook offices where I hoped Mr Jackson still held sway.

He greeted me warmly "Mrs Warmington Reed! How lovely to see you after so long! Don't look so worried, I've everything arranged for you."

"Bless you! I knew I could count on you. Is this my pass to Haifa? Thank you so much!" I clutched it tight.

"It was my pleasure. I cannot tell you how pleased I am to see you again."

"What's your news? What've you been up to?"

He smiled his deprecating smile, and I knew he had been busy. "Just the usual! I've started a Service Women's Residential Club! Just to keep me out of mischief!"

I laughed "You obviously have got too much time on your hands. I'll have to ask my husband to factor in more trips!" Mr Jackson was the first old friend I had seen since 1940 and it was a joy to pick up where I left off.

Then on by taxi to Shepheard's, my tenacity award, the famous hotel renowned for its opulence, stained glass, Persian carpets, gardens, and terraces. I walked past the great granite pillars resembling an ancient Egyptian temple and, despite the throng of officers of varied uniforms, I felt that the world had not changed so much. I remembered the first time that Teddy and I had stayed at Shepheard's and how overwhelming it was. We had treated ourselves to their famous hospitality and then been shocked at the bill when presented. We never stayed again, but this treat was mine, for me, having crossed the entire length of Africa for it.

I skirted the familiar Long Bar and was shown to a small table amidst the buzzing of late breakfasts which had overflowed on to the terrace. All was as perfectly displayed as if there was no war still being fought, no soldiers still losing their lives. The white tablecloths gleamed under the blue sky, the silver shone, and the staff were as immaculate as ever. I was happy to be on my own and indulge this slow ritual of a breakfast of many courses, taken at a pace that allowed me to mull over the journey I had accomplished and my expectations to come.

As I was completing my meal, I became aware of the unflinching focus of a pair of eyes on me. A group of five suited civilian men sitting at an adjourning table were sharing coffee after a meal. There was nothing remarkable about them, just men who had been discussing business together whilst indulging themselves with a treat. The eyes fastened on me belonged to a neat stylish man in a cream linen suit who was going through the process of trying to work out where he knew me from. Immediately I was gripped with the same impression. It was embarrassing. Mentally I went through a dozen scenarios, but none fitted as we glanced at each other. I pride myself on my memory of faces and names and it was frustrating. I was certainly not prepared to make a fool of myself by approaching him. Only at the point when the neighbouring table decided to leave the dining room, did I recall the man. As he left the table, he turned and leant forward to pick up his hat from the floor. In bending down he displayed a distinctive head of trim brown hair surrounding a patch shaped like a Franciscan monk on the crown of his head. I had studied that crown before! My memory shot back to the man lying on the floor between beds at the hotel at Victoria Falls, his foot in my hand! A further image of the same man leaping onto our barge leaving for Kandahar Island flashed before my eyes. And the same man on some forgotten railway platform where I had not expected him. This man had encroached on my life right across Africa and had now seemingly beaten me to this rendezvous at Shepheard's Hotel. As I registered the shock of recognition, something changed in his eyes also. With still deliberation he looked hard at me, and slowly brought his index finger up to his face and tapped the side of his nose. It was a moment of total non-verbal communication between two people in a crowded auditorium. Then he was gone.

I could have cried at the frustration this encounter triggered in me. What had really been going on in this man's life? What had he really been doing? What had I missed? What would I never know? I was shaken and angered at the evidence of the enormity of my ignorance.

Deliberately wandering slowly back through the grandeur of the hotel I paused to look at the Steinway, still available for guests to play on. Teddy and I had once enjoyed the opportunity of playing on this outstanding piano. I remember we had gathered quite an audience when he had accompanied me on his violin. My fingers itched to run across the keys again, but I could not allow myself the time. Placing my fingers carefully on the keys I satisfied myself with playing one clear chord. My ball and chain of luggage demanded my attention, and I was not a free woman yet.

Back at the station my spirits rose. I had my vital visa to enter Palestine and instinct about my Namibian porters had proved accurate. I was safely reunited with my luggage and located my coupe. I found I was to share it with a charming French woman. Madame Nicolaou, married to a Greek living in Alexandria, was on her way to a short holiday in the Lebanon as guest of the Mexican Consul and his wife. The train was alarmingly full, the corridors stuffed with soldiers sitting on suitcases and duffel bags. I could see that even a trip to the bathroom was going to be a major undertaking and was not looking forward to the night ahead. The train took us through the town of Ismailia which was as attractive as ever but had grown considerably larger while I had been away. Catching my eye fleetingly, I saw some huge black shapes wallowing on the ground and drew Madame's attention to them. I thought they looked like enormous hippopotami, and she enlightened me that they were balloons used in the sky to trap planes. These were the first barrage balloons I had ever seen.

Then we approached the Suez Canal. To my delight, a great improvement has been brought about only the previous year as the canal was now crossed by a swing bridge. It entailed an extremely slow and careful crossing, but I imagine it was one of the lasting improvements that the necessity of war had brought about. At Kantara we all had to dismount the train, except for Madame Nicolaou who had dispensation organised by the Mexican Consul. Our passports had to be checked at an office which meant waiting in a long queue in the late afternoon sun. The train was full to brimming with soldiers and civilians, and every one of them had to be checked through carefully. I had come so far and couldn't help but be impatient. I was nearly on my home territory and the tension of so many unanswered questions weighed heavily on me.

Seeing a familiar figure wandering down the crawling line, I called out "Mr Haifiz!" Thomas Cook's man and old acquaintance was scanning the queue.

His face broke into a broad smile, "Mrs Warmington Reed! Mr Warmington Reed told me to look out for you! A pleasure to see you again."

Mr Haifiz took me under his wing, and we immediately and embarrassingly went to the head of the line. I exchanged apologies and pleasantries with many who were being overtaken. Mr Haifiz rushed me personally through customs and then helped me further, jumping the queue in the café where I bought coffee and sandwiches for Madame and myself, to last us the night. It felt strange to be in that old familiar position of being looked after by my husband after two years of fending totally for myself. It was as if Teddy himself was now once again attempting to organise me, and I was aware of a niggle of resentment at the implication that I needed looking after.

The noise generated that evening by the soldiers in the corridor outside my coupe was unrelenting, but I forgave them as I enjoyed hearing them talk. North of England lads they were, from places I knew in a past life, Durham, Redcar, Whitby, and the like. The war effort work I had done in Cape Town had bought me in touch with honest, courageous lads like these, and it was a joy to hear the familiar voices and sense of humour. Negotiating the corridors was an obstacle race after dark with many a suitcase or bag lurking to break your ankle. Soldiers were sleeping, and others were distinctly merry and bright, worse for alcohol as the journey wore on. They said, 'It was fine to meet a real English lady again!' There were no drinks or food served on the train, and only tepid water from the wash basins if flask water had run out. There were no fans, only makeshift ventilators, so I anticipated arriving at my destination the next day looking far from my most attractive.

Madame put herself into the bed aloft early, and I was left with my own thoughts about the day to come. The day when I would be reunited with Teddy.

I was so close now to picking up my old life and allowed myself to consider the reality of the journey I had undertaken. I had survived, possibly against the odds. With hindsight I had paid a price for underestimating the wear and tear that such a journey would inflict on me. I was exhausted and I was not well. I had behaved irresponsibly. I had doggedly taken on a journey that would tax a much younger woman. I had not listened to my Cape Town friends when they had pointed out my physical shortcomings, my lack of flexibility and strength, my increasing tiredness, my age. But I had managed to survive, and I prayed that the treasure I was bringing with me had survived too.

Deep in the now battered trunk I was bringing home, lay Teddy's most profligate expenditure ever, his Stradivarius violin. His mother had been a doting accomplice in buying this extravagance. He was an accomplished musician but not outstanding and this priceless instrument, only rarely played upon, was a madness and a responsibility. Teddy's most prized possession was at this moment padded in layers of clothing in the middle of my large trunk. It was a prima donna, needing to be securely wrapped, safe from too much heat, too much cold, or too much damp. Prying eyes that knew its value, or not, had to be avoided. I was bringing the Stradivarius home to my husband. Only when I opened the trunk in the privacy of my home in Haifa, would I know whether I was carrying his treasure or nothing but a ruin. There had been times on this journey when I had hated that trunk. I could have dragged the specialist violin the entire length of Africa only to find that through ignorance, stupidity, or bad luck, I was carrying a destroyed cargo.

The violin, like my marriage, was precious and needed to be protected. I felt I would know, as soon as I saw Teddy, whether our marriage had survived these two years of separation. Teddy had always loved the company of attractive women. I was not immune to the fun of lightly flirting and had felt the lure of the unknown, but I took my marriage vows seriously. My recent afternoon with Mr Darvell came to mind. I knew the boundaries for me, and I knew that my husband had waived these boundaries twice to my knowledge. I believed him when he said his love for me was unshakable, but it had been presumptuous of me to assume that we could not be parted. In my absence he could have been seduced into forgetting that. He could have been made to feel so attractive and young that it would prove too heady a hook. Now our daughters were scattered across the world, living their own lives, he could have been persuaded that he too could live another life. When the Government in 1940 insisted that British women and children had to leave Palestine, Teddy had been haunted with fears for my safety. Had he ever questioned my faithfulness? Cape Town was his choice of a secure place for me to live, and I enjoyed the adventure of living a different life for a while.

Reality was staring me in the face that night. I would be with Teddy once again the following day, and I would make it my business to fight for my husband and the familiarity of our entwined lives. Unsurprisingly I couldn't sleep.

June 27 1943

Groggy eyed I watched as we travelled through small stations, some new in the last two years. At Lydda I got out and walked along the platform just to feel the early morning sun on my face and stretch my limbs. I felt the surge of my energy despite tiredness, and I could hardly contain myself. I was almost home.

We covered the coastal plain on the run towards Haifa and I spotted once familiar landmarks. The grand arch near Atlit had been badly damaged, part of the arch had broken off leaving it sadly unrecognisable. War damage I assumed. The large detention camp with its residential barracks was still surrounded by barbed wire and watch towers and appeared empty.

I commented to Madame, "It seems strange that the Atlit detention camp is now closed. I remember the tragedy there so well. The terrible loss of life."

"I'm sorry? I don't know what you're talking about. I know nothing about the Atlit camp." Madame's face puckered in concentration.

"It was established here ever since the `30s by the British authorities. Built to contain Jewish immigrants who didn't have the correct official entry permits. The British were acceding to Arab demands. We also used the camp for the Palestinian Germans who openly supported the Nazis, just until we could deport them. In `40 when I was living in Haifa, the British authorities decided to send five thousand Jewish immigrants to detention camps in Mauritius. The Patria was one of the deporting ships and the Jewish underground exploded a bomb in the ship's hold. It was a tragedy."

"That sounds counterproductive! Why would they do that?"

"It was a terrible miscalculation by the Jewish underground, they only meant to stop it. Of the 1,800 refugees on board, 216 drowned. It was an appalling mistake. We British had our cross to bear being stuck in the middle of this Jewish-Arab conflict, and I don't think we handled it well." How strange that I had almost forgotten that aspect of living in Haifa.

The acrid smell of burning in the air was the first thing we noticed as we slowed up to pass one station. There were signs of a very recent fire. Iron girders were twisted and smouldering, and I saw quantities of copra in sacks had been burnt. Hundreds of sacks had been pulled away from the buildings but lay opened and partly blackened. Small fires were still flicking into life and a feeling of grease hung in the air. Soldiers that were in attendance, looked tired and dispirited.

"Could this have been enemy action?" Madame looked alarmed "I was told we were safe to travel here now!"

"Yes, I was told the same thing." I shuddered at the thought that our train might have been susceptible if we had passed a few hours earlier.

We were approaching Haifa suburbs, dear and familiar to me. I could smell the familiar smell of ozone, heat, and dust, mixed with the floating perfume of the flowering trees. How distinct this smell was, this smell of my Haifa home. I had been told in Cairo that I would have to stay in the train until it reached the Old Station in Haifa where the customs offices were based. I was hanging out of the window as it approached Haifa station with no expectations, only to fill my lungs with the life of my old stamping grounds.

I saw Teddy before he saw me. I saw him suddenly as a stranger might, a tall good-looking man with a good physique standing on the platform. His wavy hair was that distinctive cream grey that had originally been a strawberry blond and his grey eyes were searching the train for me. It was a shock as I was not mentally prepared. I was a dusty mess, far from my most attractive, but the shout that left my lips would have halted an elephant. "Teddy! Dear Teddy!"

He spun, and saw me instantly, and a smile cracked his face. "Elf! My dear! I can't believe it". He paced himself along the slowing carriages, so that as we came to a halt, he had caught up with me. I opened the carriage door and fell into his big embrace. His familiar body, his familiar smell, it was all too much, and I felt tears spring to my eyes. I just wanted to stand there blocking the thoroughfare in the arms of my husband, my best friend.

"My dear, you'll have to go on to the Old Station to get through customs."

"Yes, I know. I was expecting you there!"

"I couldn't wait to see you. It's so wonderful. I'll follow in my car. We'll get you home in no time. You must be tired."

It was only when I was climbing back into the carriage, overwhelmed by feelings of pleasure at being reconnected with Teddy again, that I spotted the diminutive figure of Clara, my old maid, now married, who was hanging back behind him. Her arms were full of an enormous bouquet of white roses and Teddy swooped to collect them to hand them to me. The train was slowly gathering speed, I was waving at Clara and blowing her kisses and I gestured for him to keep the beautiful flowers.

Teddy laughed delightedly at the pantomime, and as we pulled away, I saw him waving them above his head as he headed for the car, Clara in tow.

At the Old Station a man from Cook's took me and my luggage through customs. I had expected the polite and helpful Mr Anise but was informed that he had sadly died in my absence. Customs was easy as I declared I only had personal effects and that was accepted unchallenged. Then at last, I moved out through the entrance to Teddy, Clara and the car and we drove along familiar roads up to Mount Carmel. A taxi following with my luggage, the amount and size of which Teddy had obviously not expected.

My lovely home, with its wonderful view of the harbour was reached within minutes, and I climbed the familiar steps, hand in hand with my husband with my heart in my mouth. Leila greeted me, suspicious at first and then recognising me, smelt me, and gambolled excitedly round despite her surprisingly matronly bulk! What had Teddy been feeding her? After the interval of two years and two months, my dear German Shepherd had not forgotten me. At the door, dear loyal Sarkis came out of the kitchen and repeatedly kissed my hand and held it to his forehead and shed a tear on it. I was in tears too. The house was fresh and cool, and Teddy had put flowers in every room. He proudly told me he had had the interior of the house repainted, a beautiful cooling white, and even painted my three sets of old brown doors to match. He said he had done them himself, three coats each, and a great improvement they were!

My luggage was delivered. By some miracle it had remained intact but for a complete lack of straps and handles, but every lock had held and not one thing had been opened in negotiating the many customs posts. I could not relax until I had checked how our precious possession, the Stradivarius violin, had survived. Teddy did the honours as he opened the trunk lid. He moved in slow motion as he methodically unpacked the layers within. It took an age, and I could barely watch. Finally, his smile said it all. The violin was unharmed, and my relief was tangible. The rest of the unpacking could wait. A lovely bunch of mail awaited me from Joy, Felicity, Maude, and from Cape Town friends, to be read later.

It was not till we were seated on my old green sofa, drinking tea from my familiar China set, and confronted by an over-enthusiastic mound of Sarkis's home-made cakes, that Teddy took my hand.

"My dear, I have the best possible news for you. I can't wait to tell you."

I looked deep into his eyes, and there was no disguising the excitement and love in them. "What is it, Teddy? Don't tease. What is it?"

"Elf dear! Welcome to the world of grandparents! I only heard yesterday! Ronny is alive and well, and you're a grandmother! Your granddaughter was born in Baguio, in March last year, and she's called Catherine. They're both fine and were transferred to Santa Tomas camp in Manila in April this year. They'll now be with Pat." I was howling with pent up relief, and Teddy's eyes were also full.

"That's the best news you could possibly give me. I'm so happy Teddy!"

"Why are we drinking tea? I've a bottle of real champagne that I've kept for a very special occasion. I can't think of a better reason to open it. You're a remarkable woman. I cannot believe you've travelled all this way. My Elf is safely home, my daughter and her baby are alive, and thanks to you, my violin has survived! The war can't go on much longer and we've a wonderful future to look forward to. I love you very much Elf. I've missed you more than I can say, and I can't wait to get back to our normal life together."

I had at last arrived and belonged somewhere again, in my home and with my dear husband. I was totally confident that, if there had been a wobble, my return had secured my marriage. I had survived the forty-five-day journey of far more than the roughly judged 6,814 miles from Cape Town, all the way up the length of Africa with its endless trials and tribulations, but with its stark and wonderful memories too.

I accepted the glass of champagne and toasted the future with Teddy.

Ethel (Elf) in Leipzig

Edward (Teddy) 1914

Wedding of Samuel Taylor Jones and Miss Caroline Stephens (front row central) in front of Vale House, Ebley, Gloucestershire 1876

(L to R standing) Edward Reed, Edward (Teddy) Warmington Reed, Ethel (Elf) Warmington Reed, Ethelbert Reed, Frank Stephens (L to R seated) Miss Maimie Stephens, flower girl, Bertha Reed, Maude Taylor Jones, Charlotte Reed 1903

Wedding of Edward T Warmington Reed and Miss Ethel C Taylor Jones (central) in front of Vale House, Ebley, Gloucestershire 1903

(L to R standing) Teddy, Bertha Reed, Ethelbert Reed,
(L to R seated) Elf, Charlotte Reed, Edward Reed, Mabel Reed with Arthur,
(L to R on bearskin) Joy, Ronny 1910

(L to R) Joy, Elf, Felicity, Pat Rynd, Ronny 1917

Teddy's Identity Card for Haifa, Palestine 1940

Elf and Flick in Palestine 1941

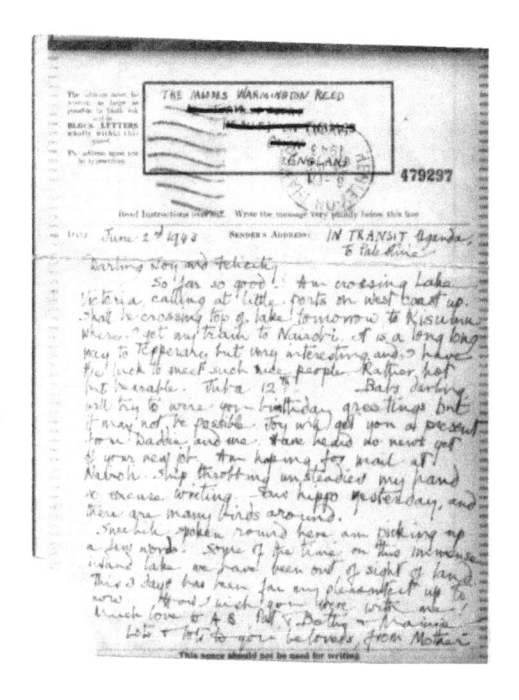

Elf letter from Uganda to Joy and Flick 1943

Author's Christening (L to R standing) Patsy Moraes, Margo Rynd,
Reg Verney, Joy, Teddy, Bertha Ostler, Clem Ostler, Betty Moraes
(L to R seated) Pat, Catherine, Ronny, baby Merilyn, Elf, Maimie. 1945

Stroud Journal 21 September 1878

WEDDING AT SELSLEY
MR SAMUEL TAYLOR JONES AND MISS CAROLINE STEPHENS

On Tuesday the marriage of Miss Caroline Stephens, second daughter of S. Stephens Esq of The Vale House, Ebley to Samuel Taylor Jones Esq of White Lee House, Crook, Durham was solemnised at All Saints' Church, Selsley. The bridal party was conveyed from the residence of the bride's father to the church in five carriages, the bride riding in the carriage of S. S. Marling, Esq M.P., who was himself present. The bridesmaids were Miss Jones (sister of the bridegroom), Misses F and N Jones (nieces of the bridegroom) and Miss Bessie Cross, the best man being Mr Henry S Stephens, and the other groomsmen Messrs S. W. and J. J. Stephens, brothers of the bride. The church was crowded, many being unable to obtain a view of the ceremony in which they took so much interest. The interior presented a very nice appearance, as the decorations used at the harvest festival on

Sunday were undisturbed, and the handsome dresses of the bride and bridesmaids made up a scene which will probably be long remembered by all those who had assembled. The ceremony was performed by the Rev. F. G. Bussell, M.A. of Leamington Parish Church, cousin of the bride, assisted by the Rev. A. S. Page, vicar of Selsley. At the wedding breakfast, at the Vale House, there were about thirty present being chiefly relatives of the bride and bridegroom. In the afternoon the happy pair left Ebley for North Wales, there to spend the honeymoon. The presents to the bride show the universal esteem in which she was held, being over ninety in number, some of which are very valuable.

Stroud News and Gloucestershire Advertiser 17 April 1891

FUNERAL OF THE LATE MRS S. T. JONES

The funeral of Mrs S. T. Jones, daughter of the late Mr Samuel Stephens, of Vale House, Ebley, took place at Rodborough Tabernacle on Tuesday afternoon last. The deceased lady was universally respected in the neighbourhood, which has been thrown into gloom by reason of her death; and expressions of regret have been numerous and sincere. As stated, the funeral took place on Tuesday; and the following was the order of procession: The bearers carrying a hand bier covered with beautiful wreaths and crosses; hearse (the top of which was hidden by floral tributes) containing the coffin, which was also partly covered by wreaths; two mourning coaches –

the occupants of the first being Mr Charles Stephens, Mr H. S. Stephens and Mr C Smith; and the second, Mr J. J. Stephens, Mr F. A. Stephens, Rev. E. Jacob and Rev. R. Nott; the private carriages of Mr J. G. Strachan J.P., Mr J. Russell Buckler, Mr. Edwin Gyde and Mr Wm. Roberts; and the general body of mourners, amongst whom were Mr John Jacob, Mr J. Latham, Mr. Smith, Mr C. Jefferies, Mr H. Jefferies, Mr. E. Harper and Mr. G. Olpin. The internment took place in the family vault at Rodborough Tabernacle, the Rev. E. Jacob and R. Nott officiating.

Stroud News and Gloucestershire Advertiser 18 September 1903

MARRIAGE AT SELSLEY
MR. EDWARD T. WARMINGTON REED AND MISS ETHEL C. JONES

On Tuesday last, at All Saints' Church, Selsley, the marriage took place of Mr Edward T. Warmington Reed, eldest son of Mr and Mrs Edward Reed; Painswick and Miss Ethel Caroline Jones, The Vale House, Ebley. The officiating clergy were the Rev. Herbert Muir M.A. (vicar) and the Rev. Bernard Jones M.A. Bristol. The church was beautifully decorated with palms and flowers and the ceremony aroused very general interest. A large company of friends of the bride and bridegroom attended both at the church and the reception held afterwards at the Vale House, where several photographs were taken of those present. The bride was given away by her uncle Mr. F. A. Stephens and was attired in a dress of white satin merveilleux, with a tucked chiffon yoke, accordion pleated chiffon sleeves, and semi-court train. Her tulle veil was arranged over a wreath of real orange blossoms. She carried a shower bouquet of white roses, white heather, and lilies of the valley. Her travelling dress consisted of a coatee and skirt of stone-coloured cloth with hat to match, trimmed with crimson velvet and dark roses. Miss Maude Jones, sister of the bride, was the principal bridesmaid and wore a dress of point d'esprit over white glace, tucked and trimmed with bebe ribbon, white panne sash and a charming white picture hat. The two bridesmaids, Miss Bertha Reed, sister of the bridegroom, and Miss Coralie J. Stephens, cousin of the bride, in their Kate Greenaway dresses with white satin Gainsborough hats and carrying shepherd's crooks trimmed with white roses, lily of the valley and smilax, were naturally the objects of genuine admiration. Mr Ethelbert W. Reed, brother of the bridegroom, was his best man. The service included the two hymns, "O perfect love" and "Love Divine" and Mr W. W. Cheriton presided at the organ. Among the pieces excellently rendered previous to the ceremony were Wagner's "Bridal March" (Lohengrin) and "Intermezzo" (Macbeth). Mendelssohn's ever fresh "Wedding

March" was played while the party and friends were leaving the church. The happy couple left by the 5.30 train for North Wales, where the honeymoon will be spent. The presents, numbering over 130, were beautiful and costly. We understand that Mr and Mrs Reed intend living at Painswick. Mr W. A. Skinner, Lansdown, Stroud, supplied the carriages.

In honour of the wedding of Mr Reed, jun., the employees of the mill at Painswick were given a half-day holiday on Tuesday, and many of them journeyed to Selsley to witness the ceremony.

HISTORICAL FOOTNOTE

Since my grandmother wrote her journal, the map of Africa has changed, both politically and to some extent geographically. I have used the original names that Elf used, but upon research using a detailed map of the period, I have found that whereas some ports of call in 1943 have now vanished off the map, others have changed their names. Palla Road is now called Dinokwe. Elizabethville is now called Lubumbashi. Jadotville is now called Likasi. Albertville is now called Kalomie.

Reed's Mill in Painswick, Gloucestershire was demolished, but The Rockery, the house abutting the mill, where Teddy's parents lived remains and is now called Painswick Mill House. Elf and Teddy's house that they designed and built in Painswick and called The Knapp, is now called Woodborough. I am delighted to say it still contains original Arts and Crafts movement features; doors, a fireplace, beams, interesting corbels and a datestone still remain. Wickstreet House, Wick Street is still a private dwelling. Elf's uncles' carpet factory, Ebley Mill, has now become the splendid Stroud District Council offices. Vale House was sadly demolished in the 1960s when the council gave permission for an industrial estate to be built on the premises.

Elf and Teddy visited England in the summer of 1945. They were reunited with Joy, Felicity, and my family which consisted of Ronny, Pat, Catherine, and me. This was only weeks after I was born there, as my mother, father and sister had been released from the Japanese prisoner of war camp in the Philippines.

After three months the Hongkong and Shanghai Bank sent my father back to work, this time in the turbulent mainland China, closely followed by Ronny, Catherine, and me.

After that visit Elf and Teddy went to live and work in Bermuda. They returned to England in 1948 to buy a family house in Sussex and from 1950 raised my eight-year-old sister, Catherine, who was flown home from China having suffered a nervous breakdown. My mother and I returned from China in 1952 to live with Elf and Teddy and Catherine, leaving my father in China. He was released in 1954.

The stories of Elf's background came mostly from my aunt Felicity who I looked after in her old age. I was easily able to verify these details on research, but the Stradivarius link is open to question. I do not find my grandfather in the list of owners of these legendary instruments. I was told that the sale of the violin funded the purchase of their thatched house in Sussex where they lived in retirement, and I like to think that that is true.

A peaceful old age in England ensued for Elf and Teddy, which was only marred by Elf developing and suffering from dementia by her mid-eighties. Teddy insisted on her remaining in his devoted care, and she died at home in 1969, aged ninety. Teddy died a year later, having suffered a heart attack whilst playing billiards. He was ninety-one.

ACKNOWLEDGEMENTS

This account of my grandmother Elf's great adventure up the length of Africa, would not have been possible without her original journal and the assistance of many supportive people.

I have been fortunate to have benefitted from the encouragement of many friends including Rob Collins, Andrea Shepherd, and my son Luke, who have given me their time, enthusiasm, and helpful suggestions. I thank Deborah Lee and Myra Joyce in particular, whose intelligence and perception were much appreciated at every step of the way. I owe a huge debt to my daughter in law Robee, who with the help of Luke, was again responsible for my lovely book cover, and the Africa map and so much more.

Terry Coughlin has once again been an outstanding editor and great support in the process of bringing another family saga to fruition. Terry was also responsible for the detailed chapter maps and the presentation of the old archive photographs, and I thank him.

Thanks to Pauline Stevens of the Stroud Local History Society who was responsible for the newspaper cuttings and invaluable local knowledge. My thanks to Peter Harris, who resides in the house Teddy built, for his knowledge and interest.

Thank you to all the staff of Troubador Matador for their care and advice whilst publishing Crossing the Rift. They combined professionalism with patient and friendly guidance at every stage of production.

My thanks to my long-suffering husband Owen Williams for his support during this lengthy writing process and my sons Ben, Adam, and Luke who gave me the motivation to tell the story of their great grandmother, Elf.

Merilyn Brason was conceived in a prisoner of war camp, in the Philippines during World War II when her mother was imprisoned by the Japanese. Merilyn's first book *The Bamboo Bracelet* was about that experience. She has lived in mainland China, Nigeria and Australia where she worked in radio journalism. She is now a retired psychotherapist, with three adult sons and lives with her husband in Gloucestershire, England. *Crossing The Rift* is Merilyn's second book, triggered by her grandmother's wartime experience. As an unaccompanied older white woman, Elf risked all by travelling the entire length of Africa overland, to be united with her husband. Merilyn has woven this extraordinary story from Elf's handwritten journals.

This book is printed on paper from sustainable sources managed under the Forest Stewardship Council (FSC) scheme.

It has been printed in the UK to reduce transportation miles and their impact upon the environment.

For every new title that Matador publishes, we plant a tree to offset CO_2, partnering with the More Trees scheme.

MORE TREES
LET'S PLANT A BILLION TREES

For more about how Matador offsets its environmental impact, see www.troubador.co.uk/about/